AFTER EICHMANN

In 1961 Adolf Eichmann went on trial in Jerusalem for his part in the Nazi persecution and mass murder of Europe's Jews. For the first time a judicial process focussed on the genocide against the Jews and heard Jewish witnesses to the catastrophe. The trial and the controversies it caused had a profound effect on shaping the collective memory of what became "the Holocaust". This volume, a special issue of the *Journal of Israeli History*, brings together new research by scholars from Europe, Israel and the USA.

This was first published as a special issue of *The Journal of Israeli History*

David Cesarani is Research Professor in Hisotry at Royal Holloway, University of London.

AFTER EICHMANN

Collective Memory and the Holocaust since 1961

David Cesarani

Routledge
Taylor & Francis Group
London and New York

First published 2005 by Routledge
2 Park Square, Milton Park, Abington, Oxfordshire OX14 4RN

Simultaneously published in the USA and Canada
by RoutledgeCurzon
711 Third Avenue, New York, NY 10017
First issued in paperback 2014

Routledge is an imprint of the Taylor and Francis Group, an informa company

© 2005 David Cesarani

Typeset in Goudy 10/12pt in Europe
by the Alden Group, Oxford

British Library Cataloguing in Publication Data
A catalogue record for this book is available from
the British Library

Library of Congress Cataloging in Publication Data
ISBN 978-0-415-36015-9 (hbk)
ISBN 978-0-415-75909-0 (pbk)

CONTENTS

Contributors

DAVID CESARANI. Research Professor in History at Royal Holloway, University of London. He was director of the AHRB Parkes Centre for the Study of Jewish/non-Jewish Relations at Southampton University 2000-04. His recent publications include *Eichmann: His Life and Crimes* (London, 2004) and as editor with Paul Levine, *Bystanders to the Holocaust: A Reevaluation* (London, 2002).

ANITA SHAPIRA. Ruben Merenfeld Professor of Zionism at Tel Aviv University. Her publications include *Berl, the Biography of a Socialist Zionist: Berl Katznelson, 1887–1944* (Cambridge, 1984) and *Land and Power: The Zionist Resort to Force, 1881–1948* (New York, 1992).

JEFFREY HERF. Professor in the Department of History at the University of Maryland in College Park. His publications include *Divided Memory: The Nazi Past in the Two Germanys* (Harvard University Press, 1997). He is currently working on *The Jewish War: The Anti-Semitic Campaigns of the Nazi Propaganda Ministry* (forthcoming with Harvard University Press).

NA'AMA SHEFFI. Senior Lecturer in the Department of Communication at Sapir College, Sderot. She is the author of *German in Hebrew: Translation from German into Hebrew in Jewish Palestine, 1882–1948* (Tel Aviv, 1998); and *The Ring of Myths: The Israelis, Wagner and the Nazis* (Sussex Academic Press, 2001). She is currently researching the image of the Jew Süss as a mirror of the German-Jewish cultural relationship.

MANUELA CONSONNI. Teaches at the Institute of Contemporary Jewry, the Hebrew University of Jerusalem. She is the co-editor, with Shlomo Simonsohn of *Biblioteca Italo-Ebraica, 1986–1995* (Tel Aviv University, Rome, 1997); and editor of *Biblioteca Italo-Ebraica, 1996–2002* (forthcoming).

MEIR LITVAK. Senior Research Fellow at the Dayan Center for Middle Eastern and African Studies and a Senior Lecturer at the Department of Middle Eastern History, Tel Aviv University. He is the author of *Shi'ite Scholars of Nineteenth Century Iraq* (Cambridge, 1998), as well as articles on Islamist movements and Palestinian history.

ESTHER WEBMAN. Research Associate at the Dayan Center for Middle Eastern and African Studies and the Stephen Roth Institute for the Study of Anti-Semitism and Racism, Tel Aviv University. She is currently writing her

Ph.D. dissertation on "The Representation of the Holocaust in the Egyptian Public Discourse, 1945–1962." Her recent publications include: *Islam and the West: Clash or Co-existence* (editor) (Tel Aviv, 2002) (in Hebrew); and *It Was Written on the Wall: Osama Bin Laden, the Man and his Deeds* (Tel Aviv, 2002) (in Hebrew).

TONY KUSHNER. Professor of Jewish/non-Jewish relations in the Department of History and AHRB Parkes Centre for Jewish/non-Jewish Relations, University of Southampton. He is the author of *Refugees in an Age of Genocide: Global, National and Local Responses* (London, 1999); *Disraeli's Jewishness* (co-editor) (London, 2002); *We Europeans? Mass-Observation, "Race" and British Identity in the Twentieth Century* (Ashgate, forthcoming); and, with Donald Bloxham, *The Holocaust: A Counter History* (Manchester University Press, forthcoming).

TIM COLE. Teaches history at the University of Bristol and co-ordinates the MA program in Contemporary History, which includes a strong focus on public history. He is the author of *Selling the Holocaust. From Auschwitz to Schindler: How History is Bought, Packaged and Sold* (New York 1999); and *Holocaust City: The Making of a Jewish Ghetto* (New York 2003). He is currently writing a social history of the Holocaust in Hungary.

SUZANNE BARDGETT. Imperial War Museum Holocaust Exhibition Project Director since 1995.

JAMES E. YOUNG. Professor and Chair of the Department of Judaic and Near Eastern Studies at the University of Massachusetts, Amherst. He is the author of *Writing and Rewriting the Holocaust* (Indiana University Press, 1988); *The Texture of Memory* (Yale University Press, 1993); and *At Memory's Edge: After-images of the Holocaust in Contemporary Art and Architecture* (Yale University Press, 2000), among other works.

Acknowledgments

This collection is based on papers presented to the conference, *After Eichmann: Collective Memory and the Holocaust since 1961*, held at Southampton University on 8–9 April 2002. The conference was organized and funded jointly by the AHRB Parkes Centre for the Study of Jewish/non-Jewish Relations, University of Southampton, the Chaim Weizmann Institute for the Study of Zionism and Israel, Tel Aviv University, and the Imperial War Museum, London. I would like to thank my co-organizers, Dr. Jo Reilly, AHRB Parkes Centre, Professor Anita Shapira, the Chaim Weizmann Institute, and Suzanne Bardgett, Imperial War Museum, for helping to make it possible. Professor Anita Shapira had the idea for the conference and provided the initial impetus. Jo Reilly was the organizational backbone of the event and gave editorial assistance at the early stages of turning a conference into a published collection. From start to finish of the publication process Anita Shapira offered wise counsel in her capacity as an editor of *The Journal of Israeli History*. Not all the papers or commentaries delivered at the conference appear in this collection, but thanks to the stimulating discussions, all the participants contributed in some measure to the final product. So I would like to express my gratitude to Dr. Peter Carrier (University of Budapest); Professor Bryan Cheyette (University of Southampton); Dr. Raya Cohen (Tel Aviv University); Professor Risa Domb (University of Cambridge); Nicholas Kinlock (UK); Professor Dan Laor (Tel Aviv University); Dr. Paul Levine (University of Uppsala); Dr. Regula Lugi (Switzerland); Professor Harold Marcuse (University of California); Dr. Joanna Michlic (Brandeis University); Professor Alan Mintz (Jewish Theological Seminary, New York); Professor Bob Moore (University of Sheffield); Rabbi David Soedendorp (UK); Dr. Dan Stone (Royal Holloway College); Teresa Swiebocka (Auschwitz State Museum); Dr. Isobel Wollaston (University of Birmingham); Dr. Hanna Yablonka (Ben Gurion University).

David Cesarani

Introduction

David Cesarani

Before the Eichmann Trial

In May 1960 Adolf Eichmann, a Lt. Col. of the Schutzstaffel (SS) who managed the deportation of Jews from all over Europe to the Nazi death camps during 1942–44, was abducted from Buenos Aires in Argentina, where he had found refuge after World War II, and taken to Israel. His capture was announced to the world on 26 May 1960 and he stood trial in Jerusalem between April and December 1961. He was found guilty and sentenced to death. Following an unsuccessful appeal to Israel's Supreme Court he was executed on 31 May 1962.[1]

The capture, trial and execution of Adolf Eichmann were sensational events that for short periods dominated the news media of the time and changed forever perceptions of the Nazi persecution and mass murder of the Jews. During the trials of leading Nazis at Nuremberg in 1946–47, the destruction of European Jewry had been only one strand in the charge sheet and was often submerged or marginalized in the course of the proceedings.[2] Eichmann was the first Nazi official to be tried primarily for crimes against the Jewish people. The evidence and testimony amassed by the prosecution, as well as the way it was shaped and delivered in the courtroom, ensured that Nazi anti-Jewish policy and the experience of those it had affected were exposed with unprecedented force and clarity. The trial began the process of correcting the peripheral treatment of Nazi crimes against the Jews in the historiography of the Third Reich and World War II. It undoubtedly increased public awareness of the fate that had overtaken Europe's Jews fifteen years earlier, although there is less certainty as to how much that awareness was raised or how deep it went.[3]

Most historians and commentators do agree that the trial marked a turning point in perceptions of the recent past. Although for many years there was a tendency to overstate the extent of ignorance about the mass murder of the Jews and to exaggerate the "silence" of survivors and others. It is true that prior to 1960 the destruction of Jewish life in Europe had been commemorated almost only amongst Jewish communities and, even then, often only by those Jews who were directly affected, such as refugees from Hitler and camp survivors. Yet the reverberations from the Nazi years echoed through politics, culture and scholarship — faint and distorted, perhaps, but present all the same to those attuned to them.

The State of Israel had begun to institutionalize memory of the catastrophe during the late 1940s and early 1950s. Between 1948 and 1960 issues connected with the Nazi persecution and mass murder of the Jews repeatedly erupted into Israeli politics and public life, while survivors made their voices heard in numerous arenas. The notion that even in Israel the survivors were "silent" has recently been subjected to significant revision. The Eichmann trial may have altered attitudes towards them and brought the persecution of the Jews to the foreground of historical awareness, but as Anita Shapira, Dalia Ofer, Yehiam Weitz and Hannah Yablonka have demonstrated it did not cause this transformation overnight and did not come *ex nihilo*.[4]

Similarly, recent research into postwar culture in Europe and the United States of America has revealed that the genocide against the Jews was a persistent theme, even if it took peculiar guises. Throughout Western Europe, fierce debates about the role of the resistance, and its postwar claims in the sphere of politics, provoked attention to the relative status of the different victims of Nazi persecution. In most countries primacy went to those who had resisted Nazism and so maintained national pride. There was little scope for accommodating the situation of the Jews: it was believed that they had gone "like lambs to the slaughter" and, anyway, their fate begged awkward questions about the role of local collaborators and "bystanders." Jews responded by submerging their specific experiences within the wider plight of the "victims of fascism." But at least this ensured that they would have some place in the pantheon of victimhood, even if what was uniquely Jewish about their plight was diluted.[5]

In West Germany restitution, reparations, and judicial processes ensured that the persecution of the Jews had to be faced, if only obliquely. Just as often, consciousness (and conscience) was displaced onto other seemingly irrelevant issues. Robert Moeller and Gilad Margalit have shown that during the 1950s West Germans who kept alive the memory of Wehrmacht POWs in Russia used the iconography of barbed wire fences and camp watch towers in posters that yoked memory about the Jewish victims of Nazi persecution to the cause of the soldiers who had made it possible.[6]

In the United States, too, there was an awareness of the atrocities perpetrated in Europe. It may not have taken the form with which we are familiar, and it was certainly more modest in scale, as befitted a quieter era, but it existed none the less. Jeffrey Shandler has revealed that throughout the 1950s American television networks featured documentaries, interviews, and live dramas that explored moral dilemmas through the medium of wartime history. A steady stream of memoirs and fictional treatments of the subject appeared in Yiddish and in English. Sidra DeKoven Ezrahi lists about 30 works published or conceived before the Eichmann trial, including bestsellers such as John Hersey's *The Wall* (1951) and *Mila 18* by Leon Uris (1961).[7]

Even in the realm of scholarship and historiography we need to rethink the extent to which the Nazi assault on the Jews was represented merely by an aporia. The collection and publication of documents, often within the context of national histories of the war or judicial investigations, and rudimentary accounts of Nazi persecution commenced much earlier than is commonly thought. The late 1940s and 1950s witnessed a spate of books on anti-Semitism, racism, prejudice, and totalitarianism that were all to some extent exploring the origins of the recent catastrophe. Eric Fromm, Wilhelm Reich, Theodor Adorno, Bruno Bettelheim, Arthur Koestler and Hannah Arendt all explored the Nazi debacle from various (often idiosyncratic) angles. While historical research was hindered by the unavailability of source materials, and Raul Hilberg's work remained *sui generis*, William Shirer produced a runaway bestseller, *Rise and Fall of the Third Reich*, that could not fail to remind readers that Nazism had been a criminal, racist and ultimately barbaric movement that had brought disaster to the Jews.[8]

Thus, by itself the trial of Adolf Eichmann did not create awareness of what we know today as "the Holocaust." The prosecution and commentators could not have handled the case unless it was framed by pre-existing concepts of the Third Reich, discourses about the "Nazi personality," and totalitarian theory. However, by presenting a mass of new information in a new format, the trial catalyzed consciousness and crystallized certain trends. This effect went through several phases. The trial had a brief, potent initial impact and then a longer-term and more subtle influence on the formation of memory and historical consciousness.

The Eichmann Trial and its Impact

The capture of Eichmann and the announcement that he would be tried in Israel triggered protests from the Argentinian government, whose sovereignty had been blatantly violated, and an international debate over the legitimacy of Israel's action.[9] Meanwhile, journalists and writers rushed to satisfy the curiosity kindled in the world public by the diplomatic row.

Between the announcement of Eichmann's capture and his execution several books were published that attempted to explain what sort of person he was, his alleged crimes and the nature of the regime he served. These potboilers presented Eichmann as a social misfit who had a troubled youth and suffered from the economic distress that afflicted Austria after World War I. Several claimed that when he was a schoolboy he was mistaken as Jewish and developed a hatred of Jews as a result of the torment he endured in the school playground. It was thereby assumed that Eichmann gravitated towards the Nazi Party and the SS because he was a misfit, a social and economic failure who resented Jews.[10]

The lurid biographies were based on a small amount of known data about Eichmann. Much information came from the testimony of Dieter Wisliceny, one of Eichmann's subordinates, and Rudolf Höß, commandant of Auschwitz, who ramped up Eichmann's Jew-hatred and authority in order to diminish their own guilt. Wisliceny's testimony, especially, seemed to offer evidence that Eichmann had a troubled childhood and youth that turned him into a fanatical hater of Jews.[11] This information was then fitted into the template provided by theorists such as Reich, Fromm and Adorno, and adjusted to accord with the body of psychological writing that emerged from psychiatric examinations of the defendants at Nuremberg. According to this line of thought fascism attracted a certain type of person suffering from feelings of inadequacy, repressed sexuality or insecurity. By 1960 it was the received wisdom that there was such a thing as "the Nazi personality," so Eichmann had to have the required characteristics and have been shaped according to the appropriate model of child development.[12]

Eichmann's ascribed personality was also fitted into the then existing concepts of the Third Reich. In 1960 it was commonly believed that Hitler was a criminal lunatic who had seized control of a modern state and ruled it with the help of a thuggish, corrupt and perverted clique. Thanks to the prevailing ideas about totalitarianism, it was thought wholly credible that one madman could have orchestrated the brutal actions of his no less warped minions and, through a combination of modern bureaucracy and technology, bent an entire continent to his will. According to this conception, power flowed exclusively from the top down and its bearers were able to deploy terror and force to implement their crazed policies.[13]

The early accounts of Eichmann's career agreed that thanks to his rise through the SD (*Sicherheitsdienst*, the SS security service) he came to share in this absolute power. He then zealously implemented the orders he received from above, notably for the "Final Solution," using all the terroristic methods at the disposal of the regime. Most authors exaggerated his authority, and at least one credited him with dreaming up the "Final Solution" and suggesting it to Himmler.[14] All agreed that Eichmann served at the apex of a ruthless dictatorship and was endowed with far-reaching powers by virtue of the concentration of authority at the top. Even though the Prosecution at Eichmann's trial presented a more realistic portrait of the man and the regime, it chose to reproduce the commonplace understanding of the Third Reich as a rigidly hierarchical, totalitarian regime. According to Gideon Hausner, Israel's Attorney General and the chief prosecutor, the Nazi leadership decided to launch a genocide against the Jews, inducted Eichmann into this plan as early as September 1939, and assigned him the task of refining the technique of mass murder during 1941. Hausner contended that from mid-1941 Eichmann was the driving force behind the implementation of the European-wide program of annihilation.[15]

The Prosecution treated Eichmann's own narrative, delivered in his prison memoirs, interrogation, and in open court, as little more than dissimulation. It dismissed his efforts to show that no plan of mass murder existed before mid-1941 and that he was repelled when exposed to the massacres committed by the *Einsatzgruppen* in Russia. His admittedly rambling and obtuse explanation of how he was eventually drawn into the genocide between mid-1941 and the Wannsee Conference in January 1942 attracted derision. Eichmann's efforts to explain that the subsequent implementation of the "Final Solution" was halting and constantly frustrated by conflicting jurisdictions within the Nazi regime met with disbelief and ridicule. This simply did not accord with what was then known about the dating of the decision to commence the genocidal program or the way the Nazi state worked.[16]

However, only a fraction of the investigation or the complex debate in the courtroom reached the general public. Coverage of the trial in the world's media became patchy once the trial opened. Unfortunately, the Chief Prosecutor, Gideon Hausner, devoted several days to a long and dull legal justification of the trial. It was necessary because Eichmann's counsel, Dr Robert Servatius, had lodged an objection that undermined the legitimacy and validity of the proceedings, but it could have been delivered in writing and summarized in open court. Instead, Hausner ploughed on diligently, the journalists grew impatient and many left. Even though in subsequent weeks the court saw dramatic and powerful testimony by witnesses and survivors, these too were surrounded by hours of tedium during which written documentation was introduced into the court record. Again, few journalists stayed the course and many missed the most shattering moments of testimony. In any case, the format of the trial reduced the narrative to numerous individual strands: the bigger picture got broken up and it was hard for newsmen to reassemble it in a way that sustained public attention. Consequently, the biggest impact on public awareness came from the instant biographies published *before* the trial and the reportage that appeared *afterwards*.[17]

Several of the post-trial publications were solid, responsible, and durable works of journalism that faithfully summarized the proceedings and interwove them with an account of Eichmann's life and crimes informed by the documents unearthed during the investigation.[18] However, the one destined to have the greatest impact was the capricious and contentious account by Hannah Arendt, *Eichmann In Jerusalem* (1963).

Arendt cast aspersions on the motives for the trial, falsely claiming that Eichmann's capture was engineered by David Ben-Gurion, Israel's prime minister, for the sake of gaining domestic and international advantage. She disparaged the determination to try Eichmann for crimes against the Jews because she believed his transgressions and the "Final Solution" were less an outgrowth of "eternal anti-Semitism" and more a symptom of generic racism inherent to totalitarian regimes. Eichmann merely exemplified how anyone would behave under totalitarianism, so the charges should have been framed universally as genocide and crimes against humanity. She was also convinced that one reason he could have acted as he did was that no one pointed out he was committing egregious acts, not even the Jews he encountered. On the contrary, Jews, especially Zionists, cooperated with him. For this reason it became essential to her thesis to show that Jewish leaders under Nazi rule had collaborated with the Nazis and she accused the court of suppressing the evidence of this collusion. Arendt also drew explosive conclusions about Eichmann's personality. To a great extent these were less empirically deduced conclusions and more confirmation of her preconceptions about the way she anticipated men would behave in a totalitarian society. She denigrated the evidence that Eichmann was anti-Semitic and had emerged from a far-right milieu. Rather, she maintained that he was an empty-headed careerist who jumped on the Nazi bandwagon and slid into the conduct of genocide because it was a job and he was a loyal, obedient civil servant — thus personifying the "banality of evil."[19]

Arendt's *Eichmann In Jerusalem*, even more than the trial, caused controversy and introduced millions to the issues surrounding the Nazi genocide against the European Jews. It stimulated hundreds of newspaper and magazine articles and dozens of books. Although scholarship on the "Final Solution" had been developing prior to the trial and the row over Arendt's thesis, it received an urgent fillip and from then on research accumulated relentlessly. It percolated into culture too, with poets and novelists reflecting on the trial and the debate. For example, Saul Bellow devoted part of *Mr. Sammler's Planet* to delivering a riposte. Sammler, a survivor, muses that "The idea of making the century's greatest crime look dull is not banal." In a pointed reference, he comments that "Everybody (except certain blue-stockings) knows what murder is." The literary historian Sidra DeKoven Ezrahi observes that it was "Hannah Arendt's interpretation of the trial which was the filter through which Americans were able to conceptualize what was otherwise a morass of indigestible, unintelligible facts." She supplied the raw material that creative figures turned into works of art.[20]

However, survivors of Nazi persecution and mass murder were outraged by Arendt's deliberate blurring of the line between victim and perpetrator. The trial and post-trial controversies marked a turning point for them, too.[21] The sight of survivors giving testimony, being treated for the most part with sympathy and respect for the tales of pain, grief, and loss that they had to tell, transformed public attitudes towards them and their own sense of self. Haim Gouri recalls: "The trial legitimized the disclosure of one's past. What had been silenced and repressed gushed out and became common knowledge." The same effect was apparent outside Israel. During the trial newspapers printed recollections by survivors and they were interviewed on radio and television. In the wake of the trial there was a discernible increase in applications to Yad Vashem by survivors who wished to record their memories. The great collections of audio and video testimony were borne out of this moment. The cyclical rise in the number of survivor memoirs also dates from this watershed.[22]

However, many of the effects of the Eichmann trial were latent and emerged only over time. International tension, such as the abortive invasion of Cuba in early 1961 and the Berlin Wall Crisis in the middle of the year, kept public attention focused on the present. In the wake of the Cuban missile scare in Autumn 1963 the universal "lessons" drawn from Eichmann's case that seemed relevant to the Cold War struck the most immediate, resonant chord. Works of scholarship and memoirs that reinforced the awareness of the singular Jewish experience took time to write and to appear in print. Survivors who would later endow chairs in Holocaust Studies, patronize research projects and the collection of testimony, or campaign for Holocaust museums and memorials still lacked the financial or political clout to achieve the goals that they now realized were possible.[23]

So, if the trial of Adolf Eichmann sowed the seeds the harvest was not reaped for another two decades. This collection of essays, based on a conference held at Southampton University on 8–9 April 2002, explores the gradual, halting emergence of "the Holocaust" in scholarship and culture after the Eichmann trial and why, when it finally crystallized, it took the form that it did.

After Eichmann

In her agenda-setting paper, Anita Shapira explains how the trial of Eichmann unexpectedly captured the imagination and the emotions of Israeli society, taking even Prime Minister David Ben-Gurion, by surprise. Hardened journalists as well as the man in the street and the field were transfixed by the courtroom drama day after day. Yet, when Hannah Arendt arrived in Israel to cover the trial she was utterly out of sympathy with its purpose or its effect. She disparaged Eichmann and had little empathy with the Jews either, be they his European victims or young Israelis. Her understanding of Eichmann and the Final Solution was consequently warped and the importance of her interpretation has waned. Ironically, it holds the greatest appeal for those critical of the Jewish leadership of the 1940s, Zionism, Israel and Ben-Gurion — the chief targets of Arendt's polemic. Arendt, who was a moral absolutist, has ended up giving succor to revisionists and relativists.

West Germans preferred to forget the Nazi years, but were never allowed to dismiss them fully. There was pressure from the Allied powers to compensate and memorialize the victims and dispense a measure of retribution against their tormentors. Konrad Adenauer understood that a degree of public remorse was politically necessary especially as the Federal Republic of Germany sought integration into the West European and international community. However, Adenauer had to balance against this the need to integrate former Nazis and their "fellow travelers." The tendency to play down Nazi crimes was courageously opposed by Fritz Bauer who, as Attorney General for the state of Hesse, initiated proceedings against Nazi criminals and contested the statute of limitations that would have frustrated further proceedings. Bauer played a significant part in bringing Eichmann to trial by passing information about his whereabouts to the Israelis and urging them to act because he feared that the West German judicial system could not deliver the fugitive to justice. The trial received extensive coverage in the West German media and thus helped to force a closer engagement with the Nazi past in the German Federal Republic.[24]

Eichmann's trial overlapped with a string of judicial reckonings against perpetrators in West Germany. As Jeffrey Herf shows, these very efforts to bring Nazi criminals to justice exposed the presence of former Nazis in the judiciary itself and revealed the liabilities of Adenauer's policy. A succession of trials and judicial scandals perpetuated the memory of Nazism and laid bare the inadequate "coming to terms with the past." Foreign politics also played a part. Willy Brandt's "Ostpolitik" inevitably brought in its train deliberation on the Nazi genocidal rampage in the east. The rebellious youth of the 1968 generation added steam to this process and continued their interest once they reached positions of power and influence in the united Germany of the 1990s. During the debates about the merits of intervention to prevent genocides abroad, Auschwitz was a natural point of reference for Germans weighing up their country's international responsibilities — a feature that would have astounded a politician of the Adenauer years.

In Italy, too, as Manuela Consonni shows, there was a reluctance to embrace the history of the war years during the first decades of peace. The country emerged from the war, and near civil war, divided into two political camps each of which championed a mythic version of the preceding era. For the right (Christian Democrats and liberals), Mussolini's rule was superficial and most of Italian society had been anti-fascist. For the left (socialists and communists), all Italy had succumbed to fascism except for the oppressed working classes who had resisted. In both camps there was an appetite for memoirs of heroic resistance fighters who had ended in the concentration camps or recollections of those sent to do forced labor in Germany. Jewish "racial deportees" did not fall into either category. Though Jews contributed to the flood of memoirs in the late 1940s they felt constraints on what they could say.[25]

As Manuela Consonni explains, there was little stomach for reminders about the anti-Jewish persecution from 1938 to 1943, or the "racial deportations" carried out by the Germans with Blackshirt collaboration, especially in northern Italy, in 1943–44. As in West Germany, during the 1950s Italy moved into a period of reconstruction and enjoyed its own "economic miracle." The past receded in importance. These were the years in which Primo Levi's memoir If This Is a Man was out of print and publishers showed no interest in reviving it. However, in the late 1950s something changed. A generation that had come of age since 1945, freed of wartime allegiances, showed a curiosity to find out what had happened then. Well before the capture of Eichmann interest in the fascist era and the war years was burgeoning, as illustrated by the opening of exhibitions on the subject, over-subscribed courses in recent Italian history, and the success that greeted a new edition of If This Is a Man. News of Eichmann's capture was injected into this receptive atmosphere. However, although the trial received extensive coverage in the Italian media, it did not provoke a direct confrontation with the wartime fate of the Italian Jews. Instead, the trial became a battleground over which the Left and the Right refought old struggles. Eichmann became a symbol of resentment against Germany rather than the cause for soul-searching about the role Italians played in the persecution and deportation of the Jews. Another three decades would pass before Italian politicians finally acknowledged the indigenous character of anti-Semitism in Italy and the role of Italians in dispatching 7,000 Italian Jews to Auschwitz.

Despite the fact that Britain avoided defeat and occupation, or perhaps because of this, during the postwar years there was limited interest in the catastrophe that befell the Jews of Europe. Britain had enjoyed a "good war" and had been on the winning side, the side that liberated the camps. Over 50,000 German and Austrian Jewish refugees found a haven in Britain before 1939, to be joined by several thousand survivors of the ghettos and camps after 1945. But beyond the Jewish communities there was little sustained or critical engagement with the fate of Europe's Jews.[26]

Suzanne Bardgett illustrates how this situation was reflected in the absence of any specific references to the persecution and mass murder of the Jews in the exhibitions of the Imperial War Museum, London, the official custodian of the history and memory of Britain at war. Interest amongst the museum's curatorial staff was first piqued by the transmission of the benchmark television history documentary series "World at War," which featured a program devoted to the genocide. In 1977, an exhibition on the history of the Third Reich was planned that was intended to contain some reference to the Nazi persecution of the Jews. The scale of this treatment proved controversial and the ensuing public row deterred the Museum from proceeding further. Nevertheless, in 1978 the Museum initiated an oral history program that embraced the experience of former Jewish refugees and survivors, and an educational project was inaugurated that made use of this important raw material. Small temporary exhibits began to tackle the Nazi genocide: in 1991 a display on the liberation of Belsen and in 1993 one on the Warsaw Ghetto Uprising. In the mid-1990s, after prolonged internal deliberation, the Museum decided to create a major, permanent exhibition devoted to the persecution and mass murder of the Jews during the Nazi years and World War II. This decision elicited a mixed response that suggested the public was still divided over the merits of recalling the misery of the Jews at the hands of the Nazis and their allies. However, the exhibition's tremendous success since its opening in 2000 has proven that there is a willingness to engage with this tragic history and to examine Britain's connection with it.

In Israel, not surprisingly, any problems that arose from commemoration of the genocide against the European Jews was not due to lack of interest. The entire country was saturated by this history. However, commemoration was always politicized and was as much about who was making the decisions about the subject and the mode of commemoration as it was about the past itself. Indeed, the politics of remembrance in Israel are complex and extend far beyond memorialization of the Shoah.[27]

Na'ama Sheffi shows how the music of Richard Strauss and Richard Wagner, which many Jews associated with Hitler and Nazis, has acted like a lightning rod for these sensitivities. After the November 1938 pogrom against the German and Austrian Jews, orchestras in the Jewish community of Palestine resolved not to play Wagner's music on the grounds that he was an anti-Semite and had been adopted as the Nazis' favorite composer. Strauss was also anathematized because he briefly served the Nazi regime as head of the Reich Chamber of Music. Feelings about Strauss soon eased, partly thanks to a benign revision of his reputation. But throughout the 1950s and 1960s, former refugees and survivors in Israel policed the informal ban on Wagner's music, bolstered by right-wing politicians and by some intellectuals. The trial of Eichmann heightened antipathies to anything bearing on the Third Reich and strengthened the hand of the survivors. Conductors, musicians, and music lovers respected their feelings but chaffed at the restriction. In the 1980s, sensing that the survivors were older and fewer in number, they sought to breach the embargo. It was their bad luck that the initiative coincided with a downturn in relations between Israel and West Germany, with Prime Minister Menahem Begin manipulating memories of the Nazi years for political advantage. Anything connected with the Third Reich was an explosive issue and the attempt backfired. As the band of survivors dwindled they increasingly used the law to enforce the ban, but conductors such as Zubin Mehta confidently expected that with the passage of time their influence would evaporate. He did not reckon with the arrival of a new cadre of activists: Orthodox Jews who used the ban symbolically to assert their agenda. They compensated for the fact that they were not themselves survivors by ratcheting up the level of rhetoric. Daniel Barenboim's efforts to play Wagner were greeted by ugly protests. To some music lovers, the answer to this continuing dilemma is to wait until the survivors all depart the scene before attempting to reintroduce Wagner into the repertoire of Israeli orchestras. But Sheffi asks if playing this waiting game is not a dereliction of the duty incumbent on Israelis to openly debate the issues raised by the Nazi genocide and precisely when it is most difficult.

In the 1990s, "Holocaust-era" issues proved capable of generating seemingly endless controversy on a global scale. Between 1985 and 2000, the news media and the political agenda of a dozen countries were dominated by a series of scandals, causes célèbres, legal disputes and "revelations" connected with the treatment of the Jews in the Nazi years. The conventional explanation attributed this to the end of the Cold War, the demise of the USSR, and the aging of the survivors. The collapse of the Soviet Bloc enabled the opening of previously closed archives in Eastern Europe and the declassification of intelligence documents in the West, prompting the discovery of incriminating documents that provided fuel for campaigns of redress and fed controversy. Meanwhile, survivors were determined to make one last push to seek justice and the redress of grievances remaining from the despoliation and exploitation that accompanied Nazi genocide.[28]

In my essay, I contest the conventional explanation, arguing that interest in moral and financial restitution for the victims of genocide had been building up steadily and was related to the burgeoning concern with genocide as a phenomena that had not gone away. In this sense the end of the Cold War and Soviet hegemony was significant because it unleashed the forces of murderous nationalism and ethnic hatred. It also allowed a recrudescence of neo-fascism and gave newly minted nationalist politicians the opportunity to revisit or revise the past. All of these developments were taken up and amplified by the new, diverse and much ramified global media. History and the experience of the survivors became commodities for the "infotainment" industry. They were explored and exploited not just because "memory studies" were in vogue, but because commercial interests could profit from them. Yet the popular response was not simply a result of ghoulishness. In postmodern societies, in which relativism had become de rigueur amongst intellectuals and those supposed to offer political and moral leadership, there was a widespread yearning for moral absolutes. "The Holocaust" with its easily grasped dimensions of good and evil seemed to offer that certainty.

Further evidence that "the Holocaust" has emerged as a "moral paradigm" since the Eichmann trial comes from Tim Cole's scrutiny of three "Holocaust museums" — Yad Vashem in Jerusalem, the United States Holocaust Memorial Museum (USHMM) in Washington, DC, and the exhibition at the Imperial War Museum, London. He demonstrates that each one of the trio is situated within a discrete national location and the moral tale it tells is inflected accordingly. At Yad Vashem the pedagogic and memorial functions of the site relate to the perception of Israel as a refuge from anti-Semitism and a power able and willing to deter another onslaught against the Jews. The USHMM symbolizes America as haven from oppression yet also interrogates the role and guilt of the "bystander" to genocide. The Imperial War Museum exhibition also examines the conduct of the "bystander" within the context of World War II and draws from it a universal message about resisting evil. In every case, memorialization is "utilized as a tool of nationalism."

Tony Kushner reaches similar conclusions in his critical evaluation of Britain's recently inaugurated Holocaust Memorial Day (HMD). The capture and trial of Eichmann obtained considerable coverage in Britain in 1960–61 and helped to lever awareness of the destruction of the European Jews out of the "private domain" of survivor and Jewish communities and into the public arena. However, attitudes did not change substantially until the 1990s when initiatives from survivor groups and Jewish activists succeeded in getting teaching about the mass murder of the Jews made mandatory in United Kingdom schools. The Holocaust exhibition at the Imperial War Museum also marked a greater willingness to examine and commemorate the specifically Jewish aspects of the war years. These developments proceeded relatively unopposed. But efforts to pass legislation for the trial of alleged Nazi war criminals in the United Kingdom were bitterly resisted and there was dissent over the merits of a day devoted to memorializing their victims. Kushner argues that HMD was ultimately established because it accorded with the ethos of a multicultural Britain and to some extent realized the aspirations of antiracist campaigners. However, he asks whether HMD really serves the needs of antiracism. As currently conducted it implies that genocide is an aberration in the modern world rather then "the norm." Certain groups assaulted and massacred by the Nazis are recalled while others are not, or occupy a subordinate level of remembrance. Above all, by implicitly celebrating Britain as a refuge, HMD evades a confrontation with the currents of racism in Britain that led to the poor treatment of survivors who reached the country after 1945. Holocaust Memorial Day thus becomes a comfortable moment of national self-congratulation.

The "nationalization," elevation, and virtual sanctification of "the Holocaust" has inevitably provoked a counter movement, especially amongst artists who see their role as challenging nostrums. James Young discusses an exhibition in New York of new artworks themed around Nazi imagery which provoked a storm because it ran against the grain of received wisdom and customary expectations. The artists explored not so much "the Holocaust" as the ways in which it was represented — or could be represented. This was a generational imperative because they had not themselves lived through that time. As Young observes: "For a generation of artists and critics born after the Holocaust, their experience of Nazi genocide is necessarily vicarious and hypermediated." Survivors and commentators who took umbrage mistook the enterprise as being about the representation of the events themselves, rather than exploring the question of how those who are distantly related to a particular, horrific past engage with the way it has been transmitted to them. This included taking a caustic look at the commercialization and commodification of history. Several artists in New York were fascinated by the highly marketable image of the perpetrator. Although representations of, and by, survivors have been legion and subjected to critical scrutiny, it is remarkable that representations of the perpetrators have escaped the same degree of inquiry. The iconic images of Eichmann in his Nazi salad days and later, in his box in Jerusalem, have been noted but hardly deconstructed. Thus a new generation of artists turned to the image of the killer as a device for interrogating the nature of evil and the question of responsibility.

While memory of the Final Solution was contended ground in Europe, America and Israel, it aroused conflicting responses amongst Arabs, too, though for very different reasons. Meir Litvak and Esther Webman argue that the persecution of Europe's Jews was always perceived by Arabs through the lens of its impact on Palestine and the Palestinians. After the war, Arabs believed that they were made to suffer the consequences of European anti-Semitism. To them, the State of Israel was established partly to assuage the guilt of the European nations. They considered that Palestinians had already paid the price for the Jewish refugees who migrated to Palestine from 1933 to 1939, allegedly displacing the indigenous Palestinian Arab population. Then came the flood of survivors after 1948, bolstering the demographic strength of Israel. In Arab eyes, the Jews were the victors of the war because they emerged with a state at the expense of the Palestinians. The details of the Eichmann case did not concern them greatly and the trial had little impact in the Arab world. Instead, Arab intellectuals pursued two, contradictory strategies in dealing with the Final Solution. On the one hand, because Jewish suffering at the hands of the Nazis was routinely used to justify the existence of a state for the Jews, they denied that it had happened at all or accused the Jews of complicity in their own destruction by collaborating with the Nazis. On the other hand, they implicitly accepted that it had happened, but claimed that the Jews deserved what they got due to undue prominence and financial domination over the societies in which they lived. From the 1970s, some Arab intellectuals in the Palestinian diaspora, notably Edward Said, who understood the disaster that had overwhelmed the Jews in the 1930s and 1940s, began to have an effect on opinion formers in the Middle East. They realized that judicious comparisons between the Nazi persecution of the Jews and the situation of displaced Palestinians, as well as those living under Israeli occupation, could supply potent propaganda. But this could only take effect if Palestinian publicists dropped vulgar Holocaust denial or crude endorsements of Nazi anti-Semitism. Sadly, this more enlightened, if calculating, attitude did not penetrate deeply and the continued conflict in the Middle East has only entrenched violently antagonistic attitudes.

Forty years after the trial of Adolf Eichmann, the wheel has turned full circle. Whereas the trial helped to shape the image of "the survivor" and promoted survivors as repositories of memory, attention amongst scholars and artists is now shifting back to explaining the perpetrators. Coverage of the trial helped to promote public awareness of the Final Solution and stimulated scholarly inquiries. Now, however, public commemoration of "the Holocaust" has led to its universalization and the progressive dilution of that which made the Nazi genocide against the Jews specific and unprecedented. Whereas it was hoped that teaching about the destruction of the European Jews would mute anti-Semitism, it has had little effect on the currents of anti-Jewish hostility emanating from certain Arab countries and from within sections of the world's Muslim population. Indeed, to them "the Holocaust" is at best an irrelevance or at worst an invention of the Jews. Many hoped in 1961 that after Eichmann the world would be a changed place, a better and safer place for Jews to live in. Sadly, those aspirations remain to be fulfilled.

NOTES

1 For accounts of the capture and trial of Eichmann, see Moshe Pearlman, *The Capture and Trial of Adolf Eichmann* (London, 1963) and Gideon Hausner, *Justice in Jerusalem* (London, 1967).

2 Raul Hilberg, "Opening Remarks; The Discovery of the Holocaust," in Peter Hayes (ed.), *Lessons and Legacies*, Vol. 1, *The Meaning of the Holocaust in a Changing World* (Evanston, 1991), pp. 13–15; Michael Marrus, "The Holocaust at Nuremberg," *Yad Vashem Studies*, No. 26 (1998), pp. 5–42. See also, Michael Marrus, *The Nuremberg War Crimes Trial, 1945–46* (New York, 1997); Donald Bloxham, *Genocide on Trial: War Crimes and the Formation of Holocaust History and Memory* (Oxford, 2001).

3 See, for example, Charles Y. Glock, Gertrude Selznick and Joe L. Spaeth, *The Apathetic Majority. A Study Based on Public Responses to the Eichmann Trial* (New York, 1966).

4 Tom Segev, *The Seventh Million: The Israelis and the Holocaust*, trans. Haim Watzman (New York, 1993). Compare, Judith Tydor Baumel, "'In Everlasting Memory': Individual and Communal Holocaust Commemoration in Israel," in Robert Wistrich and David Ohana (eds.), *The Shaping of Israeli Identity: Myth, Memory and Trauma* (London, 1995), pp. 146–70; and Yehiam Weitz, "Political Dimensions of Holocaust Memory in Israel during the 1950s," ibid., pp. 129–45; Anita Shapira, "The Holocaust: Private Memories, Public Memory," *Jewish Social Studies*, Vol. 4, No. 2 (1998), pp. 46–58; Dalia Ofer, "The Strength of Remembrance: Commemorating the Holocaust during the First Decade of Israel," *Jewish Social Studies*, Vol. 6, No. 2 (2000), pp. 24–55; Josef Gorny, *Between Auschwitz and Jerusalem* (London, 2003), pp. 127–33. Cf. Hanna Yablonka, *Survivors of the Holocaust: Israel after the War*, trans. Ora Cummings (London, 1999), pp. 274–8.

5 Pieter Lagrou, "Victims of Genocide and National Memory: Belgium, France and the Netherlands, 1945–1965," *Past and Present*, No. 154 (1997), pp. 187–222.

6 Robert Moeller, *War Stories: The Search for a Usable Past in the Federal Republic of Germany* (Berkeley, 1999); Gilad Margalit, "Divided Memory: Expressions of a United German Memory," in Dan Michman (ed.), *Remembering the Holocaust in Germany, 1945–2000: German Strategies and Jewish Responses* (New York, 2002), pp. 31–42.

7 Jeffrey Shandler, *While America Watches: Televising the Holocaust* (New York, 1999), pp. 1–69; Sidra DeKoven Ezrahi, *By Words Alone. The Holocaust in Literature* (Chicago, 1980).

8 Dan Michman, "Research into the Holocaust in Belgium and in General History and Context," in idem (ed.), *Belgium and the Holocaust: Jews, Belgians, Germans* (Jerusalem, 1998), pp. 3–38; David Cesarani "Memory, Representation and Education," in John K. Roth and Elisabeth Maxwell (eds.), *Remembering for the Future: The Holocaust in an Age of Genocide* (London, 2001), Vol. 3, Memory, pp. 231–6; Gavriel Rosenfeld, "The Controversy That Isn't: The Debate over Daniel J Goldhagen's *Hitler's Willing Executioners* in Comparative Perspective," *Contemporary European History*, Vol. 8, No. 2 (1999), pp. 249–73.

9 See Pearlman, *The Capture and Trial of Adolf Eichmann*, pp. 62–79; Raanan Rein, "The Eichmann Kidnapping: Its Effects on Argentine-Israeli Relations and the Local Jewish Community," *Jewish Social Studies*, Vol. 7, No. 3 (2001), pp. 101–30.

10 Comer Clarke, *Eichmann: The Savage Truth* (London, 1960); John Donovan, *Eichmann: Man of Slaughter* (New York, 1960); Henry Zeiger, *The Case Against Adolf Eichmann* (New York, 1960); Philip Paneth, *Eichmann: Technician of Death* (New York, 1960); Quentin Reynolds, *Minister of Death: The Adolf Eichmann Story* (London, 1961); Charles Wighton, *Eichmann: His Career and Crimes* (London, 1961); Moshe Pearlman, *The Capture of Adolf Eichmann* (London, 1961); Siegfried Einstein, *Eichmann: Chefbuchhalter des Todes* (Frankfurt/Main, 1961).

11 The available documentary evidence can be sampled in Centre de Documentation Juive Contemporaine [Joseph Billig] (ed.), *Le Dossier Eichmann* (Paris, 1960); World Jewish Congress, *Eichmann: Master of the Nazi Murder Machine* (New York, 1961); Randolph Braham, *Eichmann and the Destruction of Hungarian Jewry* (New York, 1961); Albert Wucher, *Eichmanns gab es viele: Eine Dokumentarbericht über die Endlösung der Judenfrage* (Munich, 1961); Rudolf Höβ, *Commandant in Auschwitz* (London, 1959).

12 Erich Fromm, *Escape from Freedom* (London, 1941); Wilhelm Reich, *The Mass Psychology of Fascism* (New York, 1942); Theodor Adorno et al., *The Authoritarian Personality* (New York, 1950); Gustav M. Gilbert, *Nuremberg Diary* (New York, 1947). For the continuation of this tendency, see Florence Miale and Michael Selzer, *The Nuremberg Mind: The Psychology of the Nazi Leaders* (New York, 1975), pp. 3–15; and Eric Zillmer et al., *The Quest for the Nazi Personality: A Psychological Investigation of Nazi War Criminals* (Hillsdale, NJ, 1995), pp. 4–19 and 177.

13 Otto Dov Kulka, "Major Trends and Tendencies in German Historiography on National Socialism and the 'Jewish Question'," in Yisrael Gutman and Gideon Greif (eds.), *The Historiography of the Holocaust Period* (Jerusalem, 1988), pp. 12–37.

14 Clarke, *Eichmann: The Savage Truth*, p. 81.

15 The indictment and opening speech are reproduced in [Gideon Hausner], 6,000,000 *Accusers. Israel's Case against Eichmann* (Jerusalem, 1961).

16 For the interrogation (in German) and trial record (in English), see *The Trial of Adolf Eichmann: Record of Proceedings in the District Court of Jerusalem*, 9 vols (Jerusalem, 1992–95). On the use of Eichmann's various memoirs and interrogation, see Irmtrud Wojak, *Eichmanns Memoiren: Ein Kritischer Essay* (Frankfurt, 2001); and Christian Gerlach, "The Eichmann Interrogations in Holocaust Historiography," *Holocaust and Genocide Studies*, Vol. 15, No. 3 (2001), pp. 428–53; and Christopher Browning, "Perpetrator Testimony: Another Look at Adolf Eichmann," in his *Collected Memories: Holocaust History and Postwar Testimony* (Madison, WI, 2003) pp. 3–36.

17 Shandler, *While America Watches*, pp. 118–21, 132; Lawrence Douglas, *The Memory of Judgment: Making Law and History in the Trials of the Holocaust* (New Haven, 2001), pp. 125–42. See also the remarkably perceptive Harold Rosenberg, "The Trial and Eichmann," *Commentary*, Vol. 32, No. 5 (November 1961), pp. 369–81.

18 Harry Mulisch, *Strafsache 40/61: Eine Reportage über den Eichmann-Prozeß* (Dermil, 1996) (first published in Dutch, 1961); Lord Russell of Liverpool, *The Trial of Adolf Eichmann* (London, 1962); Pearlman, *The Capture and Trial of Adolf Eichmann*; Bernd Nellessen, *Der Prozeß von Jerusalem* (Düsseldorf, 1964); Peter Papadatos, *The Eichmann Trial* (New York, 1964); Gideon Hausner, *Justice in Jerusalem* (London, 1967).

19 Hannah Arendt, *Eichmann in Jerusalem: A Report on the Banality of Evil*, revised and enlarged edn. (New York, 1964). For extensive and varied discussions of Arendt's version of the trial, see Steven Aschheim (ed.), *Hannah Arendt in Jerusalem* (Berkeley, 2001); and "Hannah Arendt and *Eichmann in Jerusalem*," special issue of *History & Memory*, Vol. 8, No. 2 (1996).

20 Randolph Braham (ed.), *The Eichmann Case: A Source Book* (New York, 1969), pp. 141–74. Saul Bellow, *Mr Sammler's Planet* (London, 1969), p. 17; Dan Michman, *Holocaust Historiography. A Jewish Perspective* (London, 2003), pp. 346–8; DeKoven Ezrahi, *By Words Alone*, p. 205.

21 Richard Wolin, "The Ambivalences of German-Jewish Identity: Hannah Arendt in Jerusalem," *History & Memory*, Vol. 8, No. 2 (1996), pp. 26–8; Dan Diner, "Hannah Arendt Reconsidered: On the Banal and the Evil in Her Holocaust Narrative", *New German Critique*, No. 71 (Spring/Summer 1997), pp. 177–90; Leora Bilsky, "Between Justice and Politics: The Competition of Storytellers in the Eichmann Trial," in Aschheim (ed.), *Hannah Arendt in Jerusalem*, pp. 232–54.

22 Haim Gouri, "Facing the Glass Booth," in Geoffrey H. Hartman (ed.), *Holocaust Remembrance: The Shapes of Memory* (Oxford, 1994), p. 154; Geoffrey H. Hartman, *The Longest Shadow: In the Aftermath of the Holocaust* (London, 2002), pp. 22 and 133–50; DeKoven Ezrahi, *By Words Alone*, pp. 109, 177–81, 205–16; Robert Rozett, "Published Memoirs of Holocaust Survivors," in Roth and Maxwell (eds.), *Remembering for the Future*, Vol. 3, pp. 167–71.

23 For sensitive studies of this time lag, see Edward T. Linenthal, *Preserving Memory: The Struggle to Create America's Holocaust Museum* (New York, 1995) and Rochelle Saidel, *Never Too Late to Remember: The Politics Behind New York City's Holocaust Museum* (New York, 1996). See also the polemical treatment in Peter Novick, *The Holocaust In American Life* (New York, 1999).

24 Jeffrey Herf, *Divided Memory: The Nazi Past in the Two Germanys* (Cambridge, MA, 1997), pp. 267–333; and Mary Fulbrook, *German National Identity after the Holocaust* (London, 1999), pp. 48–55; Harold Marcuse, *Legacies of Dachau: The Uses and Abuses of a Concentration Camp* (Cambridge, 2001), pp. 199–203, 206–7; Segev, *The Seventh Million*, pp. 324–6;

25 For the initial response to the liberation of the camps in a comparative perspective, see the essays by Annette Wieviorka, Pieter Lagrou and Daniele Jalla on, respectively, France, Belgium and Italy, in Marie-Anne Matard-Bonucci and Edouard Lynch (eds.), *La Libération des Camps et le retour des déportés* (Brussels, 1995).

26 See Tony Kushner, *The Holocaust and the Liberal Imagination* (Oxford, 1994).

27 On the politics of remembering in Israel, see Yael Zerubavel, *Recovered Roots: Collective Memory and the Making of Israeli National Tradition* (Chicago, 1995); Wistrich and Ohana (eds.), *The Shaping of Israeli Identity*; Susan Slyomovics, *The Object of Memory: Arab and Jew Narrate the Palestinian Village* (Philadelphia, 1998).
28 See Stuart E. Eizenstat, *Imperfect Justice: Looted Assets, Slave Labor, and the Unfinished Business of World War II* (New York, 2003), especially pp. 15–21; and Michael Bazyler, *Holocaust Justice: The Battle for Restitution in America's Courts* (New York, 2003).

The Eichmann Trial: Changing Perspectives

Anita Shapira

On the eve of the Jewish New Year 1960, a conversation took place, which was already an annual journalistic tradition, between the editors of the daily *Ma'ariv* and Prime Minister David Ben-Gurion. The interviewers ranged widely, exploring many diverse issues and areas. At a certain point they pointedly asked Ben-Gurion: what do you think was the most important event of the past year, internationally, in Israel and the Jewish world? When it came to the world at large, Ben-Gurion was quick to respond: decolonization would transform the face of the globe. But an outstanding single most important event of the year for Israel and Judaism? Ben-Gurion hesitated, undecided. Like a backstage prompter, Shalom Rosenfeld suggested to him: "Eichmann? ..." And Ben-Gurion answered, almost in a declamation: "Yes, that operation vouchsafes the rule of historical justice in the life of our people, thanks to the existence of the State of Israel."[1] Four months had passed since the electrifying announcement in the Knesset of Eichmann's capture in Argentina by the Mossad and abduction to Israel for trial. But Ben-Gurion had not yet grasped just how significant all this was.

The Eichmann trial was officially opened on 12 April 1961; five days later Gideon Hausner, Israeli Attorney General, read the indictment. It was one of those days when time seemed to stand still. The poet Haim Gouri wrote about an "ambience of a grand moment," a day he would remember all his life.[2] A few days later, during his Independence Day broadcast to the nation, Ben-Gurion commented on two significant events of the past year: the discovery of the remains of Bar Kokhba fighters in the Judaean desert and the Eichmann trial. Both, Ben-Gurion stressed, were the product of the independence of the Jewish people in its own sovereign land.[3] In that speech, two founding myths of the State of Israel symbolically met: the myth of the heroism of the Jewish people in its ancestral land, and the myth of the Holocaust. One underscores the historical bond between the people and the land, forging a vital link with the age-old landscape and the nation's pristine youth. The other inscribes the Jewish people's unique fate, the bloody reckoning between Jews and non-Jews, the commitment to the people, and the state that was established as a lesson from the past and pledge for the future. One draws its sustenance from antiquity, the experience of a free people in its ancient land, its struggle for freedom, its military prowess in a distant past, its national pride. The other centers on the more recent past, the reality of life in the diaspora, an endangered minority among belligerent nation-states, the sense of Jewish powerlessness in the face of violence, profound disillusionment with the civilized world. From the vantage of 1961, it is doubtful anyone could perceive the extent to which the Eichmann trial was a historic watershed marking the first phase in the waning of one myth and the ascent of the other. Yet today it is possible to see Ben-Gurion's remarks on Israel's 13th Independence Day in 1961 as emblematic of a historical conjuncture — one that had been reached unawares and which today seems almost self-evident.

At the time, during the 11 months that elapsed between the capture of Eichmann and the beginning of the trial, the questions in the eye of public debate revolved around the legal aspects connected with the abduction: was it possible to try Eichmann in Israel, a state that had not existed at the time the crimes he was charged with had been committed, and on the basis of legislation postdating the events? Many, Jews and non-Jews alike, were troubled by the question whether it was proper for Jews, as Eichmann's victims, to bring him to trial and render judgment. Ben-Gurion proclaimed that an Israeli court had every right to try Eichmann and unfold the story of the Final Solution before the Jewish people and the world, a statement that sparked hostile responses. Richard Crossman, a staunch friend of Israel, characterized the frame of the trial as a "combination ... of Old Testament ethics and modern sensationalism." Crossman was apprehensive lest Eichmann's trial give an impression of tribal vengeance: then "its net effect in the West will be to ferment a great deal of suppressed but real anti-Jewish feeling."[4] Karl Jaspers was prepared to accept Eichmann's being tried by an Israeli court, but hoped it would then pass on its conclusions to an international court for final sentencing.[5] Nachum Goldmann, the *enfant terrible* of world Jewish and Israeli politics, endorsed the idea of a United Nations tribunal. Hannah Arendt thought Germany should try Eichmann, and was upset that the Bonn government had not requested his extradition.[6] Philosophers, theologians and other leading personalities appealed to Ben-Gurion to agree to allow a "neutral" disinterested authority to bring Eichmann to justice. While all the states under former Nazi occupation had tried and sentenced war criminals and none doubted their fundamental right to do so, the Jews were suspected of vindictiveness: they were bent on vengeance, not justice. Now, 40 years after the trial, those legalistic questions seem irrelevant. Today none question the right of Israel to bring a Nazi criminal to trial for crimes against the Jewish people and crimes against humanity. The judicial aspects of the trial are no longer of importance.

The opening speech by Gideon Hausner spoke in the name of six million victims, thus appropriating to the State of Israel the right to represent the Jews who had perished and to speak in their name. Indeed, no other polity had claimed a right to represent those many millions. The countries in Europe, for the sake of whose murdered citizens the trial was conducted, did not oppose Israel's claim to representing millions of their dead citizens. Nor did Jewish communities complain they had no part in the trial or demand formal representation. Almost by default, the State of Israel had adopted the community of Holocaust victims as its own. They seemed to hover like silent shades from the world beyond gazing down at the living world below, granting it depth of meaning and justification, solace and hope.

The Eichmann trial was *the* most important media event in Israel prior to the Six Day War. During the trial's first two weeks, the Jerusalem Civic Center Beit ha-Am was packed to the rafters with foreign journalists from all over the world. They had arrived in search of shocking "news," and soon became weary of the legal routine. The prophecy of Binyamin Galai (a prominent Israeli journalist and writer) came true: "at the end of a month the foreign correspondents will pack their bags and leave, not to return until the final monologue of the final act."[7] The seats at the hall of justice were now taken by local people. Despite all the cynical and mocking comments by Israelis on the trial — such as "Hausner vs. [Robert] Servatius [the defense attorney], what's the score?" or "what's the latest word from the festival? Are they playing the anthems?" — Shulamit Har-Even noted that "the entire country is living the trial in a way that's unprecedented, there's never ever been something like this."[8] The transistor radio became consumer item number one across the country. Young and old could be seen radio in hand everywhere — in constant earshot of the broadcast from Beit ha-Am. And from among the throngs of ordinary people embarking on that horrifying trip in time and space the survivors gradually began to emerge.

While the audience in the hall of justice changed, two persons remained whose personalities represented two Jewish civilizations: Hannah Arendt and Haim Gouri. They were not acquainted and it is doubtful whether Arendt, a German-Jewish intellectual and US citizen then in her fifties, who had gained international fame with her 1951 book, *The Origins of Totalitarianism*, paid any attention to Gouri, a native-born sabra, barely 40 years old, though already well-known in Israel as a gifted poet. This was a virtual encounter between two individuals who had come to the trial from different places in search of different things. A philosopher noted for her critical approach to politics, society and humankind, highly skeptical of any establishment qua establishment, Arendt had come to Jerusalem, dispatched by *The New Yorker*, to report on the trial. She had arrived at Beit ha-Am expecting to find a carefully staged event: Ben-Gurion pulling the strings behind a show trial in which the prosecutor-cum-associates were under the prime minister's direct instructions. She expected the trial would reflect what she deemed as the provinciality and utter pettiness of the Ben-Gurion government — such as the "contacts" and nepotism alluded to at the very beginning of her book as the reason why Hausner had been assigned a translator who was inferior. In general, Hausner struck this German-Jewish political theorist with a Ph.D. from Heidelberg like a boor just arrived from the boondocks of rural Galicia, still bearing the stamp of that coarse province that had pretensions to being German. Arendt came equipped with a superficial knowledge about the relation between religion and the state in Israel. She was quick to comment on the irony inherent in the prosecution's criticism of the Nuremberg laws, which prohibited sexual relations between Jews and non-Jewish *Volksgenossen*, given the fact that the laws in Israel did not allow for marriage between persons of different faiths.[9] She had prepared to witness and report on a courtroom spectacle: one that would be as sensational as the Nuremberg tribunal, aimed at teaching the world a "lesson" relevant to relations between Jews and Gentiles, Jews and Arabs and Jewish identity.[10] In her eyes, the trial was a pretext Ben-Gurion was utilizing to stress the collusion between the Nazis and the Mufti of Jerusalem, while at the same time carefully avoiding any accusations against high-ranking government officials in West Germany of past involvement in Nazi Germany and complicity in its crimes.[11] Arendt had come to Jerusalem determined not to be swept up by the tide of sentimentality: she was resolved to keep a cool and sober head. The solitary defendant in the glass-encased dock should have a fair trial: she was opposed to any attempt to broaden the trial beyond that specific individual and the crimes for which he had been indicted. Arendt came as an investigator intent on studying the character of a mass murderer (or desk-murderer or any other suitable term for a modern bureaucrat); as she herself noted, she came to report on Eichmann's conscience.[12] And indeed, she lived up to all her expectations. And found everything she had expected to.

Haim Gouri, by contrast, came to Beit ha-Am from a totally different world: he was a native son, educated in Palestine. Born in Tel Aviv in 1921, he had attended the Kaduri Agricultural School, like Yigal Allon and Yitzhak Rabin, two of the most outstanding figures of his generation and circle. Like them he had joined the Palmah, the elite military unit of Jewish youth in the *Yishuv* (Jewish community in Palestine), and later entered Mapam, the left-wing party many Palmah fighters belonged to, which was highly critical of Ben-Gurion's leadership. He looked at the world beyond through the spectacles acquired in his native land. For him, Israel was the vital hub, both of the wider world in general and the Jewish world in particular. The State of Israel had been conceived as proof of Zionism's vision, which taught that Jews had no future except in their own sovereign state. The "new Jew" — a handsome, courageous young man, weapon in hand — was for Gouri the ideal of Israeli youth. Though he had been abroad and had even met survivors while in Europe in 1947–48, his familiarity with Jews from "over there" was superficial. It was devoid of that native intimacy which infused his bonds with members of his own generation in Israel.[13] He was somewhat familiar with the story of the Holocaust, but only in a fragmentary and selective way.[14] Despite his "Palestinocentric" approach, Gouri came to Beit ha-Am imbued with the feeling he was about to participate in a singular historic event, and a strong sense of being a part of the collective plaintiff in the trial. From the very outset, he drew a clear line between "ours" and "his."[15] This was a "class action" — the Jewish people vs. Adolf Eichmann — and he knew where he belonged.

Ultimately, the differing approaches of Arendt and Gouri were driven by different objectives. Arendt was intent on analyzing Eichmann and probing the nature of the Israeli justice system. Gouri had no predefined objectives: he was somewhat apprehensive of what he might learn in the trial, prepared for what could be disturbing revelations — but no more than that. Arendt came with set views and attitudes, so it is hardly surprising she found what she was looking for. Gouri entered the courtroom with the preconceptions and bias of the average Israeli, but left the trial a changed man. Arendt and Gouri constitute two models for different modes of response to the same event. Here I shall also explore how their perceptions of the trial influenced public dialogue over the short and longer term.

*

Arendt argued that this was the trial of a single individual, Adolf Eichmann, and that the prosecution's task was to establish his guilt. In her view, the Holocaust was not the story of what had happened to the Jews. Rather, it was what the Germans had done, their motives and the true account of the facts.[16] In Arendt's eyes, the narrative of Jewish suffering was something secondary, not directly relevant: it was one of those sentimental details that could cloud the clarity of the full picture. So she concluded that most of the witnesses were in fact superfluous: after all, they did not know Eichmann and were unable to testify directly on his role in the Final Solution, although there were some exceptions whose testimony touched her heart, such as Zindel Grynszpan and the German Anton Schmidt (whom Abba Kovner recalled in his statement).[17] She also speaks with evident respect about Zivia Lubetkin, one of the leaders of the Warsaw ghetto uprising. But Arendt remains adamant: none of those testimonies have any place in this court of law, since they have no direct bearing on Eichmann's story. The available documentation and Eichmann's testimony are, Arendt contends, the authoritative sources for adjudicating the case. Moreover, the witnesses were unable to shed light on a topic of central interest to Arendt, namely the *conscience* of Eichmann the man. For Gouri and most other Israelis, the dominant riveting experience in the trial was the stark testimony of the survivors. It is true that the documents were more incriminating; yet whenever the prosecution presented such documents, the bored journalists headed straight for the snack bar.[18]

Something in the symbiotic chemistry between the witnesses and the public transformed the Holocaust for the first time into a human tale, accessible, connected with real lives, events that happened to our neighbors next door. "None of us left here the same person," Gouri observed after a month of testimony.[19] After the witnesses had finished testifying, Gouri commented: "Only the many witnesses who came forward to speak were able to convey to us a bit [of the reality] of those times, those places."[20] What for Arendt were sentimental tales that blurred the general picture was to Gouri's mind the core of a new ethos, another conception of reality, a bid to "reach out for the whole fuller picture through a long series of encounters with the actual details of that experience." Encountering the witnesses, a new energy was generated, a sense of "yes, now I really understand."[21] The differences in how Gouri and Arendt viewed the matter of testimony reflect two different schools in research on the Holocaust: is the focus on the perpetrators' deeds or on what the victims suffered? If the actions of the evildoers are foregrounded, then it is but a short leap to examining the question of evil more generally in philosophical and universal terms. If the spotlight is on the suffering of the Jews as real flesh-and-blood human beings, not as a more abstracted generalization in the sense of "victims," then the Holocaust is a unique event, "Jewish" in its very pith and essence.

Thus, the differing approach to testimony and witnesses points to fundamental differences in perspective. These remain two distinct schools in Holocaust research down to the present. Arendt's and Gouri's differences in approach also stemmed in part from the available languages: Hebrew vs. German. Gouri learned about the Holocaust from testimony presented largely in Hebrew, and the prosecutor's statement was in his mother tongue. But his information about the documents was mediated, second- or thirdhand, since their language was for him a closed book. Arendt was in just the opposite linguistic boat. She did not understand Hebrew, and her native German was the language of Eichmann and the documents. Constant simultaneous translation notwithstanding, the understanding of the original is important, not just for rapid absorption of the experience but for the depth and breadth of its personal psychological impact.

Hausner repeatedly asked the witnesses: "Why didn't you resist?" From the remove of 40 years later, the question seems to bespeak an incomprehensible arrogance towards the survivors on the part of Jews who had lived in the relative safety of Palestine during the war. But I suspect that Hausner repeated that particular query in order to pry open the door to answers by the survivors that could cast new light on the situation in the territories under Nazi occupation. And that for the first time, they would explain to the Israeli public just how distant that question was from actual reality. Arendt and Gouri both agree: the question was inappropriate. The Jews behaved no differently than others under the Nazi boot, such as Russian POWs, Poles and Gypsies. They all went to their death without resisting, since defiance led to agonies that made the horror of death pale by comparison. Arendt, fully in character, added a word of critique: presenting the story of events exclusively from the Jewish perspective distorted that absence of resistance, which was in fact a general phenomenon.[22]

But Arendt returns to this sensitive question via another venue, harsh and offensive, by raising the charged issue of collaboration and complicity by Jewish leaders in the destruction of their communities. She stresses that her criticism here is rooted in her own background as a Jew: "To a Jew this role of the Jewish leaders in the destruction of their own people is undoubtedly the darkest chapter of the whole dark story."[23] While she has some sense of empathy for the people sent to the slaughter, she has none for these *Judenrat* leaders. She expected these men to pursue a policy of non-cooperation with the Nazis. If the Jews had not been organized, she argues, there would have been much chaos and suffering, but far fewer Jews would have been annihilated.[24] At the time, when the comments in her book on the collaboration by Jewish leaders in the extermination unleashed a storm of criticism, she defended herself by contending: "This issue came up during the trial, and it was of course my duty to report it."[25] But the actual truth is that the issue was not raised at the trial. Moreover, the issue of the *Judenräte* had no relevance for the guilt or innocence of the accused. Why did Arendt, who repeatedly criticized the prosecution for broaching irrelevant matters in the trial, find it necessary to raise this matter? In a long and convoluted sentence, she claims that the prosecution avoided presenting this the "darkest chapter" in order not to embarrass the Bonn government (though parenthetically one may wonder why this was likely to embarrass the Adenauer government more than other matters brought up in the trial's course). In that same sentence, she labels her obligation to disclose that dark chapter "almost a matter of course." This chapter, Arendt contends, "accounts for certain otherwise inexplicable lacunae in the documentation of a generally over-documented case."[26] She claims that the prosecution's case against Eichmann would have been weakened if it were established that the naming of individuals who were sent to their doom had not been his job but that of the Jewish administration. The clear distinction drawn by the prosecution between persecutors and victims would have been seriously compromised.[27] In other words, Arendt decides it is her solemn duty to narrate the darkest chapter in the whole dark story, since she believes the prosecution has sought for whatever reasons to blur, conceal and weaken the matter of the cooperation between Jewish leaders and the Nazis.

Her critique of the *Judenräte* relates to her interpretation of Eichmann's testimony. On principle, Arendt tends to take what Eichmann says at face value. She believes him when he states he persuaded the *Judenräte* in Theresienstadt and elsewhere to willingly carry out the Nazi orders: "If the person in question does not like what he is doing, the whole work will suffer . . . We did our best to make everything somehow palatable," Eichmann commented, and Arendt goes on to note ironically: "No doubt they did; the problem is how it was possible for them to succeed."[28] The source for that "gentle persuasion" is, as mentioned, Eichmann's own testimony. But did the leaders of the Jewish community actually see things in this light? The seemingly delicate symbiosis between the hangman and his victim, between the snake and its prey, which it paralyzes before the deadly bite, may appear refined and sophisticated to an outside observer who sees only the result: namely the victim's passivity, accepting with acquiescence the lethal sentence. But can one call the terror that paralyzes the victim to the point of submission to his or her destruction "cooperation"? This story is reminiscent of the question asked again and again over the years regarding the show trials in Moscow with veteran Bolsheviks, commanders in the Red Army, outstanding intellectuals in the dock: "Why did they confess?" The phenomenon of prominent persons of proven courage marching to stand before the tribunal, accepting blame for the worst of possible crimes, thus condemning themselves to death, was incomprehensible to the Western world. After all, they could have recanted in court, retracting their confession! Koestler's *Darkness at Noon* attempted to solve the riddle by explaining it psychologically: the condemned man accepts guilt because he believes his conviction and ultimate death will benefit the regime, a kind of final sacrifice for the glory of the revolution.[29] Today we know the truth: in brutal regimes such as the totalitarian societies Hannah Arendt described so well, there is no "gentle persuasion," since the fear of punishment, always physical, is ever-present. And there is little sophistication associated with this, though much humiliation and pain.[30] Even when Eichmann spoke politely to the *Judenrat* leaders, he stood before them as a master over life and death. He never gave them the option of choice: whether to cooperate or not. The scope of freedom Arendt attributes to *Judenrat* members reveals just how divorced from reality her ideas were on everyday life under a regime of Nazi terror. Her critics were correct when they argued that she was trying here to corroborate her more general notions on the collaboration between oppressors and oppressed in a totalitarian society — a form of acquiescent cooperation that for Arendt was one of the defining characteristics of such regimes.

But it appears there is another, less obvious element involved here: Arendt claims that Hausner's question "Why did you not resist" was a smokescreen designed to conceal the real question that should have been asked: "Why did you collaborate in the destruction of your own people, and, eventually, in your own ruin?"[31] This argument reveals how close these two questions are linked in her own consciousness. Arendt expresses great respect for those Jews who did indeed resist. The testimony she most praises is that of Zivia Lubetkin. She even explains that Ben-Gurion had intended to have the rebels testify that their rebellion was the work of the Zionist activists. But his plan was disappointed, since the rebels told the truth: the fighters in their ranks had come from all strata of Jewish society. Arendt repeatedly emphasizes that testimony by the rebels on Jewish resistance was not relevant to the trial. However, she nonetheless finds praise for this evidence: after all, the testimony of these rebel fighters shattered the impression of general collaboration by the Jews in their own destruction, the "stifling, poisoned atmosphere which had surrounded the 'Final Solution.'"[32] Thus Arendt, in her own way, makes the same old accusation against the Jews, who purportedly went "like sheep to the slaughter." Arendt's flight from the moral stranglehold of the *Judenräte* to the ethical purity of the rebels parallels the shame felt by young Israelis faced with Jewish helplessness. "We were ashamed of the Holocaust as of a terrible and visible deformity. And we had embraced the heroism [of the rebels] as a token of pride, allowing us to hold high our heads" — this is how Gouri described the relation of his generation to the Holocaust and heroism prior to the trial.[33] Arendt would seem to have expressed a similar attitude, although wrapped in a far more sophisticated covering. Gouri cites a survey done on the eve of the trial among Israeli youth. Many stated that had they been "there," they would have acted differently.[34] Isn't Arendt's argument similar?

Gouri takes a different tack. Initially he emphasizes the contradiction between the Jerusalem streets, vibrant with youthful vitality, and the humiliation and powerlessness described in the courtroom. The tension and conflict between the healthy and proud youngsters dancing in the streets on the eve of Independence Day but a few days after the beginning of the trial, on the one hand, and the picture of past reality emerging in the courtroom, on the other, constitute the hidden layer in the plot: he mentions an anecdote of a schoolgirl who reacts to her teacher's account of the Holocaust by asking: "why didn't the IDF [Israel Defense Forces] go to help the Jews."[35] In the light of a witness testifying on the uprising in the death camp, Sobibor, Gouri reflects on what might have happened had paratroopers of the German and Balkan sections of the Palmah met thousands of strong and bold Jewish youths like the witness.[36] As if the arrival of several dozen young combatants from Palestine could have fundamentally changed anything in occupied

Poland... Just as Eichmann was giving testimony on the "merchandise for blood" deal, word was received in the journalists' snack bar that Israel had launched a missile into space. "The telegraph offices that had become accustomed to cabling the tales of terror to the four corners of the globe suddenly began to send thousands of words that were different," Gouri observed with relief. The chasm between present strength and past weakness made him dizzy.[37] There is something soothing and conciliatory in the reality outside the courtroom walls. Israel's physical strength constitutes a kind of warranty against the horrors recounted within. Yet, as the story of the Holocaust becomes ever more familiar and accessible via witness testimony, Gouri repents his (and other young Israelis') sin of arrogance: "We must ask forgiveness from the countless many whom we so harshly judged in our hearts, we who had been outside that circle. And we judged them many times without asking ourselves what possible right we had to do so."[38]

Rejection of the accusation that Jews went like "sheep to the slaughter" brings both Arendt and Gouri to subversive conclusions. Arendt finds a common ground of guilt between the Jews and their persecutors. For Arendt, the moral ambiguity that sprang from the alleged collaboration shattered the simple dichotomy of victim and victimizer, guilty and innocent. It also transposed the question of the Holocaust onto a universal plane connected with totalitarianism more generally and the distinctive psychology such regimes generate, over and beyond the confines of any one individual nation.[39] Gouri, by contrast, limits his focus to the Jewish people. He discovers in himself a new empathy and understanding for the Jews he did not feel prior to the trial. Yet that newly acquired insight goes hand in hand with a subversive question: what did *we* do during the time of terror? "I say: while the Jewish people was being annihilated over there, back here ... the brothers of the murdered did not do what might have been expected in response to the reports they were receiving from over there."[40] The Jewish masses were now acquitted of the charge of going "like sheep to the slaughter." But that acquittal transferred the gravity of guilt from the people "there" to the people "here": "who is prepared to place their hand upon their heart and swear that the Jewish *Yishuv* in this country did all it could do to sound the alarm, to uncover the truth, to challenge, to save?"[41]

Nowhere in the 260 pages of her book does Arendt accuse herself or her colleagues who escaped from the burning ground in Europe to the safety of Manhattan's shore of having done nothing to help rescue the Jews. In response to Gershom Scholem, who had accused her of a lack of love for the people of Israel, Arendt declared that she had never felt love for a "collective," whether a people or a class, but only for those who were close to her.[42] This apparently helps to explain her lack of any sense of personal guilt. Gouri's sense of guilt springs from his identification with a national collective which bears responsibility for its different tribes. The closer the murdered Jews became to him, the nearer the blame for their death. By contrast, Arendt combats the tribalistic notion that "the whole world is against us." Hence, she is careful to emphasize any information pointing to non-Jews who helped Jews, as proof that there were points of light in the darkness that descended on Europe. And with that same determination Arendt distances herself from the Jews, turning them into a kind of "objective" model of a universal problem: she emphasizes she is part of the Jewish people, yet does her best to keep the Jews at arm's length, touching yet not touching her.

> The characteristic line that runs through Eichmann's personality is his total lack of character. He belongs to that same faceless army of bureaucrats who continued to operate the wheels of the Third Reich after it was already crystal clear that defeat was inevitable. In contrast with Himmler, Eichmann, as far as is known, had no views or beliefs whatsoever, nor did he possess any special ambitions aside from the desire to rise in official rank. Nor can we discover in him any special signs of cruelty, heartlessness or perversity that would have "qualified" him to serve as a criminal of such a high ranking.... Even in terms of Nazi criteria, there was something remarkable in the manner in which Eichmann was able to execute all the orders he received.

That paragraph was written not by Hannah Arendt but by Richard Crossman, before the trial in Jerusalem, in an essay entitled "The Faceless Bureaucrat."[43] Crossman articulated a perception that was rife among Israeli and foreign journalists regarding the petty nature of Eichmann the man contrasted with the enormity of the crimes he was charged with. In the dock sat a thin, balding, middle-aged man, with the demeanor of a petit bourgeois. There was nothing in his external appearance that might connect him with that same brutal, cunning official so clever at leading his victims astray, indefatigable in the zeal and resourcefulness with which he had hunted down Jews and sent them to their death. Eichmann was poorly cast for the lead role in the great drama of the century. He made the impression of a minor official, a colorless bureaucrat, obedient and efficient, but not a person one might associate with genocide. "Many will reflect," wrote Gouri at the time of Eichmann's testimony, "what remains of the SS man after you take off his boots and remove his gun."[44] Hannah Arendt looked at the man in the glass cage, examining him in terms of the concepts she had acquired through her earlier research, and the information she had gathered on the Holocaust, largely from her reading of Raul Hilberg's history of the Holocaust.[45] She despised Eichmann as only an upper-class educated German Jew can loathe someone from the dregs of society, in keeping with Alan Bullock's characterization of the Nazi leadership as the gutter elite.[46] Every sentence he articulated provokes her bitter scorn. She analyzes the superficialities that make up his recurrent formulations, his impoverished language, the language of the bureaucrat. In her view, his inability to speak reflects an inability to think or to grasp reality from the viewpoint of the other.[47] But precisely because of his wretched intellectual capacity, Arendt is inclined to believe him when he asserts that he is not "a dirty bastard in the depths of his heart" and that his conscience would trouble him only if he "had not done what he had been ordered to do — to ship millions of men, women, and children to their death with great zeal and the most meticulous care."[48] He did not hate Jews, Arendt insists, and continues in what is probably the key passage in her book:

> Alas, nobody believed him … the judges did not believe him because they were too good, and perhaps also too conscious of the very foundations of their profession, to admit that an average, "normal" person, neither feeble-minded nor indoctrinated nor cynical, could be perfectly incapable of telling right from wrong.[49]

This miserable creature behind the glass pane cannot possibly be the source for orders that led millions to their death. Consequently, Arendt dismissed impromptu all his statements in which he claimed he was responsible for the murder of millions. It is true that at the end of the war he bragged he would go to his grave happy in the knowledge he had five million Jews on his conscience. He continued to boast in the interview he gave to the pro-Nazi journalist Sassen 12 years later. Eichmann also bragged that he had invented the Nazi ghetto, the idea of sending the Jews to Madagascar and the ghetto camp Theresienstadt. Arendt thinks these are empty boasts and that Eichmann was a man who received orders and executed them efficiently, with the dedication of a faithful official, but nothing more.[50] The contradiction between the vileness of his actions and the ludicrousness of the man who perpetrated them awakens her sarcasm: "Despite all the efforts of the prosecution, everybody could see that this man was not a 'monster', but it was difficult indeed not to suspect that he was a clown."[51] She repeatedly returns though to her basic motif: Eichmann was not a zealot, not an ideologue. He did not hate Jews. He was a simple person who believed conscientiousness meant allegiance to the Führer and obedience to his orders, right to the end. For that reason, even after Himmler abandoned the plan of annihilating the Jews, Eichmann continued to stick to his oath and the project of murder: ultimately, he was obedient to the orders and wishes of the Führer.[52] What distinguishes Eichmann as a criminal is that he "commits his crimes under circumstances that make it well-nigh impossible for him to know or to feel that he is doing wrong."[53] That is the "banality of evil."

The conclusion to be drawn from Arendt is that under a totalitarian regime, any normal person can become a mass murderer. From there it is but a short step to the postulate that in every human heart there lurks a human beast, and under certain circumstances any person can transgress the rules of human morality. Such an assertion waters down individual responsibility: if Eichmann and his comrades are the products of a regime and are incapable of distinguishing between good and evil, then it is difficult to hold them accountable. If all are guilty, then none is really guilty. There is indeed a contradiction between Arendt's downplaying of Eichmann's direct responsibility and her unequivocal support for his execution. The expanded interpretation of Arendt served to extract the "banal murderer" from the specific context of the Holocaust and Jewish history, transposing him to the more universalized plane of totalitarian regimes and their dangers, and then to the system of relations between those who command and those who obey in any society or regime. In opposition to the specific Jewish (and pro-Zionist) lesson to be drawn from the Holocaust — against dependency on others, against weakness, in favor of a sovereign state capable of defending Jews — Arendt places the story of the Holocaust within the more universalizing frame of human evil in its modern variant, genocide. In her view, the solution does not lie in separation within the confines of a national state but within a world system of justice. That is why genocide must be viewed as a crime against *humanity*, not solely against the specific victims murdered.

*

One of Arendt's more infuriating tendencies is her didacticism. Like a born teacher, she preaches to one and all inside the courtroom and beyond on what is proper behavior and even passes out grades on performance. She tells Ben-Gurion how he should run the state; how Hausner should handle the prosecution in the trial; how Robert Servatius should defend Eichmann; what Eichmann should avoid, what he should emphasize; how the Jewish Elders should have behaved under the Nazi regime. On and on. Her discourse is full of "asides" in which *inter alia* she wallops someone in the face. The only people she praises are the judges. Her all-embracing criticism and biting style, her academic arrogance, intuitive perceptions and self-assurance, allowed Arendt to pontificate on matters she had only superficial knowledge of. Her iconoclastic approach and original insights captivated many intellectuals, while enraging others. She presented the Eichmann trial in a different light, one that contrasted with the commonplace images of good and evil.

The book is structured around a central core and frame narratives. The core centers on the figure of Eichmann, the profile of a mass murderer.

Near the center, still in the core, is her criticism of the Jewish leaders. Admittedly, this criticism occupies only a few pages in the volume as a whole, but as noted, Arendt consciously chose to focus on this topic. There was nothing accidental or off-handed about that choice, which is why I believe it belongs to the book's nucleus. Her frame stories include criticism of the State of Israel in particular and Zionism more generally, along with malicious analogies between Zionist and Nazi policies in the 1930s;[54] and also her critique of the Bonn government for failing to prosecute Nazis in West Germany. Other frame narratives involve the presentation of the trial as a show trial staged by Ben-Gurion (pulling the strings of the prosecution as if in a marionette theater) and Arendt's report on the trial's conduct and whether it met the exacting criteria she demanded of it.

How well has the book stood the test of time? Paradoxically, it is evident that its core concerns no longer interest the broader public. Yet several of the frame narratives are today at the very heart of public discussion. Most researchers are no longer interested in the issue of the complicity and guilt of the *Judenräte*, but there is considerable renewed interest in the question of the show trial and its associated hype. Outside Germany and Austria, interest in the figure of Eichmann has faded, but attempts to demonize Ben-Gurion have gained new currency as time passes. Arendt's justified argument that the "Arab connection" (the Mufti and the "Final Solution") was played up in the trial, a marginal view at the time, is today being resurrected as proof that the trial was indeed in part intended to legitimize injustices against the Arabs.

One of the most perceptive essays critical of Arendt is Norman Podhoretz's "Study in the Perversity of Brilliance." He begins by comparing the strategies in the narrating of national tragedy by two authors whose essays were published in almost sequent series in *The New Yorker*. One is James Baldwin's essay on the Black Muslims, the other Hannah Arendt's report on the Eichmann trial. Baldwin opted for the strategy of an eloquent description: "there is nothing clever in the way he tells the story of the Negro in America." It's a "black and white account, with the traditional symbolisms reversed . . ." He exploits every possible bit of melodrama, touching people through the power of his eloquence. Arendt took the opposite tack, choosing to rid her story of any bit of melodrama and to highlight every nuance of moral ambiguity, every hue of gray: "Miss Arendt is all cleverness and no eloquence." The tale she told is complex, anti-sentimental, rich in paradox and ambivalence, with a quality of "ruthless honesty." And Podhoretz explains: "Anyone schooled in the modern school in literature and philosophy would be bound to consider it a much better story than the usual melodramatic version."[55] One can apply Podhoretz's distinction to the polarity between Gouri and Arendt as well. Arendt was writing for a sophisticated, cynical readership of the later twentieth century, who were weaned on scorn for melodrama and any show of emotion, taught to suspect any avowal of innocence, to be skeptical of justice and truth. Boas Evron recently wrote that "this book came like a fresh breath of sobriety and reasoned discourse in the hysterical storm gusting around the panoply of propaganda encasing Ben-Gurion's government."[56] Evron's assessment explains some of the magnetic attraction of Arendt's book: why today, nearly half a century later, it remains at the center of public debate. Arendt chose to position herself in opposition to the political-ideological-national structure. From that critical stance towards virtually everything and everyone, she sowed the seeds of a comprehensive critique of the system. These fell on fertile soil among all those who, for their own reasons, hated Ben-Gurion's government and felt frustrated by the trial, which had allowed it a moment of grace. Over and beyond her negative critical approach to the political system, there was the element of moral ambiguity. It is that ambiguity which has made Arendt the darling of postmodernists: "nothing is as it seems." There is no truth, no lies, no victim, no murderer. No one is guilty, none are innocent, there is no hierarchy of values, no value is absolute. All exists in a fuzzy realm of indeterminate morals.

Gouri, by contrast, pursued the strategy typified by Baldwin: great personal involvement, appeal to the emotions, black is black and white is white. His is the realm of moral certainties and national identification. Yet the encounter between Gouri, the Israeli sabra, and Jewish fate was eminently historical. The two discursive foci in Gouri's writing on the trial — self-accusation for not having done enough at the time of the Holocaust and nascent recognition of the heroism of the weak — were to remain at the center of public discussion of the Holocaust in Israel for years to come. Gouri does not divorce himself from the moral advantage of self-defense.[57] Blessed is the hand that made a Molotov cocktail; yet by the same token, blessed are the simple Jews who, under impossible circumstances, were able to retain their human dignity.[58] In the irony of history, the conclusions from his description were no less subversive than those that were inferred from Arendt's account, and perhaps even more influential.

The topic of the banality of evil was fascinating both from an intellectual and scholarly perspective. The more research on the course of the Final Solution penetrated down to the level of the actual perpetrators, the more question marks there were about the nature of the murderers and their motives. To a certain extent, studies that extend guilt to encompass wider strata of the German people help bolster Arendt's thesis on the banal perpetrator: in the sense that simple people, not necessarily "born murderers," were capable of committing murder or serving as accessories to mass murder, systematically and over a prolonged period of time.[59] But that argument is unconvincing when it comes to Eichmann and his fellow evildoers.

The recent book by Yaacov Lozowick, *Hitler's Bureaucrats: The Nazi Security Police and the Banality of Evil*, deals with the question by interrogating documents produced by the bureaucrats themselves. Lozowick arrives at the unequivocal conclusion that these bureaucrats were driven by a fanatic ideological belief system and hatred for the Jews. They did what they did enthusiastically, they were overzealous in dedication to their tasks. And they understood quite well that what they did placed them beyond the pale of accepted human morality.[60] Arendt's theory of the banality of evil as applied to Eichmann is contradicted by the historical materials.

The more the events of World War II receded into the past, the more universalistic arguments gained new impetus. The Holocaust as a lesson for humankind highlighting human viciousness became a privileged focus in education for tolerance and against fanaticism, prejudice and racism. In Israel, it was drawn into a debate between two camps: those who argued for national, specifically Jewish particularistic conclusions to be drawn from the Holocaust and those who stressed its universal features. But it was *Israeli politics*, not Arendt, that was at the heart of this controversy. Her second core topic, the collaborative guilt of Jewish leaders in the destruction of European Jewry, also lost its salience.

The changes in public discourse subsequent to the Eichmann trial led to a more sympathetic assessment of the dilemmas faced by Jewish leaders during the Holocaust. In the event, the issue of the *Judenräte* faded from Israeli public discussion. It is true that the epithet "Judenrat" was occasionally hurled as a term of abuse by right-wingers at their adversaries, but no longer in the concrete context of the Holocaust. By contrast, the question Gouri had raised — "what did *we* do?" — and the importance attached since to the value of *preserving life* over against the virtues of heroic death meshed with tendencies growing ever more dominant in Israeli society. Accusations that the leadership in the *Yishuv* had been lax, not doing everything it might have in the years of terror, fused with criticism of the Mapai party leadership under Ben-Gurion, a critique that had been voiced already during the Second World War. These were then absorbed into the polemics surrounding Ben-Gurion's leadership during his life and the historical debates forever after. The second key issue that Gouri had addressed, the value of preserving one's humanity, associated with the downplaying of physical bravery, blended with newer undercurrents in Israeli mentality: a new praise for the traditional images of the Jew and the self-sacrificing martyr's death (*kiddush ha-shem*) on the one hand; a critique of Israeli machismo and the glorification of force on the other.

The Eichmann trial undermined the image of the sabra as the sole defining model of Israeli identity. Gouri exemplifies a process that many of his generation went through, and the generation educated in the state after 1948 even more. Under the impact of the trial, the Jews "there" were transformed from accused to accusers. And side by side with admiration for the heroism of the ghetto fighters, a new esteem began to emerge for the silent heroism of the weak. This was tantamount to an undermining of fundamental components in the classic Zionist conception of the "negation of exile," *shlilat ha-galut*. In an instructive essay on "Canaanism" and its metamorphoses, Dan Laor deals, *inter alia*, with the dispute between Yonatan Ratosh, Shlomo Grodzhinksi and others at the time of the trial and after.[61] The main topic of the dispute is not of interest here, but the trial was often referred to in their polemics. In an interview to the daily *Ha-Boker*, Ratosh declared that "the Jewish community was brutally ravaged by the Holocaust. But the Hebrew nation that has arisen in Israel has no connection with the Jewish community." In his view, the Eichmann trial should have dealt with Nazi racism in a broader context, not just with anti-Semitism.[62] The limitation of the trial solely to the issue of anti-Semitism is a "crude distortion of history for the sake of the needs of Jewish consciousness."[63] Some 12 years later, Ratosh went on in much the same vein in a radio interview. In response to Yaakov Agmon's question "Did the Holocaust shake up your view of the world?" Ratosh retorted: "If they were to kill you tomorrow ... would you become my cousin?" Genocide was a general Nazi policy, he contended, but we tend to block out the non-Jewish victims, stressing only the Jews who perished.[64]

This position was an extreme expression of the alienation from the Jewish people that typified the Canaanite trend. Yet while the Canaanite ideology was a genuine force within Israeli society in the 1940s and 1950s, by the mid-1970s Ratosh and his views had drifted to the very margin of the Israeli political spectrum. His uncompromising fanaticism contrasted sharply with the broader mellowing that had come in the aftermath of the Eichmann trial as awareness of the Holocaust percolated into the deeper reaches of Israeli society. Avot Yeshurun gave a biting response to Ratosh in his poem "You Poured out Lies and Deceit," decrying Ratosh's perfidy in dissociating himself from the Jewish people.[65] Benjamin Tammuz, a close friend of Ratosh, did come to his defense, though while distancing himself from the ideology of Canaanism. In his 1971 book *Yaakov*, his hero — Yaakov, a "generic" Jewish name, and not Gideon or Barak or some other name from the register of biblical heroism — initially spouts the ideology of Ratosh from the 1940s, not in order to justify it but as a rhetorical means to demonstrate his own rejection of such beliefs. Yaakov, a member of the Jewish underground, is quite indifferent to the fate of the Jews in Europe (comparing the annihilated Jews to millions of Chinese dying of hunger — neither are of any interest to us, really a paraphrase of Ratosh's statements). But at the bottom of that same page, Tammuz describes, seemingly outside the context of the tale, a killing ground in Eastern Europe.[66] Later in the novel

Yaakov has a change of heart and decides to leave the underground, with the intention of finding a new kind of communication with his grandfather: "Then the last barrier between me and my grandfather will fall. No longer the contrast: on one side diaspora Jews, their backs bent down, miserable, frightened; and on the other, a proud and valiant Hebrew, killer of the English, extolling the feats of Israel's bravery." The dialogue between him and his grandfather is in the spirit of the "return of the native": "Aren't you ashamed of me, Yaakov? grandfather asked. — I'm proud of you, granddad, I said."[67] In 1981, the poet Arye Sivan, himself a former Canaanite fellow traveler, published his poem "Recruits from Europe Who Fell in the Fields of Latrun During Operation Bin-Nun." Those who "walk in the fields" here are not "native sons" (as in the novel by Moshe Shamir it echoes, *He Walked in the Fields*, one of the emblematic novels of the Palmah generation), but rather anonymous heroes, whose only mode of identification is the number the SS tattooed on their arm; lonely survivors, with no brother or friend who will mourn their passing.[68] This return of the native sons of Palestine from the mythologized, proud-hearted Hebrew to the flesh-and-blood Jew points up a shift in mentality, a change in the popular ethos.

The response to the Eichmann trial was a delayed reaction: Israelis did not awaken the morning after the trial permeated by a new consciousness of the Holocaust, totally rejecting the concept of the "negation of exile." As mentioned, there were also cynical and ironic responses to the parade of atrocities and display of emotions; these were in marked contrast to the ethos of self-restraint, the stiff upper lip and concealment of pain that was commonly accepted in the *Yishuv* and the state. In the educational system, even much later it was still possible to find residues of the "negation of exile" in textbooks and especially in the implicit approach widespread among teachers in the schools. The difficulty of distancing oneself from ideas ingrained in childhood about diaspora Jewry can be seen exemplified in Ezer Weizmann, when president of Israel: in his speeches at the presidential mansion, Weizmann continued to speak about the wonders of the state and wretchedness of Jewish life in the diaspora. The general embarrassment felt by his audiences was testimony to the changes that had occurred in the accepted norms and their discourse. These had relegated Weizmann's notions to the level of pure anachronism, the views of a survivor from another era.[69] There are quite probably still examples of such ideas in currency. But this is a tendency on the wane. The Israeli public has returned to the real world of its history — in contradistinction to its historical mythography.

Idit Zertal has written that under the impact of the Eichmann trial, the Israeli public perceived the Arab threat on the eve of the Six Day War as analogous to the Nazi threat of total destruction.[70] I agree that that was one example of the suspended or delayed influence of the trial. But I do not share Zertal's view that Israeli public opinion was manipulated here. As I see it, the associations with World War II were quite natural, the product of warmongering declarations and wild statements in Arab capitals about throwing the Jews into the sea. Yet there is no doubt that the fear of annihilation — the sense that total destruction was not an inconceivable scenario — was widespread in the civilian population in the waiting period preceding the conflict (though not in the IDF). It also played a major role in the powerful response by American Jewry to the threat against Israel at the time. These reactions were nourished by an intensified recognition of the Holocaust as something that could happen again. There was, I would contend, no similar fear of total destruction at the time of the War of Independence, despite the fact that the objective dangers then were greater.

The Holocaust was far more central in the consciousness of the generation educated in Israel between 1948 and 1967 than among the preceding generation that was brought up in the *Yishuv*. A comparison of two "canonical" works from members of those two generations is instructive: *Parchments of Fire* (the posthumous literary and other writings of soldiers who perished in the 1948 War) and *Soldiers' Talk* (discussions among young Israeli combatants after the Six Day War).[71] In the former, references to the Holocaust are rare, while in the latter such references are pervasive, a dominant motif permeating the thoughts and consciousness of the young soldiers. That change can at least in part be accounted for by the osmosis of a new awareness of the Holocaust into the consciousness of broad strata of Israeli youth under the impress of the Eichmann trial.

Processes of change in national ethos are slow and gradual. They do not necessarily unfold in a straight line. If Ben-Gurion had been asked whether he wished the Eichmann trial to spur Israeli youth to a new awareness of Jewish history in the diaspora, weaken the myth of the past glory of the Jewish people in its land and intensify among the young "here" a sense of solidarity with and responsibility for the Jews who had perished "there," he would of course have been puzzled by this emphasis on the imputed *contradiction* between the myth of the archeological past and that of the Holocaust. Ben-Gurion understood the need to educate the young about what had befallen the Jewish people during World War II and to identify with its fate as an essential component in Israeliness. That was one of the main reasons he cited for staging the Eichmann trial. But he did not foresee the extent to which identification with the fate of the Jews in Europe would diminish the role of the ancient glorious past in Israeli consciousness. The Eichmann trial was the first giant step on Israeli identity's long and tortuous path back to the Jewish people.[72]

NOTES

This essay was translated from Hebrew by Bill Templer.

1 *Ma'ariv*, 21 September 1960.
2 Haim Gouri, *Mul ta ha-zkhukit: Mishpat Yerushalayim* (The Glass Cage: The Jerusalem Trial) (Tel Aviv, 1963), p. 11. This book was based on his reports of the trial that appeared in the daily *La-Merhav* between 12 April 1961 and 30 March 1962.
3 "Shidur rosh ha-memshalah le-yom ha-atzma'ut" (Independence Day Broadcast by the Prime Minister), *Davar*, 21 April 1961.
4 Richard Crossman, "Ha-byurokrat hasar ha-partzuf" (The Faceless Bureaucrat), *La-Merhav*, 6 April 1961 (originally published in *The New Statesman*).
5 "Da'at ha-kahal ba-olam al tfisato ve-mishpato" (World Public Opinion on his Seizure and Trial), *Yedi'ot Yad va-Shem*, No. 28 (December 1961), originally quoted in *Der Monat*, No. 152 (May 1961).
6 Hannah Arendt, *Eichmann in Jerusalem: A Report on the Banality of Evil* (London, 1963), p. 14.
7 G. Binyamin, "Ha-mishpat" (The Trial), *Ma'ariv*, 31 March 1961.
8 Shulamit Har-Even, "Tagid lo she-yakum" (Tell Him to Rise), *Al ha-Mishmar*, 16 April 1961.
9 Arendt, *Eichmann in Jerusalem*, p. 5. That charge misses the mark, since marriage between Jews and non-Jews is not forbidden in Israel. What was impossible then was a civil marriage ceremony for such purposes. At the time there was the widespread notion of a "Cyprus marriage," i.e. a marriage performed in Cyprus in order to get around the difficulties in Israeli legislation. Such marriages were of course recognized as completely legal in Israel.
10 Ibid., pp. 3, 7.
11 Such as Adenauer's ministerial director Hans Globke. Ibid., pp. 10–11.
12 Ibid., p. 99.
13 Gouri met survivors of the Holocaust in Budapest in 1947 and even struck up a friendship with some of them. Nonetheless, in contradiction with his views on the matter later in life, it seems to me that it was only after the Eichmann trial that he really began to grasp the Holocaust. Gouri spells out his position in the new introduction to his book *Ad alot ha-shahar* (Until Daybreak) (Tel Aviv, 2000), pp. 10–50. He also dedicates the book to "my students, young men and women, survivors of the extermination, in Hungary and Czechoslovakia, whom I instructed and trained in that unforgettable encounter which changed my life," and there is no doubt that is how he feels today. But it is no accident that he did not dedicate the first edition of the book in 1950 to those same young women and men.
14 For example, he heard a detailed account of the Nuremberg laws for the first time at the Eichmann trial. See Gouri, *Mul ta ha-zkhukit*, p. 32.
15 Ibid., p. 7.
16 Arendt, *Eichmann in Jerusalem*, pp. 4, 193.
17 Ibid., pp. 207–9.
18 Gouri, *Mul ta ha-zkhukit*, p. 53.
19 Ibid., p. 73.
20 Ibid., p. 134.
21 Ibid., pp. 240, 243.
22 Arendt, *Eichmann in Jerusalem*, pp. 9–10.
23 Ibid., p. 104.
24 Ibid., pp. 10–11.
25 "'Eichmann in Jerusalem': An Exchange of Letters between Gershom Scholem and Hannah Arendt," *Encounter*, Vol. 22, No. 1 (January 1964), p. 55.
26 Arendt, *Eichmann in Jerusalem*, pp. 105–6.
27 Ibid., p. 6.
28 Ibid., p. 110.
29 Arthur Koestler, *Darkness at Noon* (New York, 1941).
30 As in the closing scene of Nikita Mikhalkov's film *Burnt by the Sun* (Russia, 1994) (dealing with the sudden fall from grace of a hero of the Russian revolution).
31 Arendt, *Eichmann in Jerusalem*, p. 110.

32 Ibid., p. 109.
33 Gouri, Mul ta ha-zkhukit, p. 247.
34 Ibid.
35 Ibid., pp. 18, 19.
36 Ibid., p. 117.
37 Ibid., p. 166.
38 Ibid., p. 247.
39 Arendt, Eichmann in Jerusalem, p. 111.
40 Gouri, Mul ta ha-zkhukit, pp. 107–9.
41 Ibid., p. 249.
42 "'Eichmann in Jerusalem': An Exchange of Letters," p. 54.
43 Crossman, "Ha-byurokrat hasar ha-partzuf."
44 Gouri, Mul ta ha-zkhukit, p. 149.
45 Raul Hilberg, The Destruction of the European Jews (Chicago, 1961).
46 Alan Bullock, Hitler: A Study in Tyranny (London, 1964).
47 Arendt, Eichmann in Jerusalem, p. 44.
48 Ibid., p. 22.
49 Ibid., p. 23.
50 Ibid., pp. 40–43.
51 Ibid., pp. 48–9.
52 Ibid., pp. 130–4.
53 Ibid., p. 253.
54 Ibid., pp. 54–6.
55 Norman Podhoretz, "Hannah Arendt on Eichmann: A Study in the Perversity of Brilliance," Commentary, Vol. 36, No. 3 (September 1963), p. 201.
56 Boas Evron, "Shitot ye'ilot le-meniyat meida" (Effective Methods for Preventing Information), Ha'aretz, 6 October 2000.
57 Gouri, Mul ta ha-zkhukit, p. 247.
58 Ibid., p. 87.
59 See, for example, Omer Bartov, Hitler's Army: Soldiers, Nazis and War in the Third Reich (Oxford, 1992), and more recently his The German Army and Genocide: Crimes against War Prisoners, Jews and Other Civilians in the East, 1939–1944 (New York, 1999); Christopher R. Browning, Ordinary Men: Reserve Police Battalion 101 and the Final Solution in Poland (New York, 1992); Daniel Jonah Goldhagen, Hitler's Willing Executioners: Ordinary Germans and the Holocaust (New York, 1996).
60 Yaacov Lozowick, Ha-byurokratim shel Hitler: Mishteret ha-bitahon ha-natzit veha-banaliyut shel ha-resha (Hitler's Bureaucrats: The Nazi Security Police and the Banality of Evil) (Jerusalem, 2001). See also Dan Michman, "Ha-pitaron ha-sofi shel she'elat ha-yehudim: Hitgabshuto ve-yisumo: Matzav ha-mehkar" (The Final Solution of the Jewish Question: Its Formation and Application: State of Research), Bi-Shvil ha-Zikaron, No. 42 (Autumn 2001), pp. 21–4.
61 Dan Laor, "Me-'Ha-Drashah' le-'Ktav el ha-noar ha-ivri': He'arot le-musag 'shlilat ha-galut'" (From "The Sermon" [a famous story by Haim Hazaz] to "A Note to Hebrew Youth" [the famous declaration of the Canaanites]: Notes on the Concept of the "Negation of Exile"), Alpayim, No. 21 (2001), pp. 171–86.
62 Idit Neumann, "Mishpat Eichmann hu siluf ha-historiyah" (The Eichmann Trial is a Distortion of History), Ha-Boker, 28 July 1961.
63 Yonatan Ratosh, "Be-arba amot tzarot me'od" (Within a Very Limited Space)," Davar, 1 September 1961.
64 Yaakov Agmon, "Ha-mitos veha-metzi'ut" (Myth and Reality), Ha'aretz, 27 April 1973.
65 Avot Yeshurun, "Shafakhta kahash" (You Poured Out Lies and Deceit), Siman Kri'ah, No. 2 (1973), p. 392.
66 Benjamin Tammuz, Yaakov (Ramat Gan, 1971), pp. 44–5.
67 Ibid., p. 97.
68 Arye Sivan, Ma'ariv, 8 May 1981.

69 I myself was present at least twice at such speeches in the presidential mansion.
70 Idit Zertal, "Me-ulam beit ha-am el kotel beit ha-mikdash: Zikaron, pahad u-milhamah (1960–1967)" (From the Hall of Beit ha-Am to the Wall of the Temple: Memory, Fear and War [1960–1967])," *Teoriyah u-Vikoret*, No. 15 (Winter 1999), pp. 19–38.
71 Reuven Avinoam (ed.), *Gvilei-esh* (Parchments of Fire) (Tel Aviv, 1952); Avraham Shapira (ed.), *Si'ah lohamim* (Soldiers' Talk) (Tel Aviv, 1967), was published in English as *The Seventh Day: Soldiers' Talk about the Six-Day War* (London, 1970).
72 After finishing this study I discovered an interesting essay by Leora Bilsky, "Ke-of ha-hol: Arendt bi-Yerushalayim alpayim" (Like the Phoenix: Arendt in Jerusalem, 2000), *Bi-Shvil ha-Zikaron*, No. 41 (April–May 2001), pp. 17–25. Though there are points of similarity between us, she has a different perspective on the topic well worth examining. Of note is the recent book by Hanna Yablonka, *Medinat Yisrael neged Adolf Eichmann* (The State of Israel vs. Adolf Eichmann) (Israel, 2001), the most extensive study to date on the Eichmann trial.

Politics and Memory in West and East Germany since 1961 and in Unified Germany since 1990

Jeffrey Herf

Though the memory of the mass murder of European Jewry expanded in the Federal Republic of Germany after the Eichmann trial, it did not, contrary to some conventional wisdom, begin in the 1960s. Rather, a minority, dissonant tradition of memory of the Jewish catastrophe took root, especially in Social Democratic and liberal political circles, in the 1940s and 1950s.[1] To be sure, the most widespread response to the Holocaust in West German public opinion in the early postwar decades was avoidance and silence, combined with memory of sufferings of Germans during World War II.[2] The memory of the Holocaust in postwar West Germany, and then in unified Germany since 1990, has always been unpopular with some segments of West German society and has always competed with other memories and other narratives found more palatable by many West Germans.

Yet the interesting historical phenomenon remains that despite the fact that the Nazi regime was overthrown only by military defeat rather than by an internal revolt such a tradition of memory emerged at all. As I have argued previously, unconditional Allied military victory followed by four years of occupation and extensive war crimes trials were indispensable preconditions for its emergence. Equally important for memory's emergence were what I have called "multiple restorations" — the non- and anti-Nazi traditions that had survived and reemerged into German political life after 1945. The surviving leaders of moderate conservatism, left-liberalism and social democracy in the West, and the communist leaders in the East were able to return to political life due to Allied victory and occupation. Some of these leaders of the "other Germanys" crushed during the Nazi era inaugurated postwar traditions of memory. Third, the founders of postwar memory — Theodor Heuss and Kurt Schumacher above all — inaugurated a tradition that became a component of West German national political discourse. Where nationalists had often argued in Germany and elsewhere that speaking the truth about past crimes in public was bad for the nation, Heuss and Schumacher made doing so a matter of national honor. In so doing, they redefined the meaning of patriotism. Rather than a school for scoundrels, that sentiment should rest on the ability to look the truth about a difficult past straight in the eye.

When we turn from the period "after Hitler" to that "after Eichmann" or rather after the 1961 Eichmann trial, we shift from questions regarding origins to those of persistence and diffusion. Surely a major cause, as has been often noted, is generational change and youth protest during the 1960s and since. Yet while such protest certainly addressed the issue of "fascism," its Marxist lineages often as not led to a slighting of the specifics of anti-Jewish persecution and mass murder. Moreover, in East Germany (a key chapter beyond the scope of this essay), Marxism-Leninism legitimated active hostility to the State of Israel and to efforts to offer financial compensation to Jewish survivors. Alongside this familiar story of generational change, we should pay attention to the intersection of international and domestic politics. Just as the conjuncture of Allied victory and multiple restorations stands at the origins of West German memory, so persistence of Holocaust memory in the Federal Republic (FRG) was due to a combination of an established moral and cultural tradition with practical expressions of national interest.

In the 1950s, Western Allied intent to integrate and rearm West Germany in the Western Alliance fostered a forgetting not only of the Holocaust but also to some extent of World War II and the embarrassing — in the context of the Cold War — fact of the wartime alliance between the Western democracies and the Soviet Union. To be sure, the United States did insist that the Adenauer government be forthcoming on issues of financial restitution for Jewish survivors. Yet in the 1950s, American and Western policy was focused on integrating West Germany into the North Atlantic Treaty Orgganization (NATO) and containing the Soviet Union and thus exerted little to no pressure on Adenauer to launch trials for war crimes and crimes against humanity.[3] In this period, the impact of international politics discouraged Holocaust memory within an, albeit already quite reluctant, West Germany. Reconciliation with France, one of Adenauer's proudest accomplishments, was not accompanied by extensive public soul-searching about German policy in France during the war. Adenauer and Charles de Gaulle, leaders of an old school of diplomacy and politics, thought it best to focus on current shared interests in politics and economics rather than on the divisive memories of the recent past.

By 1958, it became evident to a number of West German state Attorneys General that a judicial scandal of enormous proportions was taking place as a consequence of Adenauer's willingness to bend to the wishes of vocal "amnesty" lobbies and his decision to staff his justice ministry with officials who had little or no interest in bringing former Nazi criminals to justice.[4] By the late 1950s, West German state prosecutors and scholars estimated that about 100,000 persons had participated in some way in the destruction of European Jewry.[5] After the formation of the Federal Republic in 1949, trials in West German courts did take place concerning crimes related to the consolidation of the Nazi regime in the 1930s, the November pogrom of 1938, euthanasia experiments, the *Einsatzgruppen* and mass murder of Jews in ghettos and camps. However, the number of West German convictions dropped from 800 in 1950 to slightly over 200 in 1951, slightly less than 200 in 1952, and about 125 in 1953. For the decade from 1954 to 1964, the number of convictions by courts in the Federal Republic hovered between 25 and 50 a year.[6]

In 1958, at the initiative of prosecutors and journalists, the Central Office for the Investigation of National Socialist Crimes was established in Ludwigsburg in the West German state of Baden-Wurtemberg. Its investigations raised troubling issues. Unless West Germany's statute of limitations of 15 years on crimes of murder were extended, tens of thousands of persons suspected of participation in war crimes and the Final Solution of the Jewish Question would escape indictment, trial and punishment merely by the passage of time.[7] This recognition was the beginning of what became known as the *Verjährungsdebatte* (debate over extension of the statute of limitations on crimes of murder), a series of four major debates in the West German parliament in 1960, 1965, 1969 and 1979. At the time of the 1965 debate, the first following the Eichmann trial, 13,892 persons were still the subjects of judicial proceedings, while proceedings against 542 persons had been stopped because the accused were abroad or in unknown locations. Cases against 41,212 persons had been closed without convictions.[8] If West Germany were to allow the statute of limitations on crimes of murder to remain at 15 years, and if the 100,000 figure was a plausible number of potential defendants, then clearly the great majority of those involved in the Final Solution would never face prosecution. The Eichmann trial in Jerusalem gave unprecedented international focus to the specifics of the Final Solution and thereby added pressure on the West German government to extend its statute of limitations.

The East German Communist government's record, despite its denunciations of "the fascists in Bonn," was no better. Between 1945 and 1949, the Soviet occupation authorities convicted 12,500 persons of war crimes in the Nazi era. Given the propensity of the Soviet occupation authorities to use the Nazi label against political opponents, these figures must be treated with great caution. The convictions delivered in the 1950 war crimes trial in Waldheim also had very dubious legal foundations.[9] After 1950, East German authorities claimed that justice had largely been done and that — with some plausibility — many former Nazi officials were among the over two million people who fled to the West between 1949 and 1961 when the Berlin Wall was built. Their Marxist-Leninist analysis of Nazism relieved pressure for prosecutions for crimes committed against the Jews in two ways. First, at a general level, its focus on fascism as a form of capitalism led to a primary focus on elites in the Nazi party, military and industry and away from the rest of the population whom the government showed little desire to prosecute for participation in these crimes; second, Marxist-Leninist orthodoxy diverted attention away from the anti-Jewish elements of Nazi policy or viewed them as tools to serve the presumably more primary focus on anti-communism. As we will see, in the late 1950s and increasingly in the 1960s, as the German Democratic Republic (GDR) was cultivating closer ties to the Arab states and then to the Palestine Liberation Organization, its interest in past crimes committed against the Jews diminished. Whatever the reason, prosecutions of Nazi-era crimes in the GDR dropped dramatically to 331 in 1951, 140 in 1952, 85 in 1953, 35 in 1954, and 23 in 1955. In any given year between 1955 and 1964 in East Germany there were at most ten convictions and as few as one. From 1951 to 1964 in the GDR, there were a total of 329 convictions for crimes committed during the Nazi era, of which 286 took place before 1956, and 46 occurred between 1956 and 1964.[10] The three to one ratio in the number of convictions between West and East Germany was roughly the same as the ratio of the populations of the two Germanys.

In West Germany, each of the *Verjährungsdebatten* kept the issue of the crimes of the Nazi past as well as the magnitude of judicial failure of the 1950s at the center of the political stage. The Social Democratic Party (SPD), along with the left wing of the liberal Free Democratic Party (FDP), led the fight to continue the prosecution of crimes of the Nazi era. The first of the West German parliamentary debates on the statute of limitations began on 23 March 1960, when SPD leaders in the Bundestag proposed that the statute of limitations on crimes which led to a sentence of ten years to life in prison be based on a starting date of 15 September 1949, rather than 8 May 1945.[11] On 24 May 1960, the full Bundestag debated the issue.[12] The Minister of Justice in the Adenauer government, Fritz Schäfer, asserted that all of the important episodes of mass murder had been researched. He disputed the assertion that there were acts and individuals who were yet to be found and tried. The SPD initiative was rejected. Nevertheless, the SPD members of the Bundestag succeeded in making the failures of West German justice in the 1950s a political issue.[13]

The first Bundestag *Verjährungsdebatte* after the Eichmann trial in Jerusalem took place in 1965.[14] It occurred in the wake of the Auschwitz Trial conducted in Frankfurt am Main in 1964, as well as trials of those who participated in murders in the *Einsatzgruppen* and at the extermination camps in Belzec, Treblinka, Sobibor, Chelmno and Maidanek. Each trial offered further details to the West German public about the Holocaust and the death camps in Poland, and made clear the extent to which justice had previously been delayed.[15] Support for extension of the statute of limitations in the Bundestag, though strongest in the SPD, now received support from moderates in the conservative Christian Democratic Union (CDU), and from Chancellor Ludwig Erhard's Justice Ministry. Research in American, German, Polish and Soviet archives now led the Minister of Justice to conclude in his report to the Bundestag of 24 February 1965 that the possibility "could not be ruled out" that as yet unknown acts and perpetrators would become known after 8 May 1965, that is, 20 years after the war.[16] On 25 March 1965 the Bundestag overwhelmingly voted in favor of changing the date on which the statute of limitations on crimes of murder would be based from 8 May 1945 to the beginning of West German sovereignty in fall 1949. In so doing, it made possible further prosecutions at least until 31 December 1969. Three hundred and forty-four members of parliament voted in favor, 96 voted against, and four abstained. The majority was composed of 184 members of the CDU/CSU (Christian Social Union), 180 members of the SPD and three members of the FDP. Voting against extension and thus for an effective end to investigations and trials were 37 members of the CDU/CSU, and 60 of the 63-member parliamentary representation of the FDP.[17] Support for extension in the SPD was almost unanimous (except for one abstention) but was also very widespread within the CDU/CSU. The core of opposition lay among right-wing representatives in the CDU/CSU, especially the Bavarian Christian Social Union, but even more so in the FDP.

The third of the *Verjährungsdebatten* took place in spring 1969. A "grand coalition" of the Christian Democrats and Social Democrats still governed in Bonn. The Justice Minister, Social Democrat Horst Ehmke, proposed that the statute of limitations for crimes of murder and genocide be eliminated. In the 11 June 1969 Bundestag session he argued that refutation of the "false reproach of collective guilt can only succeed if we find the murderers among this people and make them accept their responsibility.... If we were, intentionally or not, to express solidarity with the National Socialist crimes and for this reason.... call for an end also to their judicial prosecution, we would retrospectively justify the thesis of the collective guilt."[18] The majority of the Bundestag rejected Ehmke's proposal to completely eliminate the statute of limitations for crimes of murder but did extend the statute to 30 years, thereby enabling further investigations and prosecutions in West German courts until 31 December 1979.[19]

The fourth and last statute of limitations debates took place in 1979. More than in the previous debates, the specifically Jewish dimensions of Nazi criminality dominated the proceedings, due in part to the huge response to the American docudrama *Holocaust*, which was broadcast in early 1979.

Nevertheless, the great majority of conservative members opposed abolition of the statute, some expressing fears about a nationalist backlash should it pass. Social Democrats such as representative Herta Däubler-Gmelin responded that in 1979 as in 1965 and 1969, expiration of the statute of limitations would mean that those "Nazi murderers" who had managed to escape from the law would be freed from fear of prosecution. That, she added, would be an "intolerable situation." In 1979, she continued, it was apparent that the hopes expressed in 1965 and 1969 that justice would be done in a timely fashion had not been fulfilled. Many cases remained to be pursued. In response to concerns about protecting the rights of the accused after passage of so much time she said that legal norms would be far more seriously damaged "if due to the statute of limitations a murderer can no longer be held accountable even if his deed is obvious and even if verification of his participation in the crime posed no problem." She added that the "call from the victims must not go unheard."[20] In making such arguments in 1979, Däubler-Gmelin and the Social Democratic leadership repeated what had become since Schumacher firm Social Democratic tradition. Hildegaard Hamm-Brucher, a protégé of Theodor Heuss and a leader of the minority liberal wing of the Free Democrats, spoke in favor of abolishing the statute on limitations. She regretted that in the early postwar period the West Germans did not "decisively enough eliminate the root of the evil... and that the rapid process of material reconstruction unjustifiably abbreviated, yes repressed the slow and painful process of catharsis." She regretted that in the 1950s there was an absence of public discussion aside from "a few politicians, writers, theologians and writers," but welcomed the broader public discussion of the Nazi past that began in the 1960s.[21]

On 3 July 1979, the Bundestag voted 253 to 228 to abolish the statute of limitations on crimes of murder and genocide. Voting in favor of the extension were 38 members of the CDU/CSU faction, 219 SPD representatives, and 15 members of the FDP faction in parliament. Voting against were two members of the SPD, 24 members of the FDP (including Foreign Minister Hans-Dietrich Genscher), and 207 members of the CDU/CSU (including Helmut Kohl).[22] Compared to the votes of 1965 and 1969, conservative opposition to extension of the statute had greatly increased while support for extension had grown within the FDP. The SPD continued to be the strongest supporter for further investigations and trials.

The balance sheet of West German justice up through the 1980s was the following. From 1958 to 1986 the Central Office in Ludwigsburg opened 4,954 cases. By the end of 1985, 4,853 of those cases had been settled, and 101 were still pending.[23] In total, during the period from 1951 to 1986, West German courts, hampered by the deaths and fading memories of witnesses, the difficulty in finding evidence located in Soviet bloc countries and with limited budgets offered by unenthusiastic political leaders, still handed down 992 convictions. The trials in Frankfurt, Stuttgart, Dusseldorf and elsewhere did present the facts of Nazi criminality to that part of the public which took an interest in them and did deliver justice to some of the perpetrators. Yet thousands of persons whose cases should have been brought to trial never confronted the full force of the law.

In 1969, Willy Brandt (1913–92) and the Social Democratic Party won the office of Chancellor for the first time since the Weimar Republic on a program of "daring more democracy" at home and initiating a "new *Ostpolitik*" in foreign policy. Both initiatives rested on very different views about democracy and memory, and memory and policy, than those of the Adenauer era. Brandt was the first active participant in the anti-Nazi resistance and the first returned political exile to occupy that office.[24] Where Adenauer had linked democratization to non-discussion of Nazi crimes, Brandt argued that their public memory should be part of a program of "daring more democracy." Where conservatives had either focused on West German reconciliation with the West or argued that memory of Nazi aggression and genocide damaged the national image, Brandt and his foreign policy adviser Egon Bahr argued that public reflection on the German war on the Eastern Front in World War II was necessary to rebuild trust and normalize West German relations with Eastern Europe and the Soviet Union.[25] Conservative silence about the Nazi era bred mistrust. Memory was essential for reassurance and for hopes of Soviet agreement to ending or moderating the division of Germany.[26] With such arguments, Brandt made the case that honest confrontation with a criminal past was both a moral as well as a pragmatic necessity if the Federal Republic were to attain normal diplomatic relations with the countries of Eastern Europe and the Soviet Union.

In his 1968 book, *Peace Policy in Europe*, he wrote that "I do not ever forget that it was Hitler's 'Greater Germany' above all that brought so much unspeakable suffering to Eastern Europe."[27] Brandt's *Ostpolitik* pushed West German political memory back from the early Cold War period to the Nazi seizure of power in 1933, and the German invasions of Poland in 1939 and the Soviet Union in June 1941. Such memory could, he hoped, overcome the "under-balance of trust" that was the legacy of "criminal activities for which there are no parallel in modern history" which had "disgraced the German name in all of the world."[28] Brandt's focus was more on the crimes and aggressions that Nazi Germany had inflicted on Eastern Europe and the Soviet Union, and his critique was directed first of all at conservative anti-communism which was reluctant, to say the least, to acknowledge the historic significance and racist character of the German invasion of the Soviet Union in 1941. Although the issues of communism and anti-communism dominated the debate over *Ostpolitik*, Brandt manifested his understanding that Nazi anti-communism was inseparable from anti-Semitism when he decided to bend his knee in mourning at the memorial for Jews killed in the Warsaw Ghetto. The *Kniefall* was the first time that a West German Chancellor had so publicly expressed remorse for what the Germans had done to the Jews and the peoples of Eastern Europe and the Soviet Union during World War II.[29] Yet Brandt's rhetoric during the era of *Ostpolitik* was first and foremost about reconciliation with the countries of Eastern Europe and the Soviet Union, not primarily about the Holocaust. Just as Nahum Goldmann, the president of the World Jewish Congress, had pointed out in a speech at the Bergen-Belsen memorial in November 1952 that discussion of the Holocaust invariably recalled the "Eastern" geography in which it had occurred, so Brandt's *Ostpolitik* (or Détente), willingly or not, drew attention to the Holocaust that had taken place in the countries of Eastern Europe and the Soviet Union. That said, however, the famous photograph of Brandt's *Kniefall* at the memorial to the Jews of the Warsaw Ghetto misleadingly implies that *Ostpolitik* was primarily about remembering the genocide of European Jewry. First and foremost, it was about establishing normal diplomatic relations with the existing Communist governments in the Soviet bloc both as a goal in itself and as an endeavor to bring about, as Brandt put it, "change through rapprochement," that is, internal reform spurred by relaxation of international tensions.

Just as Adenauer's acknowledgment in 1951 of German responsibility for shouldering obligations created by the genocide of the Jews was a step in West German reintegration into the Western alliance, so Brandt's acknowledgment of the past was essential for diplomatic success in Eastern Europe and in Moscow. Just as Adenauer had sought to reassure the French, the Americans, the Jews and the Israelis, so Brandt now tried to reassure the states and peoples of Eastern Europe and the Soviet Union that West Germany was not the fascist regime bent on regaining lost territories which communist propaganda had depicted for 20 years.[30] In both instances, memory of a terrible past was an important component for serving West German foreign policy in the present.

*

From the late 1950s on, East Germany's dominant memory of the Nazi era and its foreign policy was radically different. The official memorials were moments of communist Hegelianism in which the memory of the historically unredeemed Jewish catastrophe in Europe found a marginal place, if any. Pride of place belonged to the suffering of the peoples of the Soviet Union, which had been redeemed by the victory of the Red Army and the Soviet Union, as well as an inflated story of anti-fascist communist resistance.

Otto Grotewohl, the honorific President of the GDR, summarized its ideological motif in a letter of 24 June 1957 to Gamel Abdel Nasser, the President of Egypt. Increasingly, he wrote, the political life of the Federal Republic was "determined by those forces which served criminal Hitler fascism or even were among its initiators." "Humanity still remembers," the murderous deeds of "Hitler fascism. . . . The forces of fascism and militarism" must "never again have the opportunity to seize power and again threaten peace." However, German unification under West German auspices would result in a nuclear-armed Germany along with the "restoration of those social forces in all of Germany from which fascism was born, which unleashed the Second World War, and which are preparing the Third World War." The GDR, he wrote, could not permit this to happen. Therefore, in the interests of peace and of preventing the emergence of unified, nuclear-armed, fascist Germany, it was crucial that East Germany and Egypt develop warm and friendly relations.[31] Fulfilling the legacy of anti-fascism thus meant close relations with Israel's primary adversary. Grotewohl gave public support to Egypt in the 1956 Suez Crisis.[32] He traveled to Egypt and Iraq in January 1959, after which General Consulates were established in Berlin and Cairo.[33]

From 24 February to 2 March 1965, Walter Ulbricht, the head of the government and of the ruling Socialist Unity Party (SED), capped a decade of increasingly close East German-Egyptian ties by visiting Gamal Abdel Nasser in Cairo. On 7 March 1965 the Federal Republic announced its decision to offer formal diplomatic recognition to Israel. On 14–15 March 1965, a majority of the 13 states of the Arab league voted to break diplomatic relations with Bonn, and six Arab states — Egypt, Iraq, Yemen, Algeria, Sudan, and Kuwait — indicated a readiness to offer formal recognition and diplomatic relations with East Germany.[34] The combination of the establishment of formal diplomatic ties between the Federal Republic and Israel, along with East German efforts to woo the Arabs, brought about the most important diplomatic achievement in GDR history up to that point, namely recognition by states not formally members of the Communist bloc, and thus defeat of West Germany's Hallstein Doctrine and Bonn's *Alleinvertretungsanspruch*, the claim to be the only legitimate German government. As West German foreign policy reinforced the memory of the Holocaust, East German foreign policy and its drive for recognition led away from that memory. National interests in the two cases had an opposite impact on national memory.

Walter Ulbricht traveled to Cairo in 1965, and spoke of "common struggle" against shared enemies. He denounced "all efforts of monopoly capital to build Israel as an imperialist outpost in Arab space," and use the Palestine question to heighten tensions in the area. He attacked the military cooperation between West Germany and Israel.[35] He signed a joint declaration with Nasser which recognized "all rights of the Arab peoples of Palestine, including their inalienable right of self-determination," and condemned "the aggressive plans of imperialism" to make Israel into a spearhead against the Arabs.[36] The two governments signed an agreement for dramatically expanded cultural exchanges at the level of universities, communications, cultural centers and sports exchanges.[37]

Upon returning to East Berlin from Cairo, Ulbricht accused West Germany and NATO of using "the imperialist military basis of Israel" to implement a "forward strategy" against the Arabs just as it implemented a forward strategy against East Germany. He attacked West German aid to Israel: "for the purpose of camouflaging and concealing the perpetrators, the government of the West German state delivers gifts of heavy weapons and other war materials to the imperialist outpost Israel."[38] Five days later, in a report to high-level officials about his Cairo trip, he added that East German support for the enemies of the Jewish state had nothing to do with anti-Semitism or failing to confront the Nazi past. West German restitution was a good investment which detracted attention from personnel continuities and a paucity of war crimes trials.[39] Though his government had spent nothing in restitution payments to Jewish survivors, Ulbricht argued that it was his government, not Adenauer's, that had truly learned the lessons of the Nazi past. The East Germans thus blazed a trail of *Vergangenheitsbewältigung* on the cheap. I have found no evidence to suggest that the East German leadership under Ulbricht and his successor, Erich Honecker, tried to moderate Soviet or radical Arab hostility to the Jewish state. On the contrary, they saw the "struggle against Zionism" as a fine chapter in the history of East German anti-fascism.

The Six Day War of 1967 brought longstanding East German views to the attention of a global audience. In a famous speech delivered on 15 June 1967 in Leipzig, Ulbricht denounced the United States, West Germany and "Israeli aggression" in the Middle East.[40] The East Germans repeatedly denounced "Zionist aggression," described Israel as the "spearhead" of a powerful "anti-Arab conspiracy between Bonn and Tel Aviv," and expressed their solidarity with the Arabs.[41] The regime's policies elicited neither public enthusiasm nor protest.[42] Albert Norden, a member of the SED Politburo, wrote a "Statement of Citizens of the GDR of Jewish Origin" published on 7 June 1967 which denounced Israel's military aggression. Two days later, in a memo on treatment of the war in the East German media, Norden wrote that it should be stressed

> that the Israelis are acting as Hitler did on 22 June 1941 when he attacked the Soviet Union in night and fog.... When the West German imperialist press, radio and television defame [Gamel Abdel] Nasser as an Egyptian Hitler, it can and must be pointed out, in view of

the facts of 5 June [1967] how the Israeli imperialists exactly imitated Hitler's illegal tactics and methods of invasion.[43]

Norden's efforts to enlist other prominent Jewish writers and public figures as signers of anti-Israeli manifestos met with mixed success. Yet the Jewish Communists who would have protested against East German policy had long ago fled or been driven from political life.

In 1969, East Germany established diplomatic relations with Egypt, Iraq, Sudan, Syria and South Yemen. In 1971, Yasser Arafat made his first visit to East Berlin. In August 1973, the Palestine Liberation Organization (PLO) opened a consular office in East Berlin, the first in the Soviet bloc, and signed agreements with East Germany for delivery of arms, supplies, support for students and medical treatment of PLO wounded and orphans. In the 1970s, there were frequent visits by Arafat and high-level PLO functionaries in East Berlin accompanied by declarations of solidarity between East Germany and the PLO, and statements of gratitude for assistance by PLO officials.[44]

Erich Honecker (1912–94), who replaced Ulbricht as head of the party and state in 1971 and governed until the collapse of the regime in 1989, continued to deepen East German relations with the Arab states, the PLO and Arafat.[45] In 1975, the East German delegation at the United Nations was elected to membership in the "Committee for the Realization of the Inalienable Rights of the Palestinian People."[46] At the UN and at numerous international conferences, the East Germans joined in resolutions that denounced Israeli aggression, and expressed solidarity with the Arabs, the PLO and other "third world national liberation movements." They voted for the "Zionism is racism" resolution.[47] In 1980, the PLO consulate in East Berlin was elevated to the status of an embassy. In the same year, the East Germans denounced the Egyptian-Israeli Camp David accords as an "imperialist separate peace."[48] While the details of East German support for training and equipping Arab and Palestinian terrorists remained secret, the fact of military cooperation between East Berlin and the PLO was clearly implied in articles in *Neues Deutschland* describing meetings with "military delegations" of the PLO with Erich Honecker.[49]

In part, East German support for the Arabs and the PLO from the late 1950s up to 1989 was a by-product of Soviet policy and East German efforts to find countries that would break from West Germany's policy of non-recognition. Yet a reading of the discourse and the decisions during the Ulbricht and Honnecker era indicates that the East Germans were enthusiastic rather than reluctant participants in the Soviet bloc assault on the Jewish state. They denounced Israel with gusto on many occasions and they remained loyal allies of those taking up arms against the Jewish state up to 1989. The irony of a self-described "anti-fascist" post-Nazi German government lending its support to armed attacks on the Jewish state has received strikingly less attention than has West German policy. It was not a major theme in West Germany during the era of *Ostpolitik*. Yet this was certainly the most morally problematic consequence of East German anti-fascism, one in which a universalizing discourse of revolution offered liberation from the burdens of local knowledge and memory and had a direct impact on foreign policy.

East German communism's illusion that it could separate itself from the Nazi past so easily came to a crashing end almost immediately after the government fell in 1989–90. In April 1990, the first act of the first democratically elected Volkskammer, which existed only until fall 1990 when German unification led to its elimination, was to express its regrets over past East German policy towards Israel and the Jews and to declare its readiness for a complete reversal of positions regarding policy towards the Middle East and questions of memory and restitution. On 12 April 1990 the Volkskammer voted 379 to 0 with 21 abstentions to approve a resolution accepting joint responsibility for Nazi crimes, and expressed willingness to pay reparations and to seek diplomatic ties with Israel.[50] On 14 April 1990 the headline of the left-liberal *Frankfurter Rundschau*, the West German daily which had most carefully reported on the anti-Jewish purges of the 1950s, firmly established the link between democratization and discussion of the Holocaust. It read "Volkskammer Recognizes Guilt for the Holocaust: First Freely Elected GDR-government in Office."[51] The Volkskammer statement read in part as follows:

> We the first freely-elected parliamentarians of East Germany, admit our responsibility as Germans in East Germany for our history and our future and declare unanimously before the world: Immeasurable suffering was inflicted on the peoples of the world by Germans during the time of National Socialism. Nationalism and racial madness led to genocide, particularly of the Jews in all of the European countries, of the people of the Soviet Union, the Polish people and the Gypsy people. Parliament admits joint responsibility on behalf of the people for the humiliation, expulsion, and murder of Jewish women, men, and children. We feel sad and ashamed and acknowledge this burden of German history. We ask the Jews of the world to forgive us for the hypocrisy and hostility of official East German policies toward Israel and for the persecution and degradation of Jewish citizens also after 1945 in our country. We declare our willingness to contribute as much as possible to the healing of mental and physical sufferings of survivors and to provide just compensation for material losses.[52]

The Volkskammer statement broke completely with the view West Germans alone should bear the burden of the crimes of the Nazi era, or that it was a marginal event in the history of Nazism and World War II. Gone was the arrogance and lack of historical self-consciousness with which East German political leaders had aided Israel's armed adversaries. Gone was a 40-year legacy of anti-Semitic code words clothed in Marxist-Leninist slogans, and denial that anti-Semitism could exist in an officially anti-fascist regime.[53] Gone too was the economic, political, diplomatic and military support for anti-Israeli terrorism.

*

In East Germany, the executors of the anti-cosmopolitan purge in the winter of 1952–53 had crushed a dissident communist tradition of sympathy for the Jews and support for Israel and made certain that this continuation of wartime anti-fascism never resurfaced.[54] Yet in West Germany, especially in Frankfurt am Main in the 1960s and 1970s, the debate within the Left about the Jews reemerged. Marxist-Leninist and splinter terrorist groups emerged from the West German New Left with similar interpretations of the Nazi past and the Middle East conflict as those coming from East Berlin. Milder forms of antagonism to Israel became commonplace in mainstream liberal media such as *Stern* and in *Der Spiegel*. Where the founding fathers of the democratic Left in West Germany — Kurt Schumacher, Ernst Reuter, Willy Brandt, Adolf Arndt among others — had seen support for Israel as a special duty of the German anti-Nazis, the West German New Left became increasingly hostile to Israel. The revival of Marxism with its focus on links between capitalism and fascism did little to spur interest in the particulars of the Jewish catastrophe, the nature of German and European anti-Semitism, and the causes for the foundation of the State of Israel. As is now well known, the Six Day War in 1967 marked a caesura in the attitude of many in the 1960s West German Left towards Israel. While Israel's supporters welcomed the stunning victory over the Arab attack, the victory itself proved difficult to accept for the young Left. The Jews, for many, ceased to be victims and became part of the main enemy against which the New Left was fighting: American and international capitalism and imperialism. For some groups in the West German New Left, the Palestinians became the last victims of Nazi Germany. While the Six Day War was an event of momentous significance in the history of the Middle East, for the 1960s Left, and really for public opinion generally in Germany, Europe and the United States, it was a sideshow to the main events of world politics, especially the war in Vietnam.[55] Concerning the main event for the 1960s Left, namely, the global struggle between imperialism and revolution, Israel was either irrelevant or on the wrong side as an ally of American imperialism.

In the era of the New Left and what Rudi Dutschke called "the long march through the institutions," there were scholars and intellectuals who continued to focus on the fate of the Jews in the Nazi era, but they were mostly liberals who worked outside the theoretical frameworks associated with the Marxist theory of the late 1960s. Karl Bracher and Eberhard Jaeckel, neither of whom adopted the New Left's "fascism theory," continued to write important works in the 1960s and 1970s about the specifically anti-Jewish dimensions of the Nazi regime.[56] Conservative politicians and intellectuals, with very few exceptions, showed little inclination to address the issue as well. Such memories and discussions were an unwelcome theme with conservative voters and readers who showed little desire to examine the Nazi past or the failure to confront it adequately in the early postwar years.

The end of the repression of "the Jewish question" within the West German Left began in Frankfurt am Main in the mid-1970s. It entailed fierce debates within the left-wing scene there during and after the hijacking of an Air France plane by Palestinian and West German terrorists in Entebbe in 1976. In a grotesque echo of the "selections" of the Nazi era, the hijackers separated not only Israelis from non-Israelis but Jews from non-Jews at the airport. An Israeli commando force — which included future Prime Minister Ehud Barak and the older brother of future Prime Minister Benjamin Netanyanu — shot and killed all the terrorists before they made good on threats to harm or kill their Jewish hostages. One of the West German terrorists, as Paul Berman has recalled, came from the leftist scene in Frankfurt.[57] The fact of a West German New Leftist pointing a machine gun at Jews set off a furious debate in Frankfurt's cafes, seminars, podium discussions at the university and in the pages of journals such as *Links* and *Pflasterstrand*.[58] Jewish intellectuals close to the West German New Left — Dan Diner, Micha Brumlik and Cilly Kugelmann, and a non-Jewish student of Adorno, Detlev Claussen — took the lead in challenging the way in which anti-Semitism had entered into the leftist orthodoxy of anti-imperialism and anti-Zionism. The challenge extended from Diner's attacks on the reductionist and hyper-rationalistic assumptions of Marxist theories to Claussen's denunciations of the moral obtuseness and political blindness of terrorism in general and terrorism directed by Germans against Jews in particular.[59] They argued that the theory and practice of anti-Zionism in West Germany represented at best an escape from the burdens of German history and at worst a continuation of anti-Semitism camouflaged with the Left's discourse of liberation. Daniel Cohn-Bendit, the best-known leftist political figure in Frankfurt am Main, agreed with these criticisms. So too, apparently, did a much lesser-known autodidact and future foreign minister of the Federal Republic, Joschka Fischer.

Seen in the long-term perspective of the history of public memory of the Holocaust in the era of two German states after 1945, the intra-left debate that was crushed in the anti-cosmopolitan purges in East Berlin in winter

1952–53 reemerged in Frankfurt am Main in the mid- and late 1970s. In the second instance, however, there was no Communist Party that monopolized power and was able to purge dissenters. As a result the Jewish question and the memory of the Holocaust could gradually begin to emerge among a minority of liberal intellectuals after having been obscured within the theoretical clouds of 1960s Marxism.[60]

In the 1980s, the word "Holocaust" entered West German public life in quite a different manner, namely, not in reference to the past genocide of the Jews but to a possible mass death of the Germans and Europeans in a nuclear war between the Soviet Union and the American-led NATO alliance. The occasion for this contemporary evocation of the term "Holocaust" was the political battle over medium-range nuclear weapons. The "euromissiles" dispute dominated political debate from the time of NATO's "two-track decision" in December 1979 to the deployment of American Cruise and Pershing 2 missiles in the fall of 1983.[61] The application of the term "Holocaust" to Western, especially American, policy emerged first in a 1981 book by Anton-Andreas Guha, the defense correspondent of the Frankfurter Rundschau, entitled Das Holocaust Europas, and appeared in articles in mass circulation weeklies such as Stern and Der Spiegel. Over the next two years, Soviet propaganda in West Germany included assertions that the nuclear deployments of the United States and NATO were linked to plans for a "nuclear Auschwitz" in Europe. On 30 January 1983, the 50th anniversary of Hitler's seizure of power, Günter Grass spoke at the Paulskirche in Frankfurt am Main on the "right of resistance." He granted that the NATO deployments were not the same as the death camp in Auschwitz.

> But there is no great difference between the cynical disregard of the basic ethical values at the infamous Wannsee Conference, which decreed the Final Solution, and the cynicism that in our day produces war games simulating nuclear combat with projections of here fifty, there eighty million dead. Every German should know that we would be first to feed our numbers into the fighting machine.[62]

The terms "Auschwitz" and "Holocaust" had first burst the bonds of their historical referent during the euromissile dispute, not during the subsequently infamous Historikerstreit (Historians' Debate).

Of all the bitter moments of the battle of the euromissiles none was more so than in the Bundestag debate of June 1983 when a relatively recent Bundestag deputy in the Green Party named Joschka Fischer debated with the General Secretary of the Christian Democratic Union, Heiner Geissler. The bitterness had everything to do with the way the memory and implications of Auschwitz, but also "Munich," entered into contemporary West German politics. Was the Holocaust made possible by modernity's instrumental rationality or by the mentality of appeasement that resulted in the Munich agreement? The argument began when Fischer, though insisting that the uniqueness of the Nazi crimes against the Jews "cannot be covered up with quick analogies," still expressed his horror that

> apparently in the system-logic of the modern, even after Auschwitz, it is not yet taboo to continue to prepare means of mass annihilation — this time not on the basis of racial ideology but on the basis of the East-West conflict. I am not making an analogy with Auschwitz, but I say that Auschwitz warns us to denounce this logic where it surfaces and to fight it politically.[63]

Just as the "system-logic of modernity," so Fischer argued, had contributed to Auschwitz, so now it was contributing to a possible contemporary mass extermination. In the Bundestag, Geissler rejected what he called Fischer's association of Western defense policy with "a second Auschwitz" and escalated the political temperature to the boiling point when he said that "the pacifism of the 1930s [in Britain] which in its foundations in an ethic of conviction is distinguished very little from the [West German] pacifism of today, this pacifism of the 1930s first made Auschwitz possible." While the deputies of the conservative parties rose to applaud, Otto Schily, currently leading the battle against terrorism in Germany as the Interior Ministry of the Federal Republic but then a member of parliament in the Green Party, called out to Geissler "that is an absolutely shameless statement." Undeterred, Geissler referred to debates between Winston Churchill and Neville Chamberlain in the House of Commons and recalled the disastrous consequences of appeasement at Munich. "The whole horrible and murderous development in the National Socialist regime with the death and murder of millions of people would not have been possible if the weakness of the free democracies had not made it easier for the National Socialist regime to begin the war." Horst Ehmke, the Minister of Justice in the still governing Social Democratic/Free Democrat coalition led by Helmut Schmidt, pointed out that Neville Chamberlain was not a pacifist but a "British right-winger" who had hoped to turn Hitler against the Bolsheviks. "It was," Ehmke continued, "the German Right in Weimar that made Auschwitz possible by helping put Hitler in the saddle."[64] Helmut Kohl, soon to become German Chancellor, urged his fellow parliamentarians to read Churchill's *Gathering Storm* to understand how appeasement in the 1930s had made, in Churchill's words, "the unnecessary war" possible.[65]

As this debate made apparent, German memory of the Holocaust divided not only between East and West Germany but also between Left and Right within the Federal Republic. On the whole, at the end of the era of *Ostpolitik*, the political implications of Holocaust memory on the left were anti-militarist and opposed to the realist interpretation associated with Churchill's critique of appeasement. For West German conservatives, on the other hand, memory of the Nazi era focused less on Auschwitz than on the attempt to see parallels between appeasement of Nazism in the 1930s, on the one hand, and "appeasement" of the Soviet Union in the 1980s expressed in opposition to the NATO deployments in the 1980s. The issue here was less whether or not to remember the Nazi era but rather what the proper lessons of that era were.

The Bitburg controversy was a chapter in German memory that followed from the disputes of the euromissile period. Chancellor Kohl's insistence that President Reagan visit the graves of members of the Waffen SS in Bitburg was part of a conservative reaction to the political culture of the Détente era of Willy Brandt and Helmut Schmidt. This *Tendenzwende* overshot the mark of plausible critique of the erosion of liberal and left-liberal anti-communism and, whether intentionally or not, became an effort to displace the growing prominence that the memory of the Holocaust had assumed in West German political culture. It also represented an attempted return to the memorial discourse of Kohl's political hero, Konrad Adenauer, in which distinctions between perpetrators and victims gave way to reference to vague, unspecified and generalized victims that made no such distinctions.[66] Kohl's determination to have the American president honor the memory of soldiers who had fought in the Wehrmacht and even the Waffen SS seemed to offer symbolic confirmation of an unbroken continuity between the Wehrmacht's war against the Soviet Union and the Cold War that followed. Was this not what communist propaganda about "Nazis in Bonn" had been saying for decades?

In the Adenauer era, Theodor Heuss had used the pulpit of the *Bundespräsident* to counter the pressures to place a distorted image of the past in the service of present politics. In the Kohl era *Bundespräsident* Richard von Weizsäcker used the same pulpit to reinvigorate the beleaguered traditions of West German national political retrospection. The soon world-famous speech in the Bundestag on 8 May 1985 in ceremonies marking the 40th anniversary of the end of World War II was the most important speech about the crimes of the Nazi era delivered in the national political arena since Heuss's address in Bergen-Belsen in November 1952.[67] The central theme of Weizsäcker's speech was the need for Germans to "look truth straight in the eye — without embellishment or distortion." He responded directly to the conservative politicians and pundits who declared in newspaper advertisements that 8 May 1945 was the beginning of flight, expulsion and dictatorship in the East. Weizsäcker insisted that the cause of Germans' postwar problems "goes back to the start of the tyranny that brought about war. We must not separate May 8, 1945, from January 30, 1933." Rather than to remember the sufferings of one group at the expense of another, he urged Germans to mourn for "all the dead of the war and the tyranny." In a clear indication of how the memory of the Holocaust had entered into the center of his national narrative, he placed the "six million Jews" at the beginning of a list of the dead which also included "countless citizens of the Soviet Union and Poland"; German soldiers, German citizens killed in air raids, captivity or during expulsion; the Roma and Sinti; the homosexuals and the mentally ill; those killed due to their religious or political beliefs; hostages; members of resistance movements "in all countries occupied by us," and also "the victims of the German resistance — among the public, the military, the churches, the workers and trade unions, and the Communists."[68] This was the most comprehensive listing yet made by a West German Chancellor or *Bundespräsident* of the victims of Nazism, and was one that crossed the Cold War fault lines that had distorted memory in Bitburg. The narrative structure of the speech dispensed with a happy ending, whether it be Ulbricht's victorious socialism in Sachsenhausen in 1961, or the effort by Reagan and Kohl to seek reconciliation in Bitburg, thereby striving to use Cold War alliances to put aside the memory of the antagonisms of World War II. Memory meant the ability to mourn and to grieve about "the endless army of the dead" and the suffering of those who survived.[69] Like Heuss, Weizsäcker presented a most un-Hegelian narrative of unredeemed suffering and tragedy.

In contrast to efforts to marginalize the issue, he said that "at the root of the tyranny was Hitler's immeasurable hatred against our Jewish compatriots." As opposed to those seeking to diminish the uniqueness of the event, he insisted that "the genocide of the Jews is, however, unparalleled in history." Though "execution of this crime was in the hands of a few people" and was concealed from the public, "every German was able to experience what his Jewish compatriots had to suffer, ranging from plain apathy and hidden intolerance to outright hatred. Who could remain unsuspecting" after the persecutions of the Jews in the 1930s? Anyone who "opened his eyes and ears and sought information could not fail to notice that the Jews were being deported." The claims of many of his own generation not to have known anything about the ongoing crimes would not withstand critical scrutiny.[70] In place of the distancing reference to crimes committed "in the name of Germany" used by Adenauer and others, Weiszäcker used the first person plural — "we" and "us."

His acknowledgment of collective responsibility did not mean acceptance of collective guilt. "There is," he said, "no such thing as the guilt or innocence of an entire nation. Guilt is, like innocence, not collective, but personal." The young could not profess guilt "for crimes that they did not commit. No discerning person can expect them to wear a penitential robe simply because they are Germans." But they did have a responsibility to "keep alive the memories . . . anyone who closes his eyes to the past is blind to the present. Whoever refuses to remember the inhumanity is prone to new risks of infection." Remembering the past was both a moral obligation as well as a political necessity. Furthermore, no matter what the Germans remembered, "the Jewish nation remembers and will always remember. We seek reconciliation . . . there can be no reconciliation without remembrance."[71] Reconciliation with "the Jewish nation" had to pass through memory of the Holocaust.

In contrast to the neat divisions between the memories of Auschwitz and Munich that surfaced during the euromissile dispute, Weizsäcker brought them together. The failures of other powers did "not mitigate Germany's responsibility for the outbreak of the Second World War." Moreover, he traced the postwar division of Germany to the policies of Nazi Germany. Though events following 1945 cemented the division of Europe and Germany, "without the war started by Hitler it [the division] would not have happened at all."[72] Weizsäcker's speech showed the impact of Brandt's challenge to the political culture of the Adenauer era. By insisting that 8 May 1945 must not be separated from 30 January 1933, Weizsäcker placed postwar history into a longer chronological causal sequence. Both within and outside West Germany, the response to his speech was overwhelmingly favorable.

Following German unification led by the Chancellor who had organized the Bitburg fiasco, observers of German Vergangenheitsbewältigung worried that Helmut Kohl would inaugurate a new era of Holocaust amnesia in an era of German nationalism and Western triumphalism.[73] To be sure, there was a terrible resurgence of neo-Nazi violence against Jews and foreigners, and the hard Right did make some regional electoral gains in the years of nationalist euphoria. Some of the worst fears of a forgetful and xenophobic Germany did indeed come to pass in the violent attacks on asylum seekers, Helmut Kohl's tepid responses to the victims and the difficulty of prosecutors and police in bringing the perpetrators to justice. Though the collapse of East German official anti-fascism eliminated state sponsorship from the Marxist-Leninist forms of avoidance and the regular attacks on "Zionist aggressors," the aftereffects of four decades of at times thinly veiled state-sponsored anti-Semitism were apparent in the xenophobia in post-unification Eastern Germany. Yet Kohl also demonstrated that he shared Thomas Mann's vision of a European Germany integrated into a peaceful Europe. To attain that goal, he had to demonstrate that a unified Germany would retain and even strengthen its official memory of the crimes of the Nazi era. Forgetfulness was a formula for sowing mistrust and fear among Germany's European neighbors, not to mention in Israel and the United States. So reasons of state coincided with a moral and cultural tradition that Kohl had failed to appreciate only a decade earlier in Bitburg.

On the other hand, on 9 May 1995 Ignatz Bubis, the Chairman of the Central Council of Jews in Germany, proposed that either 20 January, the day of the Wannsee Conference, or 27 January, the anniversary of the liberation of Auschwitz-Birkenau, become a German national day of remembrance for the victims of Nazi persecution and genocide.[74] On 1 June 1995, a majority in the Bundestag approved the 27 January date.[75] In June 1999, following seemingly interminable but also very thought-provoking debate and discussion in Berlin, Chancellor Kohl and the German parliament supported the construction of a memorial to the murdered Jews of Europe on a plot of land located close to the key government buildings in the new capital of Berlin. With that decision a unified Germany literally anchored the memory of the Holocaust into the landscape of the new capital in Berlin. In these years as well, Germany's citizenship laws were reformed to replace biology with residence and place of birth as primary considerations. Forty years after Eichmann, the tradition of memory that began in the late 1940s with Theodor Heuss and Kurt Schumacher had now come to encompass the mainstream political and intellectual establishment as a whole. As unpopular and uncomfortable as this tradition of memory had been since it began, every effort from the Right and the Left to displace it had failed.

The collapse of communism in Europe and the end of the Cold War also brought an important change within the German Left, a change most evident in the remarkable political evolution of Germany's Foreign Minister Joschka Fischer. The rethinking that began in the cafés in Frankfurt am Main in 1976 and found only a waystation in the bitter confrontation over the euromissiles came into full view in the 1990s. It was then that the leftist opposition and then the Social Democratic/Green government confronted the issue of what to do in response both to Iraq's invasion of Kuwait and later to Serbia's program of ethnic cleansing in the Balkans. Where the memory of the Holocaust during the euromissile dispute had led Fischer to argue against the missile deployments, now that containment of the Soviet Union and communism was no longer at issue, Fischer, Cohn-Bendit and the novelist and essayist Peter Schneider all turned the implications of memory of the Holocaust upside down. They both revived the spirit of liberal anti-fascism of the 1930s and 1940s and combined it with the spirit of human rights of recent decades. The history of this transformation remains to be written, but its outlines are clear enough. The arguments about the dangers of appeasement, which in 1983 had been the exclusive property of West German conservatives, in the 1990s entered into the public discourse of German liberals and left-liberals such as Fischer. Just as Elie Wiesel, speaking at the opening ceremonies of the United States Holocaust Memorial Museum in Washington, DC, had urged President Clinton to intervene militarily in the Balkans in 1993, so Fischer displeased many of his Green fellow party members by arguing that the memory of the Holocaust in Germany should spur the German government to intervene to prevent human rights abuses in the Balkans. The political implications of left-wing memory had been transformed from the anti-militarist, pacifist messages of the 1960s into a kind of revival of liberal and leftist anti-fascism of the 1940s, one that connected the force of arms to defense of human rights. Whereas in 1983 the memory of Auschwitz seemed so obviously to justify non-intervention and opposition to the use of military force, in the transformed post-Cold War era it now lent added urgency to the argument that Germany should do what it could to prevent a repetition of anything similar. This change constituted the most important alteration of the political implications of Holocaust memory in the German Left since the 1960s.

*

The traditions of Holocaust memory, which first emerged in the postwar years "after Hitler" and which have been assaulted from right and left for half a century, survived "after Eichmann." Eras of amnesia may in time return, but the remarkable feature of German political culture in recent years remains the degree to which Holocaust memory persists. Memory had its origins in a conjuncture of international and indigenous causes, namely defeat and occupation, on the one hand, and multiple restorations, on the other. A continuing conjuncture of international and indigenous causes contributed to memory's persistence "after Eichmann." On the one hand, West Germany and then unified Germany learned that a return to international respectability, regaining of trust, reassurance of past adversaries and then expansion of diplomatic relations to the West and to the East were enhanced, not damaged, by a vivid and truthful memory of the crimes of the Nazi era. Silence or obfuscation was bad diplomacy and yes, probably also bad for German exports. Germany had and has too many neighbors and their memories, as well as the memories of the Jews, will not go away no matter what the Germans wish to do. Along with these practical interests there remained the autonomous impact of what had become a tradition with strong roots in German political culture. Indeed, for a part of the German political and opinion-making establishment that tradition had become a duty as well as a source of pride and honor. This interaction of practical interests and moral tradition, so familiar to historians of the conjuncture of ideology and politics, was key to the persistence of German Holocaust memory "after Eichmann." It remains to be seen whether this centrality will persist or be attenuated in the face of demands for the memory of the suffering of others, reactions to the Israeli-Palestinian conflict or generational change and fading memories.

NOTES

1 Jeffrey Herf, *Divided Memory: The Nazi Past in the Two Germanys* (Cambridge, MA, 1997).
2 On this see Harold Marcuse, *Legacies of Dachau: The Uses and Abuses of a Concentration Camp, 1933–2001* (New York, 2001); and Robert G. Moeller, *War Stories: The Search for a Usable Past in the Federal Republic of Germany* (Berkeley, CA, 2001).

3 The literature on this subject is extensive. See Herf, *Divided Memory*; Norbert Frei, *Vergangenheitspolitik: Die Anfänge der Bundesrepublik und die NS-Vergangenheit* (Munich, 1996); Thomas Alan Schwartz, *America's Germany: John J. McCloy and the Federal Republic of Germany* (Cambridge, MA, 1991); Ulrich Brochhagen, *Nach Nürnberg: Vergangenheitsbewältigung und Westintegration in der Ära Adenauer* (Hamburg, 1994).

4 The German historian Norbert Frei examines the history of premature amnesty and cynical pleas for "forgiveness" in the early years of the Federal Republic in his *Vergangenheitspolitik*. During the Nuremberg era (1945–49), the Allies convicted 80 percent of the approximately 6,000 persons convicted of crimes in the Nazi era in the Western zones and then in the Federal Republic. As figures for prosecutions in the Eastern zones and East Germany included political opponents of the regime who were denounced as "fascists," the figures for East Germany remain to be firmly established. On this see Herf, *Divided Memory*.

5 Peter Steinbach, *Nationalsozialistische Gewaltverbrechen: Die Diskussion in der deutschen Öffentlichkeit nach 1945* (West Berlin, 1981), p. 74.

6 Deutscher Bundestag, *Zur Verjährung nationalsozialistischer Verbrechen: Dokumentation der parlamentarischen Bewältigung des Problems 1960–1979* (hereafter *Zur Verjährung nationalsozialistischer Verbrechen*) (Bonn, 1980), Part 1, p. 110.

7 Albrecht Götz, *Bilanz der Verfolgung von NS-Straftaten* (Cologne, 1986), p. 149; also see Adalbert Rückerl, *Die Strafverfolgung von NS-Verbrechen: 1945–1978* (Heidelberg-Karlsruhe, 1979). From 8 May 1945 to the mid-1980s, Allied and then West German courts accused 90,921 persons of participating in war crimes or crimes against humanity. Of this number 6,479 persons were convicted; 12 were executed; 160 were sentenced to life in prison; 6,192 received extended prison terms; 114 paid fines; 1 youth received a warning; and 83,140 cases were closed without convictions due to findings of innocence, non-opening of the proceedings by the court, or death of the accused. Of these 6,479 convictions, *over 80 percent (5,487) were handed down by Western occupying powers between 1945 and 1951*. The 1,819 convictions in 1948 constituted the high point of the postwar judicial proceedings. Also see Steinbach, *Nationalsozialistische Gewaltverbrechen*, pp. 51–3.

8 *Zur Verjährung nationalsozialistischer Verbrechen*, Part 1, pp. 109–10.

9 On the use of Nazi war crimes charges to convict political opponents see Michael Klonovsky and Jan von Flocken, *Stalins Lager in Deutschland* (Munich, 1993).

10 Figures from *Zur Verjährung nationalsozialistischer Verbrechen*, Part 1, pp. 103–4.

11 "Antrag der Fraktion der SPD," in ibid., pp. 10–13.

12 Götz, *Bilanz der Verfolgung*, p. 143.

13 "Die Debatte im Plenum," 24 May 1960, in *Zur Verjährung nationalsozialistischer Verbrechen*, Part 1, pp. 15–47.

14 See *Verhandlungen des deutschen Bundestages 4. Wahlperiode, Stenographische Bericht Band 58, Sitzung 178–186*, 25 March 1965, pp. 8788–90. Also see Karl Jaspers, "Für Völkermord gibt es keine Verjährung," reprinted in idem, *Wohin Treibt die Bundesrepublik* ([1966]; Munich, 1988).

15 Steinbach, *Nationalsozialistische Gewaltverbrechen*, pp. 75–7.

16 Cited in Götz, *Bilanz der Verfolgung*, p. 144.

17 *Verhandlungen des deutschen Bundestages 4. Wahlperiode, Band 58, Sitzung 178–186*, 25 March 1965, pp. 8788–90.

18 Horst Ehmke, in *Zur Verjährung nationalsozialistischer Verbrechen*, Part 2, pp. 381–90. Also see "Dr. Ehmke," in *Verhandlungen des deutschen Bundestages 5. Wahlperiode (1965) Band 70, Sitzung 230–247*, 11 June 1969, pp. 13053–8.

19 "Bundesgesetzblatt," in *Zur Verjährung nationalsozialistischer Verbrechen*, Part 2, pp. 436–7; Götz, *Bilanz der Verfolgung*, p. 144.

20 "Frau Dr. Däubler-Gmelin," in *Verhandlungen des deutschen Bundestages 6.Wahlperiode (1976) 163–175 Sitzung,166 Sitzung*, 3 July 1979, pp. 13239–43.

21 "Frau Dr. Hamm-Brucher," in ibid., pp. 13282–4.

22 Ibid., pp. 13292–4. Also see Jeffrey Herf, "The "Holocaust" Reception in West Germany: Right, Center, and Left," in Anson Rabinbach and Jack Zipes (eds.), *Germans and Jews since the Holocaust: The Changing Situation in West Germany* (New York, 1986), p. 226; Steinbach,

Nationalsozialististiche Gewaltverbrechen, pp. 64–7; and *Zur Verjährung nationalsozialistischer Verbrechen*, Pts. 2 and 3.

23 Götz, *Bilanz der Verfolgung*, p. 149.

24 Willy Brandt, *In Exile: Essays, Reflections, Letters 1933–1947*, trans. R. W. Last (London, 1971).

25 See Willy Brandt, *Friedenspolitik in Europa*, 3rd edn. (Frankfurt/Main, 1971).

26 Ibid., p. 37. See Timothy Garton Ash, *In Europe's Name: Germany and the Divided Continent* (New York: Vintage, 1994).

27 Willy Brandt, *Friedenspolitik in Europa*, p. 148.

28 Ibid., pp. 34–5.

29 See Willy Brandt, *Erinnerungen* (Frankfurt/Main, 1989), pp. 213–15.

30 *Ostpolitik*, not the Middle East, was the focus of Brandt's diplomacy. Nevertheless, his sympathies with Israel, and its Labor Party, were strong. He was the first West German Chancellor to visit Israel while in office. On this see Rolf Vogel (ed.), *Der deutsch-israelische Dialog*, Part 1, *Politik*, Vol. 1 (Munich, 1987), pp. 349–81, and 458–75.

31 Otto Grotewohl to Gamel Abdel Nasser, 24 June 1957, *Stiftung Archiv der Parteien und Massenorganizationen der DDR im Bundesarchiv* (hereafter SAPMO-BA), ZPA NL Otto Grotewohl 90/497, pp. 70–71. Also see Grotewohl's letter to Nasser of 24 October 1958, in which he praised the "anti-imperialist liberation struggle of the Arab peoples," in ibid., p. 87.

32 "Glückwunschtelegramm des Ministerpräsidenten Otto Grotewohl an den Präsidenten der Vereinigten Arabischen Republik, Gamal Abdel Nasser, anlässlich des Nationalfeiertages am 23. Juli 1958," in *Dokumente der Aussenpolitik der Regierung der Deutschen Demokratischen Republik, 1949–1986* (hereafter *DARDDR*), Band VI 1958 ([East] Berlin, 1959), pp. 481–2.

33 "Erklärung des Ministerpräsident der DDR, Otto Grotewohl über seinen Besuch in der Vereinigten Arabischen Republik," SAPMO-BA, ZPA NL Otto Grotewohl 90/491, pp. 408–9.

34 See Inge Deutschkron, *Israel und die Deutschen: Das Schwierige Verhältnis* (Cologne, 1991), pp. 287–314; and Vogel (ed.), *Der deutsch-israelische Dialog*, pp. 253–305.

35 Walter Ulbricht, "Interview der VAR Zeitung 'Al Ahram'," 23 February 1965, in *DARDDR Band XIII* ([East] Berlin, 1969), pp. 847–8.

36 Walter Ulbricht and Gamel Abdel Nasser, "Gemeinsame Erklärung," 1 March 1965 (Cairo) in ibid., p. 855.

37 "Abkommen zwischen der Regierung der Deutschen Demokratischen Republik und der Regierung der Vereinigten Arabischen Republik über kulturelle und wissenschaftliche Zusammenarbeit vom 1. März 1965," in ibid., pp. 858–63.

38 Walter Ulbricht, "Rundfunk- und Fernsehinterview… mit Gerhart Eisler," 7 March 1965 (East Berlin), in ibid., pp. 872–3.

39 Walter Ulbricht, "Kommunique über die 16. Sitzung des Staatsrates der Deutschen Demokratischen Republik am 12. März 1965," in ibid., p. 881.

40 Walter Ulbricht, *The Two German States and the Aggression in the Near East* (Dresden, 1967). Also see Walter Ulbricht, "Rede… im Leipzig am 15. Juni 1967 zu Fragen der Lage im Nahen Osten und zur westdeutsche Expansionspolitik im Rahmen der USA-Globalstrategie," in *DARDDR Band XV* ([East] Berlin, 1971), pp. 515–38. Also see "Interview mit dem Minister für Auswärtige Angelegenheiten der Deutschen Demokratische Republik, Otto Winzer, nach seiner Rückkehr von der Aussenministerkonferenz europäischer sozialistischer Staaten in Warschau am 21. Dezember 1967," in *DARDDR Band XV 2. Halbband* ([East] Berlin, 1970), pp. 570–71.

41 "Erklärung eines Sprechers des Ministeriums für Auswärtige Angelegenheiten der Deutschen Demokratischen Republik vom 11. November 1967 zur Reise des früheren westdeutschen Bundeskanzlers Ludwig Erhard nach Israel," *DARDDR Band XV 2. Halbband*, p. 566. Also see *Halbband 1* for 1967 for East German statements on the Six Day War. The use of words such as "conspiracy" to describe Western support for Israel may have been on the mind of the historian Walter Laqueur when he observed that East German anti-Israeli denunciations made Moscow's *Pravda* seem "moderate and statesmanlike." Cited in Peter Dittmar, "DDR und Israel" (II), *Deutschland Archiv*, Vol. 10, No. 8 (August 1977), p. 850.

42 On this see Karen Hartewig, "Jüdische Kommunisten in der DDR und ihr Verhältnis zu Israel," in Wolfang Schwanitz (ed.), *Jenseits der Legende: Araber, Juden, Deutsche* (Berlin, 1994), pp. 130–36; and Helmut Eschwege, *Fremd unter Meinesgleichen: Erinnerung eines dresdener Juden* (Berlin, 1991).

43 Albert Norden to Werner Lamberz, 9 June 1967, in SAPMO-BA, ZPA NL Walter Ulbricht 182/1339; cited by Hartewig, "Jüdische Kommunisten," pp. 218–19.

44 See Dittmar, "DDR und Israel" (II), pp. 849–61. One of the leading figures of East German foreign policy in these years was Herman Axen (1916–92). Axen, who had been interned in Vernet, then Buchenwald and Auschwitz, was editor-in-chief of *Neues Deutschland* (1956–66), a member of the SED Politburo from 1970, and from 1966 Secretary in the Central Committee responsible for International Affairs. See "Herman Axen," in Jochen Cerny (ed.), *Wer war Wer — in der DDR* (Berlin, 1992), pp. 19–20. Also see Herman Axen, *Starker Sozialismus — sicherer Frieden: Ausgewählte Reden und Aufsätze* ([East] Berlin, 1981); idem, *Kampf um den Frieden — Schlüsselfrage der Gegenwart: Ausgewählte Reden und Aufsätze* ([East] Berlin, 1986).

45 The many joint communiqués, reports of press conferences in East Berlin and Arab capitals, and official government statements are published in the annual documents of the foreign policy of the German Democratic Republic (*DARDDR*) for the years from 1971 to the mid-1980s. Also see "Erich Honnecker," in Cerny (ed.), *Wer war Wer*, pp. 201–2.

46 Peter Florin, "Rede in der Nahostdebatte des Sicherheitsrates der Vereinten Nationen," in *DARDDR Band XXIV 2. Halbband 1976* ([East] Berlin, 1980), pp. 908–11.

47 See Peter Florin's representative contributions to debate on "the Palestine question" at the United Nations on 4 November 1975, in *DARDDR Band XXIII 2. Halbband* ([East] Berlin, 1979), pp. 1037–40.

48 "Mitteilung über den Besuch des Mitglieds des Exekutivkomitees und Leiter der Politischen Abteilung der Palästinensischen Befreiungsorganisation (PLO), Farouk al-Kaddoumi, in der Deutschen Demokratischen Republik," 9 September 1980; and "Mitteilung über das Gespräch zwischen dem Generalsekretär des Zentralkomitees der SED und Vorsitzenden des Staatsrates der DDR, Erich Honecker, und dem Vorsitzenden des Exekutivkomitees der Palästinensischen Befreiungsorganisation (PLO), Yasser Arafat, in Berlin," 29 December 1980, in *DARDDR Band XXVIII 1. Halbband* ([East] Berlin, 1980), pp. 525–7, and pp. 528–30.

49 See, for example, "Mitteilung über den Empfang einer Militärdelegation der Palästinensischen Befreiungsorganisation (PLO) beim Generalsekretär des Zentralkomitees der SED und Vorsitzenden des Staatrates der DDR, Erich Honecker," 17 November 1981, in ibid., pp. 224–5; also see *Neues Deutschland*, 18 November 1981.

50 "The East Germans Issue an Apology for Nazis' Crimes," *The New York Times*, 13 April 1990, pp. 1 and A7.

51 "Volkskammer bekennt Schuld am Holocaust: Erste freigewählte DDR-Regierung im Amt," *Frankfurter Rundschau* 14 April 1990, pp. 1–2.

52 "Excerpts from East Berlin Statement Apology," *The New York Times*, 13 April 1990, p. A7.

53 See "Truth and Healing in Eastern Europe," ibid., 14 April 1990, p. 22; and "East Germany accepts burden of Holocaust," *The Jerusalem Post*, 13 April 1990, pp. 1 and 11. For the text of the Volkskammer declaration see "Dokumentation: Gemeinsame Erklärung der Volkskammer," *Deutschland Archiv*, Vol. 23, No. 5 (May 1990), pp. 794–5.

54 On the anti-cosmopolitan purges, see Herf, *Divided Memory*, chs. 4–5.

55 On the tendency to read the past as the prehistory of major events, see Michael André Bernstein, *Foregone Conclusions: Against Apocalyptic History* (Berkeley, 1994).

56 See Karl Bracher, *The German Dictatorship* (New York, 1970); Eberhard Jaeckel, *Hitler's World View: A Blueprint for Power*, trans. Herbert Arnold (Cambridge, MA, 1981).

57 Paul Berman, "The Passion of Joschka Fischer," *The New Republic*, 27 August and 3 September 2001; also see Jeffrey Herf, "To the Editors," ibid., 15 October 2001, p. 4.

58 See the discussion in Herf, *Divided Memory*, pp. 348–9; also see Martin W. Kloke, *Israel und die deutsche Linke: Zur Geschichte eines schwierigen Verhältnis*, 2nd edn. (Frankfurt/Main, 1994); Micha Brumlik et al., *Der Antisemitismus und die Linke* (Frankfurt/Main, 1991); Dan Diner,

Zivilisationsbruch: Denken nach Auschwitz (Frankfurt/Main, 1988); Rabinbach and Zipes (eds.), *Germans and Jews since the Holocaust*.

59 See Detlev Claussen, "Terror in der Luft, Konterrevolution auf der Erde," in *Links*, Vol. 9, No. 78 (1976), p. 6; Dan Diner, "Linke und Antisemitismus: Uberlegungen zur Geschichte und Aktualität," in Karlheinz Schneider and Nikolaus Simon (eds.), *Solidarität und deutsche Geschichte: Die Linke zwischen Antisemitismus und Israelkritik* (West Berlin, 1984), pp. 61–80; Dan Diner, *Beyond the Conceivable: Studies on Germany, Nazism and the Holocaust* (Berkeley and Los Angeles, 2000); Detlev Claussen, *List der Gewalt: Soziale Revolution und ihre Theorien* (Frankfurt/Main, 1982); and Jeffrey Herf, "The Struggle Continues," review of *Beyond the Conceivable* in *The New Republic*, 5 and 12 August 2002, pp. 34–6. For an excellent bibliography of articles about Jews, anti-Semitism and the West German Left covering the period of the 1960s to the Gulf War in 1991, see Kloke, *Israel und die deutsche Linke*, pp. 331–87.

60 Sigrid Meuschel, *Legitimation und Parteiherrschaft in der DDR* (Frankfurt/Main, 1992).

61 For a history of this episode, see Jeffrey Herf, *War by Other Means: Soviet Power, West German Resistance and the Battle of the Euromissiles* (New York, 1991).

62 Cited in Herf, *War by Other Means*, p. 171.

63 Cited in ibid., p. 186.

64 Ibid., p. 187.

65 Ibid., pp. 188–9.

66 On the lack of differentiation in postwar West German memory, see Jeffrey Herf, "Abstraction, Specificity and the Holocaust: Recent Disputes over Memory in Germany," *Bulletin of the German Historical Institute*, London, Vol. 23, No. 2 (November, 2000), pp. 20–35.

67 "Speech by Richard von Weizsäcker, President of the Federal Republic of Germany, in the Bundestag during the Ceremony Commemorating the 40th Anniversary of the End of the War in Europe and of National Socialist Tyranny, May 8, 1945," in Geoffrey H. Hartman (ed.), *Bitburg in Moral and Political Perspective* (Bloomington, IN, 1986), pp. 262–73 (hereafter "Speech"); and Richard von Weizsäcker, "Der 8. Mai 1945 – 40 Jahre danach," in idem, *Von Deutschland aus: Reden des Bundespräsidenten* (Munich, 1987), pp. 9–36.

68 "Speech," pp. 263–4. On politics and the memory of the German Resistance, see David Clay Large, "'A Beacon in the German Darkness': The Anti-Nazi Resistance Legacy in West German Politics," in Michael Geyer and John W. Boyer (eds.), *Resistance Against the Third Reich, 1933–1990* (Chicago, IL, 1994), pp. 243–56; and Jeffrey Herf, "German Communism, the Discourse of "Antifascist Resistance," and the Jewish Catastrophe," in ibid., pp. 257–94.

69 "Speech," p. 264.

70 Ibid., pp. 264–5.

71 Ibid., pp. 265–6.

72 Ibid., p. 267.

73 On this see Andrei S. Markovits and Simon Reich, *The German Predicament: Memory and Power in the New Europe* (Ithaca, NY, 1997).

74 "Bubis dringt auf Gedenktag für die NA-Opfer," *Süddeutsche Zeitung*, 9 May 1995. On his trip to Israel with members of the Green Party, see "Davidstern neben Pälästinensertuch: Joschka Fischers Israel-Besuch als grüne Aussenpolitik," *Süddeutsche Zeitung*, 24 May 1995.

75 "Auschwitz Anniversary to be German Remembrance Day," *Agence France Presse*, 1 June 1995.

Between Collective Memory and Manipulation: The Holocaust, Wagner and the Israelis

Na'ama Sheffi

> No need for fine distinctions here. There is no doubt that in the popular mind Wagner has become the classic symbol of anti-Semitism and the spiritual father of Nazism. There is nothing to argue about here, and we could line up a thousand proofs, but even if we don't agree, this is what happened and it is an inalienable part of the culture of the State of Israel. The first boycott of Wagner was begun by the people in the art world themselves, by the Philharmonic Orchestra of the State of Israel, when, after *Kristallnacht*, it canceled its performance of a Wagner piece. This means that the musicians themselves felt they just could not do it.[1]

This pronouncement by Member of Knesset (MK) Shaul Yahalom at the opening of a special meeting of the Knesset Education and Culture committee in May 2001 highlighted Wagner's unique status in Israeli culture as a symbol of anti-Semitism in general and National Socialism in particular — and, accordingly, as a part of the Israeli collective memory of the Holocaust. The subtext of Yahalom's speech was as interesting as the speech itself. The fact that such a debate was even taking place in the Knesset was a measure of the degree of political involvement in the subject, and Yahalom's membership of the National Religious Party suggests that the debate over Wagner reflected broad cultural characteristics of Israeli society. Even the date of the speech, 8 May 2001, was significant, inviting reflections on the fraught relationship between Israel and Germany. On the day that Europe was celebrating the 56th anniversary of the Allied victory over Nazi Germany, the organizers of the Israel Festival to be held in Jerusalem in late May–early July were asked to cancel a concert at which the Berlin State Orchestra, conducted by its musical director, Daniel Barenboim, was to play the first act of Richard Wagner's *Die Walküre*.[2]

In this context, I would like to examine and analyze the process by which Wagner became a symbolic part of the commemoration of the Holocaust in Israel. After reviewing some of the stages in that process, many of which coincided with climactic moments in the public discussion of the Holocaust, I will argue that the means by which Wagner became a symbol was closely related to the nature of Holocaust commemoration in Israeli culture.[3] Moreover, I see a definite parallel between the character of the Wagner debate and the way that the public debate on the Holocaust has been conducted. In both cases the debate began among Holocaust survivors and the relatives of those murdered, and then expanded to the general public. Thus, each debate involved a transition from the private memories of those personally affected by the Holocaust to the collective memory of all Israelis, who see the Holocaust as a shared national experience. The issue is also a focus for yet another significant correlation, that between the development of ideology and the gradual formation of national identity — in other words, the Wagner debate has served as a catalyst in the creation of that specific part of the Jewish-Israeli identity that is related to the collective experiences of Holocaust survivors and their impact on Israeli society.[4] Similarly, the public debate concerning the status Israel should assign German culture in general and Wagner in particular sometimes overflowed into concerns over the shaping of Israeli culture. In this respect it is notable that Israeli society tends to see ideological opposition to the Nazi heritage and the duty to remember the Holocaust as a unifying element in modern Hebrew-Jewish culture. Finally, I will examine Wagner's status as part of the Israeli collective memory of the Holocaust today, and try to determine whose memory it really is.[5]

Most of the rounds of the Wagner debate in Israel have coincided with other debates concerning the Holocaust and relations between Israel and Germany or between Israelis and Germans. Criticism of Wagner focused primarily on his anti-Semitic attitudes, which he expressed both privately and in a vituperative article entitled "Das Judentum in der Musik," published initially under a pen name and later under his own name.[6] In addition, the nationalistic interpretation given to his musical works both during his lifetime and after his death, his adoption by the Nazis and his characterization — refuted only in recent years — as the composer whom Hitler admired were the main reasons for his lasting rejection by Israel.[7] These points against him were further reinforced over the years by the testimony of Holocaust survivors, for whom the sounds of Wagner's music could never be dissociated from the image of Jews being marched to their deaths in the concentration camps.[8]

As Yahalom mentioned, Wagner was taken off the program of the Palestine Symphony Orchestra (which would later become the Israel Philharmonic Orchestra [IPO]) for the first time immediately after Kristallnacht in November 1938. The program of the concert that was to open the season three days after Kristallnacht was changed at the request of the orchestra's management. The conductor, Arturo Toscanini, himself a voluntary exile who had refused to put his art at the service of the Fascist regime in Italy, replaced the overture to *Die Meistersinger von Nürnberg* — a work popular at Nazi Party conventions — with another piece.[9] Plans to play Wagner compositions in Israel were subsequently canceled on many occasions, always for ideological reasons.

In the 1950s and 1960s the Wagner issue became linked to the controversy over performing music by Richard Strauss, the first director of the Nazi Propaganda Ministry's Music Division. Towards the end of 1952, about ten months after negotiations over German reparations to Israel were announced, the country was rife with rumors that the IPO was going to perform pieces by Wagner and Strauss, an idea that stirred up great public turmoil.[10] In the spring of 1953, in the same week as the Holocaust and Heroism Remembrance Day, the Jewish violinist Jascha Heifetz played Strauss's Sonata for Violin in the course of a series of recitals he was giving in Israel. He was fiercely attacked by the press, and ultimately physically assaulted on the street.[11] In the summer of 1966, a year after the establishment of diplomatic ties with West Germany and five years after the Eichmann trial, the IPO printed an article in its concert programs announcing its intention of playing works by Wagner and Strauss. The ensuing public uproar led it to cancel this plan.[12]

Another similar declaration of intent rekindled the conflict in the winter of 1981, a time when Prime Minister Menachem Begin was embroiled in a grim battle with West German Chancellor Helmut Schmidt over a political statement made by the latter. Visiting Saudi Arabia earlier that year, Schmidt had taken responsibility for the Palestinian refugee problem, explaining that since the establishment of the State of Israel was the consequence of the Holocaust, the refugee problem it had created should be taken care of by the Germans. This phase of the controversy also featured elements of xenophobia and general pronouncements on the implications of adopting Western culture in the State of Israel.[13] A new attempt to lift the boycott exactly one decade later again elicited protests. This time an aggravating factor was the recent Gulf War, during which newspapers in Israel had often compared Saddam Hussein to Adolf Hitler, and the modern threat of gas warfare to the horrifying use of Zyklon B in the past.[14] In the spring and summer of 2001, the issue was not only the performance of Wagner's music in itself, but also the fact that it was to be performed by a German orchestra in the Israeli capital.

On all these occasions, and on others not directly linked to other debates on the Holocaust and Israeli–German relations, the voice of Holocaust survivors was a central factor. Despite the process of fragmentation that Israeli society has undergone over the past 20 years, in which emphasis has been placed on the disparities between secular and religious Jews, Jews and Arabs, urban areas and peripheral settlements — in contrast to the unity and solidarity that characterized it until the late 1960s — the hallowed nature of the memory of the Holocaust is still a common denominator in Israeli society. The survivors insisted that performing Wagner's works was an insult to the memory of the dead who had been marched to their doom to the strains of his music. At the very least, Wagner was beyond the pale by virtue of his proto-Nazi ideology, which had influenced National Socialism itself. The degree of Wagner's anti-Semitism has been seriously discussed in Israel only in the last 20 years, since the renewal of the controversy in 1981 and the publication of the first Hebrew translation of Wagner's diatribe against Jews, "Das Judentum in der Musik," in 1984.[15] Long before that quite a few caustic articles had been published associating Wagner with anti-Semitism in such terms as "the horrible influence that Wagner's music exercised on the German beasts of prey,"[16] or, with respect to Strauss, "The sounds of spiritual and moral degeneracy arose from the magical violin [of Jascha Heifetz] and entered Jewish ears that *remained* attached to their heads after 10 years of total annihilation."[17]

Some of the authors of these harsh articles were themselves Holocaust survivors or relatives of those who had been murdered. In recent years, as their active lives as journalists and politicians draw to an end, some of them have been moved to appeal to Israeli courts for injunctions against the performance of Wagner's music in Israel. From September 2000 to May 2001, survivors took court action against Wagner's music both as individuals and through the umbrella organization of Holocaust survivors no fewer than five times.[18] This development would seem to be a natural extension of the significant increase in legal actions in Israel in the last decades, and of the heavy involvement of the courts — especially the Supreme Court — in Israeli public life. Now, however, other survivors broke the traditional unified stand of the past to complain that they would no longer serve as tools in the hands of those who saw themselves as the representatives of all survivors.

This declaration underlined a very problematic factor in the Israeli attitude to Holocaust survivors: up to that point, and despite the theoretical recognition that every survivor had his or her own personal story, survivors had been perceived as a monolithic body in Israeli society. But now, in letters sent primarily to musical institutions and, less frequently, to the press, some survivors expressed contempt for those who had

> made a career out of being a Holocaust survivor. They exploit every opportunity to shout and cry ... I, too, am a Holocaust survivor, left disabled after Nazi persecution. The Nazis murdered part of my family. Yet, despite that, I keep myself sane, distinguish between past and present, emotion and sense, and politics and art.[19]

Thus, it appears in fact that survivors' declining public activity and the courts' increasing involvement in public life were not the only reasons for their more frequent recourse to the law. To a large extent, the open dissension among the survivors, their decreasing numbers and their fear of radical erosion in the special status Israeli society had accorded them for so many years were their real reasons for taking legal action. These may also be the reasons for the increasing involvement of politicians in the issue, an idea I will return to later.

Survivors had reacted strongly to the Wagner issue before this. In 1981 Dov Shilansky, the deputy minister in the prime minister's office and a Holocaust survivor himself, made some very insulting remarks about Zubin Mehta, the IPO musical director, who was determined to conduct Wagner's music in Israel. In a radio interview, Shilansky recommended that Mehta go back to where he had come from — India.[20] This xenophobic message was in tune with some of the articles in the press, one of which, by another Holocaust survivor, asked:

> how would Zubin Mehta and his people react if, for example, they were all brought into some place in which there were sacred cows, and someone stood up and said: "We are about to slaughter the cows. Anyone who doesn't want to see it should leave." Does that seem all right to Zubin Mehta?[21]

Thus, on the public level Holocaust survivors and relatives of the dead seemed to be insisting on an Israeli monopoly on the right to make decisions concerning Wagner, and they were not willing to entrust this right to a foreigner — even a faithful friend of Israel, as Mehta was described in other articles.[22]

Ten years later it became apparent that it was not only foreignness that disturbed the survivors. When Daniel Barenboim, identified as an Israeli, took up the daunting challenge of breaking the boycott on Wagner, he discovered that there were other factors that disqualified people from discussing the subject. Barenboim had led the anti-boycott movement since 1989, and, ultimately, after conducting a special concert of Wagner's works at the end of 1991, he was attacked on account of his excessive youth — as someone who had been only a child at the time of the Holocaust and was therefore unqualified to debate issues connected with it, in this case the performance of Wagner's music in Israel.[23] Only then was it evident that nationality was not enough to entitle anyone to discuss Wagner; you had to be part of the right generation as well. In this respect, the 1991 conflict reflected Holocaust survivors' eagerness to appropriate an exclusive franchise on decisions concerning Wagner and, perhaps, to retain the great power they had held during the initial debates over the Holocaust and Heroism Remembrance Day in Israel. It should be remembered, however, that most of the publicists writing on the subject at the time were too young to have gone through the Holocaust themselves, and some of them did not even have any relatives who had. At this point an interesting contradiction was visible between the ambition to turn the Holocaust into a collective historical experience and the desire to maintain it as a private, personal experience.

Yet Holocaust survivors are not the only people who have tried to prevent Wagner's infiltration of Israeli society, nor are they the only ones accused of emotional manipulation with respect to this issue. The controversy has been fueled to a huge extent by politicians across the political spectrum. In the 1950s and 1960s members of both the right-wing Herut and the left-wing Mapam parties played the most prominent role, bitterly opposing Prime Minister David Ben-Gurion's diplomatic gestures towards Germany — or "the other Germany," as he called it. Since the 1980s they have been joined by Labor and National Religious Party MKs. All of them have pursued the matter in the Knesset by means of interpellations or debates in the Knesset Education and Culture Committee. All of them have made authoritarian, manipulative use of the Holocaust to resolve the Wagner-Strauss issue and to take it off the public agenda once and for all. Following a 1956 interpellation by MK Esther Raziel-Naor (Herut) on the subject of Strauss, during which she demanded that the orchestra lose its state funding if it played a work by Strauss, Menachem Begin, the head of her own party, intervened. He argued that the Education Ministry's policy of non-intervention in the issue undermined the commemoration of the Holocaust.[24] Subsequent discussion in the Knesset followed the same lines, except that from the 1980s onwards personal notes were injected — for example, by survivor Dov Shilansky, and by Labor MK Hagai Meirom, who cited his mother's persecution by the Nazis in order to justify the ban on Wagner's music in Israel.[25] As Begin had pointed out back in the 1950s, Israeli education ministers' basic policy on Wagner was non-intervention. Every education minister, regardless of political party affiliation, tried to avoid taking a stand on the issue, the sole exception being Professor Ben-Zion Dinur, one of the founders of Yad Vashem, the Holocaust and Heroes' Remembrance Authority in Jerusalem; he appealed to Jascha Heifetz personally to stop playing Strauss in Israel.[26] In general, the Wagner issue has given politicians a conduit for ideas and feelings that they usually have to suppress at the political level for pragmatic reasons. Thus, Israeli politics are responsible both for the rational measures taken with respect to Germany and for the emotional responses to German culture.

Of course, political pragmatism and cultural emotionalism cannot be compared. Economic or diplomatic decisions exist on a different plane from cultural rapprochement, which is emotionally based. Yet the perception of culture as unique in this respect merits further examination. Almost from the beginning the Wagner controversy has also symbolized a struggle over the nature of Israeli culture, and to a large degree it has shown that an internalized resistance to German heritage has played an essential role in the formation of the new Jewish-Hebrew identity. An excellent definition of this role was written in 1991 by an Israeli publicist, Ariel Hirschfeld, who argued: "Abstaining from Wagner is one of the few truly cosmopolitan acts carried out here in the musical field, an act that does not resemble the provincial, imitative sycophancy typical of musical life here and of the Philharmonic in particular."[27]

This attitude dovetailed with the ideas that had already been expressed generally in the 1950s and 1960s, and which were recycled from the 1980s on, mostly at the initiative of religious Jews. In the 1950s and 1960s the managers of the IPO were not only compelled to defend the orchestra's decisions with respect to Wagner and Strauss, on the grounds that artistic considerations were involved; they were also called upon to address other issues directly connected with the shaping of a modern, national Israeli culture. Thus, they were directly involved in the decisions made during the 1950s and 1960s in response to the controversies over vocal concerts in the German language — a language whose use on stage had been banned by the Film and Theater Review Board — and performances of Christian liturgical music.[28] During those years, it was very clear that cultural affairs were closely linked with national issues, including the significance of the Holocaust in Israeli public discourse. The clearest evidence of this in the context of our subject was the censorship exercised against public use of the German language.

It may have been the demise of that censorship in the late 1960s, or fears that the slowly receding memory of the Holocaust would vanish altogether, that reawakened the polemic in the 1980s. This time the standard-bearers of the cause were mostly publicists and politicians from the religious sector. Religious papers presented the controversy over Wagner as evidence supporting their demand that every effort be made to foster the Hebrew character of the state. They also used it to attack secular Jews who complained that the Ultra-Orthodox did not heed the siren signaling the minute of silence on Holocaust Remembrance Day; generally their attitude was, "how dare you accuse us, when you listen with enjoyment to the music of an anti-Semite, Wagner?"[29] In the latest clash, during the summer of 2001, the religious dimension of the debate achieved new prominence in a letter to the editor by a member of "Professors for a Strong Israel," a group identified with the Israeli Right. After remarking that "[u]ndoubtedly Germany, with all its institutions, is trying to cleanse itself of the sins of the Holocaust, and there is no place like Israel to do that," the author added:

> How symbolic it is that precisely on the eve of 17 Tammuz, the date on which a fast-day was declared to commemorate the destruction of

the walls of Jerusalem, the representatives of German culture managed to undermine the walls of Jewish culture and honor, and, by playing Wagner, placed a German cultural icon on an Israeli stage.[30]

The increasingly shrill tone of the debate concerning the general cultural context of playing Wagner's music in Israel seems to be linked not only to the growing combativeness of public expression in Israel in general, but also to the fears I have already mentioned. The increasing remoteness of the Holocaust, which might have been expected to moderate emotional attitudes towards it, is producing the exact opposite effect. This can probably be attributed to the fear that memory and the mechanisms of its conservation, imprinted in Israeli society and culture, are being eroded. Evidence of such fear can be found in the wide range of activities focusing on the Holocaust, which are based not only on a multifaceted approach to the subject, but also on the need to preserve the Holocaust as a living memory, regardless of the danger of over-saturation.

Another issue, no less central, concerns both the changing composition of Israeli society and the processes of commemorating the Holocaust that this society has internalized to date. In the 1950s, a quarter of all Israelis were Holocaust survivors; but today their numbers are naturally declining in society in general and in public life in particular. Yet in the 60 years that have passed since the beginning of the Final Solution up to today, the commemorative process has changed character twice. Initially Holocaust awareness erupted from the personal memories of survivors into the Israeli collective memory — and in this respect the central role played by the Eichmann trial testimony is well known. Later, the memory of the Holocaust returned to the personal level, with the invocation of individual Holocaust victims in the framework of the projects grouped under the slogan "Unto Every Person There Is a Name."[31]

In these respects, the debates on Wagner in Israeli society and the changes they have undergone over the years are very similar to the debates on the nature of Holocaust commemoration in Israel. Thus, for example, in the 1950s — the decade when the Knesset twice enacted laws defining the character of the national Holocaust Remembrance Day as well as the Law for the Punishment of Nazis and their Collaborators, when the Yad Vashem museum was founded, and when Israeli society was watching the Kapo trials and the more publicized Grünwald-Kasztner case — the Wagner-Strauss issue came up three times, and in one instance went all the way to the Knesset.[32] In the 1960s, when the Israeli public was coping with both the chilling testimony of the Eichmann trial and the establishment of full diplomatic relations with West Germany, there was talk of relaxing the ban on the performance of Christian liturgical music and vocal works in German even before the perennial Wagner controversy broke out again. Israel's changing self-perceptions — conditioned by the Six Day War in 1967 and the Yom Kippur War in 1973, oscillating between fear of annihilation and an intoxicating sense of power — also had implications for Holocaust memory, leading to a certain moderation of the Wagner controversy as well. However, everything that had seemed to be part of a rational process paralleling the increasing temporal distance from the Holocaust itself was undermined in the 1980s with respect to both Holocaust remembrance in Israel in general and the Wagner controversy in particular.

Since the 1980s, and particularly in the 1990s, there has been a growing awareness of the processes of Holocaust commemoration. Although the standard official ceremonies have remained unchanged, other forms of remembrance have multiplied alongside them: survivors are invited to school classrooms and special seminars to tell their stories; trips to the death camps are organized; intensive media attention is paid to the feelings of second-generation survivors; and there has been an outpouring of works in various artistic media on the subject of the Holocaust. Meanwhile, particularly fierce rounds of the Wagner conflict took place in 1981 and again in 2001. As mentioned, I attribute the intensive renewed activity in the field of shaping Holocaust memory both to the anxiety aroused by the increasing remoteness of the Holocaust experience and to the sweeping involvement of the entire Israeli society in the process of remembrance. Wagner, who had become a symbol in Israel in the early days of statehood because of his ideas, his writing on art, and the way he was viewed after his death, has, in more recent years, also served as a brick in the edifice of Holocaust remembrance; these years have shown that not only survivors see him as a symbol, but also the wider public, some of whom view the Holocaust as a collective historic experience rather than a personal one. Thus, the Wagner debate has come to reflect a strange and interesting juxtaposition of ideology and the part of Israeli identity that is based on the Holocaust.

In conclusion, I would like to raise a question concerning what participants in the Wagner debate view as "the ownership" of the decision to lift the boycott or not. As noted above, the last 20 years have seen an increasingly evident determination on the part of Holocaust survivors to keep the decision-making power in their own hands, on the grounds that only someone who lived through the horror can understand the musical and ideological implications of what Wagner represents. In the public debate that took place in November 2001 in Tel Aviv, a Holocaust survivor expressed this poignantly: "Wait a few more years, until we've left the world, and then go back to discussing the Wagner issue among yourselves," she said with a simple candor that even the great cynics sitting in the auditorium could not withstand.[33]

Nevertheless, this attitude raises a number of important questions. One of them is whether, after going through the whole process of instilling the memory of the Holocaust in the entire Jewish population of Israel, it is reasonable to leave the task of coping with the painful past solely to the survivors who live among us. Do we not doom ourselves to that same threatening process of amnesia and oblivion once the Holocaust survivors pass away, as they are bound to do? Moreover, since it is clear to everyone that the Wagner issue cannot be divorced from the memory of the Holocaust, will waiting another 10 or 20 years to discuss it permit a different kind of debate? Is this a problem inherent in Israeli society, a problem closely linked to the way it wants to form its identity?

Undoubtedly the answers to these questions — like the entire Wagner debate — depend on our perspective. We might believe that preserving the memory of the Holocaust need encompass no more than it does right now — familiarity with the events of the Holocaust, honoring the memory of those murdered, and treating survivors with special marks of distinction — or we might believe that this is not enough, and that further essentials include understanding the very short road that links the blatant verbal anti-Semitism exemplified by Wagner with acts that can lead to genocide, or the even shorter path that permits a democratic society to change overnight into a violent, totalitarian society. To my mind, suppressing discussion of the Wagner issue repeats the same mistake that Israeli society has made by artificially separating discussion of the lessons offered by German history from discussion of the lessons that Jewish society learned from industrialized genocide. In addition, having given Holocaust survivors a special place in Israeli society, how can we then brazenly wait for their deaths in order to discuss more freely the difficult experiences that they have carried around with them all their lives? We must consider whether Wagner is indeed the right symbol for maintaining Holocaust awareness in Israel.

NOTES

This essay was translated from Hebrew by Martha Grenzeback.

1 Protocol No. 268, session of the Knesset Education, Culture and Sports Committee, 8 May 2001.
2 Following the Committee's meeting, the Israel Festival Board and conductor Daniel Barenboim decided to replace the Wagner concert with another. At the end of it, Barenboim and the Berlin State Orchestra played a short excerpt from *Tristan und Isolde*, provoking yet another fierce debate about public performances of Wagner in Israel. Finally, the Knesset Culture and Education Committee declared Barenboim to be a "cultural persona non grata" in Israel. See Protocol No. 316, meeting of the Knesset Education, Culture and Sports Committee, 24 July 2001.
3 For a detailed discussion on the Wagner debate in Israel, see Na'ama Sheffi, *The Ring of Myths: Wagner, The Israelis, and the Nazis* (Brighton, Sussex, 2001).

4 The last two decades have seen numerous studies on the shaping of national identities. Outstanding examinations of particular Jewish identity and modes of commemoration can be found in Amos Funkenstein, *Perceptions of Jewish History* (Berkeley, 1993); and Yosef Hayim Yerushalmi, *Zakhor: Jewish History and Jewish Memory* (Seattle, 1982). I wish to thank Yosefa Loshitzky for her interesting comment on the formation of national identity.

5 For the public discourse on Holocaust in the early days of statehood, see Yechiam Weitz, "Political Dimensions of Holocaust Memory in Israel during the 1950s," *Israel Affairs*, Vol. 1, No. 3 (1995), pp. 129–45.

6 The essay was first published in 1850 under the pseudonym K. Freigedank, and again in 1869 under Wagner's own name, when he was already a successful composer. See Richard Wagner, "Judaism in Music," in idem, *Stories and Essays*, trans. C. Osborne (London, 1973), pp. 23–39.

7 This general impression, harbored by many Israeli publicists, is supported by research. See, for example, Joachim Köhler, *Wagners Hitler: Der Prophet und sein Vollstreker* (Munich, 1997); Paul Lawrence Rose, *Wagner: Race and Revolution* (New Haven and London, 1992); and Marc A. Weiner, *Richard Wagner and the Anti-Semitic Imagination* (Lincoln and London, 1997). See also Gottfried Wagner, *Wer nicht mit dem Wolf heult: Autobiographische Aufzeichnungen eines Wagner-Urenkels* (Cologne, 1997).

8 Despite general testimony by survivors indicating that Wagner's music was played in the concentration camps, two important witnesses give evidence to the contrary. See Fania Fenelon, *Playing for Time* (New York, 1977); and Moshe Hoch, *Hazarah meha-tofet* (Return from the Inferno) (Hadera, 1988).

9 On Toscanini, see the biography by Harvey Sachs, *Toscanini* (New York, 1988), especially pp. 196–269.

10 On the reparations agreement, see Nicholas Balabkins, *West Germany and the Reparations to Israel* (New Brunswick, NJ, 1971).

11 The attack caused a radical change in press attitudes towards Heifetz. See, for example, *Ha-Dor* and *Ma'ariv* on the day after the incident, 17 April 1953. It is important to note that most of the Hebrew press in Israel had taken part in the debate (*Davar, Ha'aretz, Herut, Ha-Olam ha-zeh, Ma'ariv, Ha-Boker, Ha-Dor* and *Yediot Aharonot*), as had the non-Hebrew press (*Jediot Hadashot, Emeth, Jerusalem Post, Yedi'ot ha-Yom*). Reports had also appeared in foreign papers such as *New York Post, New York Herald Tribune, Herald Tribune* (Paris), and *Buenos Aires Herald*.

12 The debate erupted after the publication of an article by first flutist and board member Uri Toeplitz on the IPO's plans to play Wagner and Strauss. His original article claimed that: "a change has taken place in the nation's attitude to the exterminators of our people." The public uproar that followed the article's publication led him to revise the passage to read: "We feel the time has come for a change, not only because of the paramount demands of artistic freedom, but also because the opposition to Wagner has become a mere gesture. Why should we go on denying ourselves some of the greatest music by forbidding the playing of Wagner, a loss that cannot be replaced by the works of any other composer, while a mere convenience like the German Volkswagen, with all its associations from the Hitler era, is allowed to crowd our streets? ... Accordingly, this time we must take a rational and courageous stand and allow Wagner's music to be played, thereby reopening the door to works included among the best of the music composed in the nineteenth century." See Uri Toeplitz, "Al hashivuto shel Wagner" (On the Importance of Wagner), IPO program, June 1966.

13 This time the press discussed the matter for several weeks, and even more extensively; local and special-interest magazines, flourishing at the time, jumped on the bandwagon, as did the electronic media, which had previously avoided the subject.

14 Moshe Zuckermann, *Shoah ba-heder ha-atum: Ha-"Shoah" ba-itonut ha-yisraelit bi-tkufat milhemet ha-mifratz* (Shoah in the Sealed Room: The "Holocaust" in the Israeli Press during the Gulf War) (Tel Aviv, 1993).

15 The essay appeared in Rina Litvin and Hezi Shelach (eds.), *Mi mefahed me-Richard Wagner: Hebetim shonim shel dmut shnuyah be-mahloket* (Who's Afraid of Richard Wagner: Different Aspects of a Controversial Figure) (Jerusalem, 1984), pp. 203–18.

16 "Im ha-Richardim o biladehem" (With or without the Richards)," *Davar*, 1 December 1952.

17 D. Yishai, "Tzlilei ha-nivun bak'u be-yom ha-shoah" (Degenerate Music Burst Forth on Holocaust Memorial Day), *Herut*, 16 April 1953 (original emphasis).

18 See *Arie (Louis) Garb v. Israel Broadcasting Authorities*, Supreme Court Appeal No. 6032/00, 24 August 2000; *Alther Podlowsky and Gedaliahu Appel v. Rishon Letzion Symphony Orchestra*, Miscellaneous Civil Appeals (MCA) 27053/00, 18 October 2000; *Alther Podlowsky, Gedaliahu Appel and Israel Silberberg v. Rishon Letzion Symphony Orchestra*, MCA 27228/00, 24 October 2000; *Alther Podlowsky, Gedaliahu Appel, Israel Silberberg, Center of Organizations of Holocaust Survivors in Israel, and Simon Wiesenthal Center Fund v. Rishon Le-Zion Symphony Orchestra*, Supreme Court Appeal No. 7700/00, 25 October 2000; *Alther Podlowsky, Gedaliahu Appel, Israel Silberberg, Center of Organizations of Holocaust Survivors in Israel, and Simon Wiesenthal Center Fund v. Rishon Le-Zion Symphony Orchestra*, MCA 6280/01, 4 March 2001.

19 This undated letter was sent by Shmuel Santo, a Holocaust survivor living in Rishon Le-Zion, to the managers of that city's symphony orchestra, right after the performance of the *Siegfried Idyll* in October 2000. See also Moshe Zuckermann, "Zilut zekher ha-shoah" (The Abuse of Holocaust Commemoration), 7 May 2001, at http://www.y-net.co.il.

20 Dov Shilansky, in an interview to Radio 1, The Voice of Israel, 23 October 1981.

21 Noah Kliger, "Hitehashvut be-regashot" (Consideration for Feelings), *Yediot Aharonot*, 21 October 1981.

22 See the comment made by the editor-in-chief of *Yediot Aharonot*, Herzl Rosenblum, in "Le-Zubin Mehta, be-khol ha-kavod" (To Zubin Mehta, with All Due Respect), *Yediot Aharonot*, 19 October 1981: "This whole problem is an internal problem of our own, a problem that must be discussed inside our own house, and no foreigners, even if they are our friends, should enter into it.... This is also true for our dear friend Zubin Mehta, who loves us with all his soul, and we him, but he *read* about Auschwitz, and we were *taken* there.... He must leave us to ourselves, and not try to tell us what to do."

23 "Higi'ah ha-sha'ah she-Wagner yahzor lihiyot rak muzikah" (The Time Has Come for Wagner to Be Just Music Again), *Ha'aretz*, 16 December 1991.

24 Interpellation 670, 26 November 1956. A copy of the question and its answer can be found in the IPO Archives, Tel Aviv, Wagner and Strauss file.

25 In his proposal Meirom detailed the history of Wagner's anti-Semitism, noting that the composer had "lived in Germany between the years 1813 and 1883. He was born and grew up in the city of Leipzig. One hundred years later in the city of Leipzig my mother was born, and persecuted." He went on to explain that the idea of playing Wagner in Israel was wrong, criticizing those "who try to take us out of our provincial attitude and to bring into our home the geniuses who lay the foundations for the racist creed." Agenda Proposal 1699, submitted by MK Hagai Meirom, *Divrei Ha-Knesset*, Session 110, 12th Knesset (1990), Vol. 1, pp. 334–6.

26 Heifetz was described as a guest with poor manners, and the editor of *Ma'ariv*, Dr. Azriel Carlebach, expressed his displeasure in an editorial: "The education minister, Professor Dinur, requested that no Strauss be played. And the justice minister, Dr. Rosen, seconded that request (despite his different personal views on the identification of an artist with his art).... Yet Jascha Heifetz received the request from two ministers of Israel, shoved it into his pocket, said whatever he said about opposing musical censorship — and refused to comply. He played Strauss in Haifa, and afterwards in Tel Aviv as well." "Nimusei ore'ah" (Manners of a Guest), *Ma'ariv*, 13 April 1953.

27 "Pashtuto ha-gluyah shel ha-kavod ha-zeh" (The Overt Simplicity of That Honor), *Ha'aretz*, 27 December 1991.

28 The Film and Theater Review Board (the state's cultural censor) intervened in the question of whether to allow performances in the German language on Israeli stages following a concert by singer Kenneth Spencer in 1950. The board also sent a memorandum to the IPO before the production of *Das Lied von der Erde* by Gustav Mahler. The Kenneth Spencer affair is described by Itzhak Gilead, "Da'at ha-kahal be-Yisrael al yahasei Yisrael ve-Germaniyah ha-ma'aravit ba-shanim 1949–1965" (Public Opinion in Israel on Relations between the State of Israel and West Germany in the Years 1949–1965)

(Ph.D. diss., Tel Aviv University, 1984), p. 32. On the censorship board's request, see letter from the Film and Theater Review Board to the IPO management, 6 May 1952, IPO Archives, "Miscellaneous" file.

29 This sentiment was evident in several articles appearing in the religious press. See, for example: "Ha-hayim bli Wagner" (Life without Wagner), *Yom ha-Shishi*, 27 December 1991; "Akhshav pog'im gam be-regashot shel hilonim" (Now the Feelings of Secular Jews Are Being Hurt, Too), *Yated Ne'eman*, 20 December 1991.

30 Israel Nevenzal, "Tzelem germani be-heikhal ha-muzikah" (German Icon in the Temple of Music), *Ha'aretz*, 15 July 2001.

31 The gradual personification of Holocaust survivors is notable in many art works of the last two decades. See, for example, the growing numbers of personal documentaries, such as *Hugo* (Yair Lev, 1989); *Al tigu li ba-shoah* (Don't Touch My Holocaust) (Asher Tlalim, 1994); *Ha-banot mi-Libau* (Girlfriends) (Yoel Kaminsky, 1994); *Abbale bo la-lunah-park* (Daddy, Come to the Fair) (Shmuel Vilozhny and Nava Semel, 1995); *Shalosh Ahayot* (*Drei Schwestern*) (Tsipi Reibenbach, 1998); and *Perla Ahuvati* (*Liebe Perla*) (Shahar Rozen, 1999). This trend is also evident in literature, the most recent example being Amir Guttfreund's *Shoah shelanu* (Our Holocaust) (Tel Aviv, 2000).

32 On the Grunwald-Kasztner trial, see Yehiam Weitz, "Changing Conceptions of the Holocaust: The Kasztner Case," in Jonathan Frankel (ed.), *Reshaping the Past: Jewish History and the Historians, Studies in Contemporary Jewry*, Vol. 10 (1994), pp. 211–30. On the 1950 Law for the Punishment of Nazis and their Collaborators, see Hannah Yablonka, "Ha-hok le-asiyat din ba-natzim uve-ozreihem: Hebet nosaf be-she'elat ha-nitzolim veha-shoah" (The Law for the Punishment of Nazis and their Collaborators: Another Aspect of the Issue of Israelis, Survivors, and the Holocaust), *Cathedra*, No. 82 (January 1997), pp. 135–52. See also "Law of Holocaust Martyrs' and Heroes' Remembrance" (various debates and versions), in *Divrei Ha-Knesset*, Vol. 11 (12 April 1951), pp. 1655–7; Vol. 26 (10 March 1959), pp. 1385–90, and (8 April 1959), pp. 1992–3. For Knesset debates on the establishment of Yad Vashem, see ibid., Vol. 14 (12 May 1953), pp. 1310–14; (18 May 1953), pp. 1331–53; and (19 August 1953), pp. 2402–9.

33 The open debate took place on 15 November 2001, at the Felicja Blumental Music Center and Library in Tel Aviv. Some of the papers delivered at the conference appeared in Moshe Zuckermann (ed.), *Tel Aviver Jahrbuch für deutsche Geschichte* (Tel Aviv, 2003).

Holocaust Controversies in the 1990s: The Revenge of History or the History of Revenge?

David Cesarani

During the 1990s it was often remarked that controversies about the persecution and mass murder of the Jews between 1933 and 1945 had acquired an unprecedented volume and vehemence. Indeed, the escalation of public attention to the events known, often with little definitional rigor, as "the Holocaust" gave rise to several studies and polemical works — notably by Peter Novick and Norman Finkelstein — that sought to explain the phenomenon, often in conspiratorial terms.[1] However, while it is incontestable that this decade saw an unprecedented number of books, films, memorials, commemorative events and public debates centered on the Nazi genocide against the Jews and its legacy, many of the reasons adduced for this crescendo remain within a closed explanatory circle and leave certain questions unanswered.

The typical explanation pivots on the end of the Cold War. This, it is said, resulted in the opening of archives in the East and the West, the investigation of formerly closed issues, and enabled countries to take a more critical view of their past. Survivors in their twilight years were now eager to tell their stories and there was a more receptive audience than previously, partly because Jewish communities were deliberately cultivating knowledge of the Holocaust as a way to instill in young Jews a sense that it was important to remain Jewish instead of traveling the path of total assimilation.[2] Greater awareness of the Jewish catastrophe spurred researchers, and those seeking redress on behalf of the victims, to take advantage of the transformed political conditions in Eastern Europe and to exploit the newly opened document collections there. The consequence was a flood of "revelations," commissions of inquiry, legal battles, apologies and controversies. These were piled onto the run of anniversaries from 1985 onward marking the 50th and then the 60th anniversary of crucial points in the history of the Third Reich and its treatment of the Jews.[3]

Elsewhere I have offered a critique of this explanation and drawn attention to the autonomous role of the media and globalization in foregrounding "Holocaust-era" issues. Cultures of compensation and the new, international politics of redress and apology, identified by Elazar Barkan in his important book *The Guilt of Nations*, also contributed to stimulating the unprecedented sequence of campaigns for restitution, reparation and compensation, as well as the string of apologies by, for example, French bishops, French policemen, and finally the French state and, with rather more equivocation, the Vatican.[4] The notion that the prominence of Nazi-related stories in the world's media can be attributed to Jewish influence and power, although this is undoubtedly a contributory factor, is simplistic.[5] For one thing, bouts of media and political concern about the legacy of the Third Reich preceded the alleged accumulation of Jewish power in these spheres. Much criticism of the "Holocaust industry" is predicated on the assumption that inquiry into and discussion of the persecution and mass murder of the Jews were either neglected or repressed between 1945 and 1960.[6] However, research on the postwar era by Annette Wieviorka, Pieter Lagrou, Robert S. C. Gordon, Anita Shapira and Dalia Ofer has revealed a denser and far more complex pattern of *lieux de mémoire*: commemorations, publications, memorial institutions and artistic representations — including, as Jeffrey Shandler has shown, television.[7]

In this essay I want to add a further layer of explanation for the wave of "Holocaust-era" issues and controversies that swelled so remarkably in the 1990s. Much of this explanation is tentative, even speculative. It is part of a larger project which, when completed, will add flesh to the skeletal summary outlined here. I will begin with a question: why did the Eichmann Trial in Israel and the Ulm and Frankfurt Trials in Germany between 1960 and 1965 fail to have a similar effect? Was it simply that the Cold War constricted the investigation and appreciation of Nazi Jewish policy?

There is no doubt that the bipolar ideological and political organization of the world hindered comprehension of the "Final Solution" from the late 1940s to the early 1960s. It is notorious that Hannah Arendt's account of Eichmann was shoehorned into a theory of totalitarianism that blurred the distinctions between Soviet repression and Nazi terror.[8] Her reductive and partial analysis, in which the role of ideology and anti-Semitism was marginalized, was then appropriated by theorists such as Richard Rubinstein, and later Zygmunt Bauman, who saw Eichmann as typifying a certain form of rational and bureaucratic modernity. This interpretation was given a pseudo-scientific underpinning by the "experiments" on obedience to authority conducted by Stanley Milgram.[9]

Consequently, the Nazi murder program which was conducted by the *Einsatzgruppen* in Eastern Europe was overlooked in favor of Eichmann and the bureaucratic, "sanitized" forms of killing he supposedly represented. This neglect was aggravated by the lack of easily available sources concerning Nazi policy in the East. Even though in 1960–61 the Polish Commission for the Investigation of Hitlerite Crimes supplied Israel with many documents, these were used sparingly thanks to the reluctance of Eichmann's Israeli prosecutors to give more than a token treatment to his crimes against non-Jews, especially in Poland in 1939–41. It would not be until the early to mid-1990s that a significant number of German and American historians paid greater attention to the waves of killing in which Eichmann played little or no part, and the vast reordering of ethnic groups in which he did have a substantial role.[10]

Yet there were other reasons why Nazi policy became so fascinating to a world public 30 years after Eichmann was hanged. At the time of his execution, Eichmann could be safely treated as an aberration of an aberration: the last major representative of a genocidal regime that had been consigned with its ideology and practices to the dustbin of history. Although the years immediately after the end of World War II saw vast and violent movements of population in several regions around the world, by 1949–50 this convulsion had subsided. In Germany, the Middle East, India and China millions of people had migrated under duress accompanied by vast loss of life, but for the next decade, there was relative stability and reconstruction. Despite the Korean War and the Suez/Sinai conflict there was no large-scale mass murder or internationalized displacement of population. However, the early 1960s saw the beginning of a genocidal wave that gradually traveled round the globe, with catastrophic consequences. This genocidal wave is intimately connected with the end of the overseas European colonial empires. The *annus mirabilis* of decolonization was 1960, the year Eichmann was kidnapped. In that year France left 14 colonies, Belgium evacuated the Congo, and the British prime minister announced that the "winds of change" were blowing through Africa, inaugurating Britain's retreat from the continent. Within three years, newly independent African states were wracked by civil war and genocide, notably Congo, Rwanda and Nigeria. Indonesia was the site of mass murder in 1965, while from that year onwards the US-led war in South Vietnam, itself a legacy of decolonization, had vastly murderous consequences. During the 1970s, genocide occurred in Bangladesh, Burundi and Cambodia.[11]

The Nazi mass murder of the Jews came to be seen as a prototype for these massacres and genocides, but as Nazi policy was still associated with Eichmann and Auschwitz the comparisons rarely led anywhere new. Other than proving man's proclivity for intra-species murder — "man's inhumanity to man" — the genocidal wave was seen as premodern and barbaric, or related to deformed Marxism (Maoism) and so only tangentially related to the supposedly sophisticated European project coordinated by Eichmann. It would not be until the genocidal wave lapped at Europe's doorstep and Eichmann was dethroned as the monarch of mass murder that connections would be made between past and present policies of "ethnic cleansing" and the destruction of populations. Moreover, anti-colonialism and the civil rights struggle in the USA diverted much energy and awareness of Nazi atrocities into a different channel of activism. The "lessons" of Hitler were harnessed to the promotion of Black civil rights in the 1960s. It was not until the civil rights movement had run its course, and Jews had fallen out with Blacks, that Jewish energies refocused on the history and the experience of Jewish suffering and dispossession.[12]

Still, it is a puzzle why the so-called "Holocaust industry" did not "take off" in the 1970s outside of America. Of course, in many ways it did: the 1970s saw a stream of important and innovative historical studies on the Third Reich and Jewish policy — although eventually this was stymied by the polarization of research into the two rival modes of intentionalism as against functionalism.[13] The Bitburg controversy of 1985, sparked by President Ronald Reagan's participation in a wreathlaying ceremony at the graves of German soldiers — including members of the SS — at Bitburg, which was itself tied into events marking the 40th anniversary of the end of the war, was a global media event.[14] The *Historikerstreit* (Historians' Debate) in 1986–88 spread from Germany to involve the intelligentsia worldwide.[15]

These precursors foreshadowed the cacophony of the 1990s, albeit with significant differences. Both controversies remained within the framework of Cold War politics: indeed, they cannot be fathomed outside this context. The element of the *Historikerstreit* which resolved into a debate over the "uniqueness" of the Holocaust was triggered by Ernst Nolte as part of a strategy by right-wing, nationalist German intellectuals, aligned with the Christian Democratic government of Chancellor Helmut Kohl, to "normalize" Germany's past by relativizing Nazi crimes. Nolte compared Nazism to Stalinism and deemed the former a mere copy of the original. He also invoked Cambodia as a comparator to the Holocaust, declaring that the Cambodian genocide illustrated how the twentieth century was a "century of genocide" and concluding that it was therefore wrong to single out the crimes of the Third Reich. Cold War alliances and antipathies were at the core of this strategy.[16]

If many of the key issues that typify the controversies of the 1990s had already been broached in the preceding decade, what was new and different? The end of the Cold War was crucial, though frequently in indirect and unremarked ways. It opened an unprecedented debate over national identity, in which history and politics collided. Reunited Germany was not alone in facing a dilemma over how and where to insert the fate of its Jewish citizens into the national story. Throughout Europe the cessation of bipolarism and the end of the Soviet Empire after 1991 created dramatic new possibilities, and in some cases necessities, for revising national myths. In Italy, for example, the collapse of communism triggered the erosion of support for Christian Democracy, the main *raison d'être* of which had been to keep the Communist Party out of power. One result of this realignment was an upsurge of neo-fascism. These developments in turn called into question Italian political culture and national identity, and inevitably wrested attention back to the war years. It was against this background that Roberto Benigni made *Life Is Beautiful* — one of three Italian films on the persecution of Italian Jews that were made in a space of five years at the end of the 1990s.[17]

In former Eastern Bloc countries that had experienced Nazi occupation and collaboration a reckoning with the past could hardly be avoided. In the wake of communist rule decisions had to be taken about the rehabilitation of anti-communist and nationalist figures — most of whom were tainted by collaboration with the Nazis. Restitution issues added to these contentious debates. In their efforts to enter the EU and NATO, Poland, the Czech Republic, Slovakia, Hungary, the Baltic states, Slovenia, Croatia, Romania and Bulgaria have not only been obliged to satisfy the externally mandated criteria for observing human rights in the present, but to atone for the violation of human rights in the past. All have attempted to do so, more or less, and have engaged in public relations campaigns to convince Jewish communities, West European countries and the North Atlantic alliance that they have succeeded. An example of the methods and what is at stake may be gleaned from a recent review by Brendan Simms of Tzvetan Todorov's, *The Fragility of Goodness: Why Bulgaria's Jews Survived the Holocaust* (2002). Simms concludes that: "It should be required reading for those western politicians and diplomats unaware that this contender for admission into the European and western club has a stronger democratic and humanitarian pedigree than some of those who have already slipped under the wire."[18]

More grimly, genocide returned to Europe. After the collapse of the Soviet bloc, Europe became the location for a series of bloody ethnic conflicts that reintroduced the mass displacement of populations and genocide after a gap of 50 years. As we have seen, genocide in the context of the Cold War had raised interest in the fate of the Jews, but it had been foreclosed by the model of Eichmann as killer and the imposition of the totalitarian mode of explanation. The effort to understand and explain the atrocities that occurred in Europe (Croatia, Bosnia, Kosovo) and also in Rwanda after 1990 occurred at the same time as new research in East European archives was producing studies that displaced the model of the "desk-killer." War crimes investigations into Nazi collaborators that commenced on a large scale in the USA, Canada, Australia and Britain, and the opening of archive collections that shed light on Nazi occupation policy, ousted Eichmann from preeminence and replaced him with the *Einsatzgruppen* killer, the East European auxiliary and the reserve policeman. Much pioneering research into Nazi occupation policy and the role of East European collaborators was actually the by-product of war crimes investigations. Konrad Kwiet, Bettina Birn, Jürgen Matthäus, Martin Dean, Peter Longerich and Robert Waite are just a few of the historians who worked for judicial investigations in the USA, Australia, Canada, Germany and Britain. In this sense their contribution resembles that of Hans Buchheim, Helmut Krausnick and Martin Broszat in Germany in the 1960s, with the salient difference that unlike their German predecessors, Kweit, Birn, Matthäus, Dean, Longerich and Waite found a political appetite and a worldwide audience for their findings.[19]

As a consequence of this new documentation and new approaches, research moved from the "banality" of Eichmann to the behavior of "ordinary men" and then, following Daniel Goldhagen's critique of Browning, it alighted on "ordinary Germans." The refiguration of the perpetrators did not end with Goldhagen's provocative assertions. Thanks to war crimes trials in France, Britain and elsewhere, by the end of the 1990s the Goldhagen thesis was being challenged by the argument that the murderers were "ordinary Europeans."[20]

The incidence of genocide in the 1990s thus keyed into the study of Nazi mass murder in a way that academic research and current affairs had not become enmeshed in the 1980s. Current affairs buttressed scholarly research: academic interest and media interest became mutually reinforcing and cross-pollinated. Whereas there seemed little to tie Eichmann to genocide in Biafra, there was a startling resemblance between the "ethnic cleansers" of the Balkans and their Nazi predecessors who had operated in the same region half a century earlier. French President François Mitterrand's surprise flight into the besieged city of Sarajevo on 28 June 1992 followed a desperate plea for aid from the Bosnian head of state Alija Izetbegovic in which he compared his embattled capital to the Warsaw Ghetto. The message, conveyed by the philosopher Bernard-Henri Lévy, may have been couched in hyperbole, but the analogy illustrates the dynamic between history and contemporary affairs that distinguished the 1990s. If it was a contentious parallel, the debate it aroused, like other similar heated exchanges over the singularity or comparability of the Final Solution, typified the decade.[21]

These controversies were globalized because of the involvement of several world powers in the Balkan mêlée and the coverage it was given by the world's media. To a large extent, then, the shift in the 1990s appears to be a matter of scale, scope and intensity. Global news networks and newspaper empires increased the sheer volume of debate and ensured that controversies over the convent at Auschwitz, for example, were of as much interest in Quebec, Chicago and London as they were in Warsaw. *Média-ization* needed a market, though, and the migration of peoples provided it. The settlement of Jews, Holocaust survivors, perpetrators and East Europeans in North and South America, Western Europe, Israel, South Africa and Australasia created a global interest in Nazi-era stories. However, it is not self-evident that this audience *should* have been there. It is rarely noted that increasing life expectancy has preserved survivors, witnesses and perpetrators for far longer than might have been expected for those involved in previous atrocities. It would be an interesting exercise to work out how many survivors of the Armenian genocide were alive in 1945 or 1955 and whether their life span had an impact on the preservation of memory.

Jewish survivors of Nazi persecution and mass murder were fortunate to survive in considerable numbers into an era when memory mattered and when the technologies of memorialization had multiplied and grown in sophistication.[22] Even if there were a lot of Armenians around in the 1950s, how many had access to cumbersome tape recorders or film cameras? In any case, would there have been an interest in what they had to say or sufficient incentive to record and disseminate it? Jewish survivors of Nazi atrocities have been doubly fortunate to enjoy greater life expectancy and to live into an era when ethnic memory, especially the memory of suffering and victimhood, was politicized and instrumentalized.[23]

It must be noted, too, that memory was also commodified and marketed to an unprecedented degree. There had always been an appetite for stories of heroism and resistance against the Nazi assault, but it could only be satiated by a relatively small number of survivors such as the ghetto fighters and former partisans. Furthermore, these individuals were often ideologically driven and averse to personalized statements, preferring to eschew individual valor and sublimate their experiences into the struggle of the political movements or youth groups to which they had belonged. For two decades this mismatch conspired to reduce the volume of publications by or about survivors. With the widening interest in "ordinary" survivors, however, and the elevation of this much larger cadre to revered status, the appetite for the memory of survival could be fed by films and publications which now proliferated to an extraordinary degree.[24]

Jews also benefited from being urban. By the late twentieth century almost the entire world Jewish population inhabited cities. These urban locations have become the focus for memory activity: they are the site of national memorials, museums, archives, ceremonies, educational institutions, publishing houses, media enterprises. If Jews had been a rural people, scattered throughout the countryside of a dozen countries, how much impact would their memories have made in the modern world?

Not only have Jews lived longer, in cities to which they migrated from zones of suffering, they also migrated into the media and the institutions of representation. Jews have played a leading role in the media, museums and art world. They helped to create "representation" as an academic subject and a field of competition. The Jewish historical experience thus entered a virtuous cycle of amplification. As memory and representation attracted interest, Jewish memory and the representation of Jewish experience were pushed to the foreground. It is indicative of this relationship that one of the most oft-quoted books in the field is Yosef Yerushalmi's *Zakhor* (1982). Pierre Nora, who is himself Jewish, has acknowledged the centrality of Jews, particularly secular Jews, to the memory project.[25]

The interest in memory per se was relatively uncontroversial, but it led to an excitement about memorials that was anything but. The debates over the convent at Auschwitz and how best to preserve the site, the US and British Holocaust museums, the Berlin Jewish museum and Holocaust memorial are all products of a hyperactive memory industry rather than the "Holocaust industry."[26]

It may also be significant that the new areas of academic endeavor were also visually exciting and hence suitable for televisual presentations or richly illustrated books that had an appeal beyond the academy. Memory hinged on survivors and their testimony, which could be filmed and then screened to a mass audience, while debates about representation have frequently centered on exhibitions, art works and museums. Thus a synergy developed between the media, publishing and academic research into this new aspect of the Holocaust — a synergy that is hard to find paralleled anywhere else. The design for the proposed Holocaust memorial in Berlin and the 1995 exhibition on the crimes of the Wehrmacht became nodal points for debates in which issues of representation, history, memory, national identity and politics coincided in such a way as to greatly increase the amplitude of each separate controversy.[27]

Ironically, the burgeoning interest in representation of "the Holocaust" is associated with discourse studies, the linguistic turn in philosophy and historiography, and postmodernism, which initially were all regarded as potential enemies of memory and scholarship.[28] Yet, instead of eroding interest in the Nazi persecution and mass murder of the Jews, postmodernism had the opposite effect. While grand narratives embodying providence or materialistic forces were dissolved, and moral codes were liquefied in the acid of relativism, there was an ever more pressing need for a secular replacement for theological notions of evil. Hitler and the genocide against the Jews provided that surrogate. As Yehuda Bauer remarked at the Stockholm International Forum on the Holocaust in January 2000: "An amazing thing has happened in the last decade — in fact, during the last few years: a tragedy that befell a certain people, at a certain time and certain places, has become the symbol of radical evil as such, the world over."[29]

If the Enlightenment killed God and postmodernism killed off the Enlightenment project, this left an enhanced role for "the Holocaust" as "radical evil." In which case, its facticity was at more of a premium than ever before. Paradoxically, postmodernism encouraged tougher action against Holocaust deniers, while the practitioners of postmodernism felt themselves obliged to place debates about representation of "the Holocaust" at center stage, treating it as a test case for their conceptual apparatus.[30]

Holocaust deniers and Holocaust fraudsters (such as David Irving, Helen Demidenko, Benjamin Wilkomirski) added to the rancor of the 1990s, at the same time as postmodernism added new subject matter and reinvigorated old debates, not least about memory.[31] Such controversy over Holocaust denial, hoaxes and the fragility of genuine memory were not unprecedented but they occurred in a new context. On the one hand, the postmodern disposition generated greater sympathy for the issues they evoked.[32] On the other, discourse studies and the "linguistic turn" had an important effect on oral history and the historiography of the "Final Solution", too.

A second wave of oral history, drawing on sophisticated readings of testimony, has added texture to what was said, and perhaps more importantly what was unsaid, about the Jewish experience of Nazi persecution. Looking back on earlier decades it is striking that historians were so concerned with what was said and present in testimony, memoirs, and documents, rather than the significance of lacunae, elipses and silences. Mark Roseman's A Past in Hiding exemplifies the heightened ambitions and sensitivity of the new form of inquiry.[33] What is remembered or what can be recalled has also changed. Recent oral history projects have teased out of the past such themes as childhood, gender, sexuality and other subjects that were previously disparaged or taboo. The recovery of memory proceeded simultaneously with the revolution in mores, so that investigators naturally asked questions about subjects that interested them in their present lives. The result has been a surge of studies on children and women.[34] The new configuration of interests and the relief of inhibitions resulted in the appearance of a "new" Anne Frank based on a startling new edition of her diary.[35] This gendered and generational reading of the "Final Solution" was not uncontroversial.[36]

Another contentious subject that has been retrieved from the memory hole is revenge. As Berel Lang has pointed out, revenge was a great unspoken subject in survivor literature and testimony immediately after the war.[37] In a comparison of Eli Wiesel's Yiddish memoir and Night, Naomi Seidman has shown that Wiesel was not silent after his release, nor was he reticent about expressing his desire for and satisfaction in revenge upon the Germans. The forgiving Wiesel of Night was an adaptation in French designed to gratify his mentor François Mauriac and satisfy a Catholic readership in 1950s France.[38] In the 1990s, a small torrent of books appeared that documented and celebrated Jewish revenge (sometimes in the context of wartime resistance) while retribution was retrieved from earlier texts — such as Wiesel's first memoir. The public image of Abba Kovner was suddenly, and controversially, transformed from the gentle, dreamy partisan-poet and Zionist pioneer into the avatar of vengeance more attuned to expectations of Jewish men as macho, forceful and potentially homicidal.[39] As always with the historiography and memory of "the Holocaust", context was crucial.

In deconstructing the incidence of revenge in the record of Jewish responses to Nazi persecution and mass murder we can see the revenge of history. It shows the force exerted by context over what can and cannot be said or represented at certain times and in particular places, for reasons far removed from such neat explanations as the existence of an alleged "Holocaust industry." It also hints at the inherent dynamic of history and memory, their unruliness and their constant ability to escape control and constraint. The recurrence of revenge reveals how the subjects of history, the bearers of memory, can get their own back, both literally and metaphorically; how they can repossess that which they saw as their property and at the same time wreak vengeance on the expropriator.

NOTES

1 Peter Novick, *The Holocaust In American Life* (London, 1999); Norman Finkelstein, *The Holocaust Industry: Reflections on the Exploitation of Jewish Suffering* (London, 2000).

2 William Slaney (ed.), *US and Allied Efforts to Recover and Restore Gold and Other Assets Stolen or Hidden by Germans During World War II* (Washington, DC, May 1997), p. 58; Novick, *The Holocaust In American Life.* See also the editor's introductory remarks in Hilene Flanzbaum (ed.), *The Americanization of the Holocaust* (Baltimore, 1999), pp. 9–15.

3 Over 25 historical commissions have investigated or are due to report on the record of countries, banks and corporations with respect to the spoliation of the Jews, the treatment of Jewish refugees, Jewish and non-Jewish slave labor. World Jewish Congress, *Policy Dispatches*, No. 54 (September 2000), lists Argentina (1992, 1997), Austria (1998), Belgium (1997), Brazil (1997), Croatia (1997), Czech Republic (1999), Estonia (2000), France (4 in 1997), Israel (1999), Italy (1998), Latvia (1999), Lithuania (1999), Netherlands (3 in 1997), Norway (1997), Portugal (1996), Spain (1997), Sweden (2 in 1997), Switzerland (4 in 1996–97), UK (1996, 1997), USA (several since 1997), Turkey (1998), Paraguay, and Uruguay (on fugitive Nazis). For some of the books charting aspects of the banking scandal, looted art and compensation for slave labor, see Adam LeBor, *Hitler's Secret Bankers: The Myth of Swiss Neutrality during the Holocaust* (London, 1997); Tom Bower, *Blood Money: The Swiss, the Nazis and the Looted Billions* (London, 1997); Jean Ziegler, *The Swiss, The Gold, and the Dead*, trans. John Brownjohn (New York, 1998); Gregg J. Rickman, *Swiss Banks and Jewish Souls* (New Brunswick, NJ, 1999); George Carpozi, *Nazi Gold* (Far Hills, NJ, 1999); Itamar Levin, *The Last Deposit: Swiss Banks and the Holocaust Victims' Accounts*, trans. N. Dornberg (Westport, CT, 1999); Hector Feliciano, *The Lost Museum: The Nazi Conspiracy to Steal the World's Greatest Works of Art* (New York, 1997); Elizabeth Simpson (ed.), *The Spoils of War: World War II and Its Aftermath: The Loss, Reappearance, and Recovery of Cultural Property* (New York, 1997); Peter Harclerode and Brendan Pittaway, *The Lost Masters: The Looting of Europe's Treasurehouses* (London, 1999); Christopher Simpson, *The Splendid Blonde Beast: Money, Law and Genocide in the Twentieth Century* (New York, 1995); Reinhold Billstein et al., *Working for the Enemy: Ford, General Motors and Forced Labour in Germany during the Second World War* (Oxford, 2000), esp. pp. 229–47; Jonathan Steinberg, *Deutsche Bank and Its Gold Transactions during the Second World War* (Munich, 1999); Harold James, *The Deutsche Bank and the Nazi Economic War against the Jews* (Cambridge, 2001).

4   Elazar Barkan, *The Guilt of Nations: Restitution and Negotiating Historical Injustices* (New York, 2000). David Cesarani, "The Holocaust Is/As News," in Stephanie McMahon-Kaye (ed.), *The Memory of the Holocaust in the 21st Century: The Challenge for Education* (Jerusalem, 2001), pp. 109–28.

5   See David Cesarani, "Is There, and Has There Ever Been a 'Holocaust Industry'?" in Latvian Commission of Historians (eds.), *The Issues of the Holocaust Research in Latvia* (Riga, 2001), pp. 83–99.

6   David Cesarani, "Memory, Representation and Education," in Elizabeth Maxwell and Franklin Littell (eds.), *Remembering for the Future 2000*, Vol. 3, *The Holocaust in an Age of Genocide* (London, 2001), pp. 231–6.

7   Annette Wieviorka, *Déportation et genocide: Entre mémoire et l'oubli* (Paris, 1992); Robert S. C. Gordon, "Holocaust Writing in Context: Italy 1945–47," in Andrew Leak and George Paizis (eds.), *The Holocaust and the Text: Speaking the Unspeakable* (London, 2000), pp. 32–50; Pieter Lagrou, *The Legacy of Nazi Occupation: Patriotic Memory and National Recovery in Western Europe, 1945–1965* (Cambridge, 2000), pp. 251–61. See also the important revision of assumptions about the key case of Israel in the 1940s and 1950s by Anita Shapira, "The Holocaust: Private Memories, Public Memory," *Jewish Social Studies*, Vol. 4, No. 2 (1998), pp. 40–58; Dalia Ofer, "The Strength of Remembrance: Commemorating the Holocaust during the First Decade of Israel," *Jewish Social Studies*, Vol. 6, No. 2 (2000), pp. 24–55; Jeffrey Shandler, *While America Watches: Televising the Holocaust* (New York, 1999), esp. pp. 41–79.

8   Hans Mommsen, "Hannah Arendt's Interpretation of the Holocaust as a Challenge to Human Existence," in Steven E. Aschheim (ed.), *Hannah Arendt in Jerusalem* (Berkeley, 2001), pp. 224–31; Richard E. Cohen, "Breaking the Code: Hannah Arendt's *Eichmann in Jerusalem* and the Public Polemic: Myth, Memory and Historical Imagination," *Michael*, No. 13 (1993), pp. 30–41. See also Sharon Muller, "The Origins of *Eichmann in Jerusalem*: Hannah Arendt's Interpretation of Jewish History," *Jewish Social Studies*, Vol. 43 (1981), pp. 237–54.

9   Stanley Milgram, "The Compulsion to Do Evil," *Patterns of Prejudice*, Vol. 1, No. 1 (1967), pp. 3–7; Richard Rubinstein, *The Cunning of History: The Holocaust and the American Future* (New York, 1974); Zygmunt Bauman, *Modernity and the Holocaust* (London, 1989), ch. 6. Cf. Ian Parker, "Obedience," *Granta*, No. 71 (2000), pp. 99–126.

10 See the prefatory remarks by Volker Berghahn in Hannes Heer and Klaus Naumann (eds.), *War of Extermination: The German Military in World War II, 1941–1944* (Oxford, 2000), pp. xvi–vii. For this element of the new historiography, see Christopher R. Browning, *Ordinary Men: Reserve Police Battalion 101 and the Final Solution in Poland* (New York, 1992); and idem, "Nazi Resettlement Policy and the Search for a Solution to the Jewish Question, 1939–1941," in his *The Path to Genocide: Essays on Launching the Final Solution* (Cambridge, 1992); Götz Aly, *The Final Solution: Nazi Population Policy and the Murder of the European Jews* (London, 1999), first published in German in 1995.

11 David Reynolds, *One World Divisible: A Global History since 1945* (London, 2000); Samuel Tottens et al. (eds.), *Genocide in the Twentieth Century* (New York, 1975).

12 Edward Shapiro, *A Time for Healing: American Jewry since World War II* (Baltimore, 1992), pp. 223–5; Deborah Lipstadt, "The Failure to Rescue and Contemporary Jewish Historiography of the Holocaust: Judging From a Distance," in Michael J. Neufeld and Michael Berenbaum (eds.), *The Bombing of Auschwitz: Should the Allies Have Attempted It?* (New York, 2000), pp. 233–4.

13 For the classic summary, see Ian Kershaw, *The Nazi Dictatorship*, 4th edn. (London, 2000), pp. 93–133.

14 Geoffrey H. Hartman (ed.), *Bitburg in Moral and Historical Perspective* (Bloomington, 1986).

15 Peter Baldwin (ed.), *Reworking the Past: Hitler, the Holocaust and the Historians' Debate* (Boston, 1990); Charles S. Maier, *The Unmasterable Past: History, Holocaust, and German National Identity* (Cambridge, MA, 1988); Richard J. Evans, *In Hitler's Shadow: West German Historians and the Attempt to Escape from the Nazi Past* (London, 1989).

16 Gavriel D. Rosenfeld, "The Politics of Uniqueness: Reflections on the Recent Polemical Turn in Holocaust and Genocide Scholarship," *Holocaust and Genocide Studies*, Vol. 13, No. 1 (1999), pp. 28–61.

17 James Walston, "History and Memory of the Italian Concentration Camps," *Historical Journal*, Vol. 40, No. 1 (1997), pp. 169–83.

18 *Times Higher Education Supplement*, 5 April 2002.

19 Bettina Birn, "Austrian Higher SS and Police Leaders and their Participation in the Balkans," *Holocaust and Genocide Studies*, Vol. 6, No. 4 (1991), pp. 351–72; Jürgen Matthäus, "What About the 'Ordinary Men'? The German Order Police and the Holocaust in the Occupied Soviet Union," *Holocaust and Genocide Studies*, Vol. 10, No. 2 (1996), pp. 134–50; Konrad Kwiet, "From the Diary of a Killing Unit," in John Milfull (ed.), *Why Germany? National Socialist Anti-Semitism and the German Context* (Oxford, 1991), pp. 75–90; and "Rehearsing for Murder: The Beginning of the Final Solution in June 1941," *Holocaust and Genocide Studies*, Vol. 12, No. 1 (1998), pp. 3–26; Martin Dean, *Collaboration in the Holocaust: Crimes of the Local Police in Belorussia and Ukraine, 1941–44* (London, 2000); Peter Longerich, "From Mass Murder to the 'Final Solution': The Shooting of Civilians during the First Months of the Eastern Campaign within the Context of Nazi Jewish Genocide," in Bernd Wegner (ed.), *From Peace to War: Germany, Soviet Russia and the World, 1939–1941* (Oxford, 1997), pp. 253–75; Robert Waite, "'Reliable Local Residents': Collaboration in Latvia, 1941–1945" in *Latvia in World War II*, symposium of the Commission of Historians of Latvia (Riga, 2000), pp. 115–44.

20 Daniel Jonah Goldhagen, *Hitler's Willing Executioners: Ordinary Germans and the Holocaust* (New York, 1996), is implicitly and explicitly an assault on the earlier work of Christopher Browning: see Browning's response in the 2nd edn. of *Ordinary Men* (London, 2001), pp. 191–223. For the full debate on Goldhagen's thesis, see Robert R. Shandley (ed.), *Unwilling Germans? The Goldhagen Debate*, trans. J. Reimer (Minneapolis, 1998); and Gavriel Rosenfeld, "The Controversy That Isn't: The Debate over Daniel J. Goldhagen's *Hitler's Willing Executioners* in Comparative Perspective," *Contemporary European History*, Vol. 8, No. 2 (1999), pp. 249–73. For Browning's response, positing the idea that the assault on the Jews was a European phenomenon, see his "Ordinary Germans or Ordinary Men? Another Look at Perpetrators," in Donald Schilling (ed.), *Lessons and Legacies*, Vol. 2, *Teaching the Holocaust in a Changing World* (Evanston, IL, 1998), pp. 13–25.

21 *The Independent*, 29 June 1992; *Le Monde*, 30 June 1992.

22 See, for example, Luisa Passerini (ed.), *Memory and Totalitarianism* (Oxford, 1992); James E. Young, *The Texture of Memory: Holocaust Memorials and Meaning* (New Haven, 1993); Andreas Huyssen, *Twilight Memories: Marking Time in a Culture of Amnesia* (London, 1995); Martin Evans and Ken Lunn (eds.), *War and Memory in the Twentieth Century* (Oxford, 1997); Jay Winter and Emmanuel Sivan (eds.), *War and Remembrance in the Twentieth Century* (Cambridge, 1999).

23. See Barkan, *The Guilt of Nations*.

24. See *The Last Days*, directed by James Moll (1998); *Into the Arms of Strangers: Stories of the Kindertransport*, directed by Mark Jonathan Harris (1999). For an example of the marketing of survivor memory, see the growth of the list published by Frank Cass in England, the series produced by Beth Shalom and the lists of all major US university publishers.

25 Pierre Nora, "General Introduction: Between Memory and History," in Pierre Nora (ed.) *Realms of Memory: Rethinking the French Past*, Vol. 1, trans. Arthur Goldhammer (New York, 1996), p. 11. See Yosef Hayim Yerushalmi, *Zakhor: Jewish History and Jewish Memory* (Seattle, 1982).

26 Wladyslaw Bartoszewski, *The Convent at Auschwitz* (New York, 1991); Michael Steinlauf, *Bondage to the Dead: Poland and the Memory of the Holocaust* (Syracuse, 1997), esp. pp. 117–21, 135–9; Michael Marrus, "The Future of Auschwitz: A Case for the Ruins," in Peter Hayes (ed.), *Lessons and Legacies*, Vol. 3, *Memory, Memorialization, and Denial* (Evanston, 1999), pp. 169–77; Lea Rosh, *"Die Juden, das sind doch die anderen": Der Streit um ein deutsches Denkmal* (Berlin, 1999); Caroline Wiedmer, *The Claims of Memory: Representations of the Holocaust in Contemporary Germany and France* (Ithaca, 1999), pp. 120–63; James E. Young,

"Daniel Libeskind's Jewish Museum in Berlin" and "Germany's Holocaust Memorial Problem — And Mine," in idem (ed.), *At Memory's Edge: After-Images of the Holocaust in Contemporary Art and Architecture* (New Haven, 2000), pp. 152–83, 184–223; Tony Kushner and Donald Bloxham, "Exhibiting Racism: Cultural Imperialism, Genocide and Representation," *Rethinking History*, Vol. 2, No. 3 (1998), pp. 349–58.

27 See n. 20 above, and Heer and Naumann (eds.), *War of Extermination*. The profusely illustrated catalogue to the exhibition testifies to the sheer visual impact of the exhibition: *The German Army and Genocide*, trans. S. Abott (New York, 1999). In general, see Young, *At Memory's Edge*, and Barbie Zelizer (ed.), *Visual Culture and the Holocaust* (London, 2001).

28 Saul Friedländer (ed.), *Probing the Limits of Representation: Nazism and the "Final Solution* (Cambridge, MA, 1993), especially the editor's introduction, pp. 1–21. Also, the editors' introduction to Alan Milchman and Alan Rosenberg (eds.), *Postmodernism and the Holocaust* (Amsterdam, 1998), pp. 1–15.

29 *Proceedings of the Stockholm International Forum on the Holocaust* (Stockholm, 2000), p. 34.

30 See n. 28 above, and the extracts from journal debates in Keith Jenkins (ed.), *The Postmodern History Reader* (London, 1997), pp. 384–433.

31 Richard J. Evans, *Lying About Hitler: History, Holocaust, and the David Irving Trial* (New York, 2001); Sue Vice, *Holocaust Fiction* (London, 2000).

32 See, for example, Sue Vice "The Demidenko Affair and Contemporary Holocaust Fiction," in Leak and Paizis (eds.), *The Holocaust and the Text*, pp. 125–41.

33 Mark Roseman, *A Past in Hiding: Memory and Survival in Nazi Germany* (London, 2000). See also Lawrence L. Langer, *Holocaust Testimonies: The Ruins of Memory* (New Haven, 1991); Henry Greenspan, *On Listening To Holocaust Survivors: Recounting and Life History* (Westport, CT, 1998);

34 Deborah Dwork, *Children with a Star: Jewish Youth in Nazi Europe* (New Haven, 1991); Jane Marks, *The Hidden Children* (London, 1993); Dalia Ofer and Lenore J. Weitzman (eds.), *Women in the Holocaust* (New Haven, 1998); Judith T. Baumel, *Double Jeopardy: Gender and the Holocaust* (London, 1998).

35 Anne Frank, *The Diary of a Young Girl: The Definitive Edition*, ed. Otto H. Frank and Mirjam Pressler (London, 1997). Reflecting the renewed wave of interest in Anne Frank, three biographies of her (by Mirjam Pressler, Melissa Muller and Carol Ann Lee) and an acclaimed TV documentary by Jon Blair for the BBC appeared in English in 1998–99.

36 Gabriel Schoenfeld, "Auschwitz and the Professors," *Commentary*, Vol. 105, No. 6 (June 1998), pp. 42–6; and letters, *Commentary*, Vol. 106, No. 2 (August 1998), pp. 14–25.

37 Berel Lang, "Holocaust Memory and Revenge: The Presence of the Past," *Jewish Social Studies*, Vol. 2, No. 2 (1996), pp. 1–20.

38 Naomi Seidman, "Elie Wiesel and the Scandal of Jewish Rage," *Jewish Social Studies*, Vol. 3, No. 1 (1996), pp. 1–19. See also the discussion of Jean Améry's tergiversation on revenge and resentment in Nancy Wood, "The Victim's Resentment," in Bryan Cheyette and Laura Marcus (eds.), *Modernity, Culture and "the Jew"* (Stanford, 1998), pp. 257–67.

39 Henry Armin Herzog, ... *And Heaven Shed No Tears* (London, 1995); Joseph Harmatz, *From the Wings* (London, 1998); Rich Cohen, *The Avengers: A Jewish War Story* (London, 2000). For shifting images of the Jewish male, see Paul Breines, *Tough Jews: Political Fantasies and the Moral Dilemma of American Jewry* (New York, 1990); and David Biale, *Eros and the Jews: From Biblical Israel to Contemporary America* (New York, 1992).

The Impact of the "Eichmann Event" in Italy, 1961

Manuela Consonni

The fall of fascism, the military defeat and, above all, the Resistance with all its myths shattered the ideological model that had defined life in Italy for over 20 years — the paradigm of identity that the fascist regime had created — and replaced it with an anti-fascist ideological model that was equally strong. What these events failed to accomplish, however, as Ernesto Galli Della Loggia stresses, was to inflict basic harm on the fortunes of the middle class that had been the mainstay of the fascist dictatorship.[1]

The "Eichmann event," as I shall call the abduction, trial, conviction and execution of Adolf Eichmann by the Israeli authorities, was received in a particular way in the context of a country such as Italy, which, at the end of the 1950s, still oscillated between heroic, Resistance-style anti-fascism — which was steady, with all its overly celebrative aspects — and a seemingly strong fascist element. The latter continued to obfuscate the memory of the war and the deportation and extermination of Italian Jews by disseminating anti-liberal propaganda that preyed on people's forgetfulness and widespread ignorance of the facts to dim the historical truth. It is from this perspective that the impact of the Eichmann event in Italy should be evaluated.

This confrontation between two ostensible poles, a "totally anti-fascist" Italy and another Italy, a "totally fascist" one that was somewhat similar to it, began in 1945, immediately after the end of the war. In 1955, Piero Caleffi, a survivor of Mauthausen, explained its political terms very clearly: "In our country, immediately after the liberation, there quickly came together not only an indulgence, which could be to a certain extent noble, but an oblivion of what was and remains criminal."[2]

During the decade between the end of the war and the year in which Caleffi explained the nature of the confrontation, the Jewish memory of the deportation started to emerge, even though the memory of the deportation and the extermination was represented mainly by political survivors. The Jews did not enunciate a precise request for a specific kind of memory; that would come later. Instead, they made a shy attempt to station the Jewish memory alongside the other memory, that of the political deportation, as a worthy and separate Jewish memory of resistance to Nazism and fascism.

To justify this solution, the active participation of Italian Jews in the war of liberation, among other things, was cited:

> Today it would be salutary to document the participation of Italian Jews in the war of liberation, lest our silence make us responsible for another mistake, one that we define as opposite to and nearly as dangerous as the other — the mistake of considering the Jews passive participants only, persecuted opponents of the persecutors, the Fascists and the Nazis, but excluded by the others who knew how to resist the Nazi fascism.[3]

As stated, this was not yet an explicit demand for difference. However, it was definitely the affirmation of a presence, a will that wished to become a voice. It is a fact that Primo Levi's book, *Se questo è un uomo* (If this is a man), was published by Einaudi at this time amidst a massive advertising campaign. The idea of Jewish resistance had already been suggested during the war by the Italian Jew and literary critic Giacomo Debenedetti, who was more than convinced that the Jewish claim for recognition, i.e. the demand that Jews who had died of violence and starvation should be recognized as war victims, fighting victims, like others who had died in the cause of liberty, was fundamental.

> Their ordinary clothes served them as uniforms but were tattered by the torments and hung empty on their bare bodies.... Under these conditions, they marched toward their fronts, the places of their pain and sorrow... falling face-down.... These soldiers ask only that their [casualties] be remembered as [having fought on the] battlefields of this war. They ask that their names be read out among the names of other soldiers who fell in this war... without any extra pity — pity for the poor Jews — that would demean their sacrifice.[4]

So much for the level of principled declarations. At the practical level, the Italian national memory of the deportation and destruction during those years expressed the opposite message: the failure and, ultimately, the collapse of national solidarity. The truth is that the Resistance and its history became, during the 1950s, a silent chapter that the anti-fascist drive had rendered meaningless.[5]

These regressive events in Italian politics, unexpected in a country based on the republic that had been established after the downfall of fascism, had a very strong influence on what was said and how it was received.

> In a country where the Fascists, the ones you fought until yesterday and who caused you to suffer the camps and the torture, have returned to the opposition; in a country where the democracy for which you fought is always on the verge of forming an alliance with the enemies of yesterday

and considers it a virtue to resist this temptation; in such a country, belief in sincerity is destroyed and the true need for communication is broken. Nobody pleads guilty in front of the enemy.[6]

The memory and its expression in "silent writing" — survivors' writings that were created but not published in 1947–54 — are among the contrasts and contradictions of a political tradition that was not allowed to free itself of the fetters of the past, a political tradition interrupted by hopes for an auspicious postwar renewal that did not take place. Armanda Guiduicci has attributed the history of this writing, or non-writing, to the climate that followed the 1948 elections, brought about by the absence of a political ethos based on democratic conviction and confidence in the future. The utter absence of commemorative writing during those years, she claimed, was the outcome of the method and forms that had been adopted in 1945–47, when the end of the war was followed by a torrent of writing. She construed this spurt as a natural but limited fact — a flood of random writings created in the immediate aftermath of a traumatic experience.[7]

The early producers of memoir literature were neither journalists nor publicists but simple people who had survived the inferno. Publishers thwarted the appearance of this literature on artistic and commercial grounds, precipitating a crisis and squandering an opportunity for change. In the 1950s, however, the memoir literature evolved into a more professional and polished genre that had literary aims as well. It positioned itself in the domain of important literary, aesthetic, and artistic research that responds, more than anything else, to the contemporary and social trend. The second phase of memory had begun. Now memory was no longer an act and a will of political morality but an inert, strained outburst. Once, it could have furthered the construction and formation of a cultural consciousness and could have made a personal contribution. By the mid-1950s, however, this potential no longer existed. Amidst the cacophony of voices with which it seemed to express continued collective participation in the war against Nazi fascism on the basis of the Resistance, it no longer expressed the hopes of the Jewish and non-Jewish survivors. The lengthy silence that separated 1947 from 1954 — the year in which L'oblio è colpa, a special issue of the survivors' journal, Triangolo Rosso, appeared — shows how difficult it was for all sides — Jews, partisans and military internees — to talk. By that time, not only had an opportunity to hear them been squandered, but the words themselves had lost their power and symbolic existence.[8]

These were Italy's years of reconstruction, the years that truly represent the country's postwar period. They were marked indelibly by a general tendency to treat the events of the war as a closed chapter and to dismiss the suffering. With this, a chapter was closed as well. A larger cultural phenomenon occurred instead: the emergence of people from the war of liberation, from the world war, and from the concentration camps with the intention of reestablishing democracy.

As stated, the impact that the initial writing could have made was squandered. There are various ways of interpreting this silence in memory, which persisted into the late 1950s amidst domestic social tension. Perhaps survivors always tend to distance themselves from the agony that they experienced, to take a necessary pause for silence, before grasping the strands of memory and reflection again. "One must forget in order to remember," said Jorge Semprun.[9] Many survivors "cleared their desks" in order to have room for the future, for careers, or for politics. This is an especially valid statement for those who, having written or told their stories, were certain that they had done their duty. Others went to work for survivors' associations. Still others, who had returned from the camps in worse condition and in deeper loneliness, were driven by the indifference of society to marginality and even greater loneliness.

This loneliness is represented in the greatest postwar drama, *Napoli milionaria*, written by the Italian playwright and actor Eduardo De Filippo. At the end of the play, the hero, Gennaro Jovine, an unemployed tram driver who has just returned from a concentration camp to his hometown, Naples, utters a sentence that has become legendary: "The night must pass." This expression, the voice of a difficult hope, of a naïve expectation of someone who suffered, captures the general tendency of the period succinctly. Once the night passes, however, why stir up old matters, reopen the scars and wounds, and shatter the small certainties, individual and collective, that ordinary people have just reestablished?[10] Then, as happens in the eyes of these ordinary people, testimony becomes sheer lamentation, an obstinate will to remember and recall the past in order to obtain by repetition a form of reparation that would otherwise be unobtainable. Many survivors were deterred from continuing to bear witness by the justified rage of some survivors who wished to keep placing society's attitudes and behaviors on trial, a kind of Pirandellian torture chamber, a pitiless *mise en scène* of their possibilities of starting to live again, and intolerance and judgmentalism.

Another aspect of the 1950s was the appearance in 1959 of a different publication for a different age and attitude. It came in the aftermath of the first exhibition about the deportation, sponsored by the Aned-Piemont (the National Association of Survivors) in Turin. The exhibition was prepared entirely by survivors, including Primo Levi. It was

> an important date.... The bitter and painful silence that the survivors were very often obliged to maintain... and the careless silence of historiography were finally broken by the will of the same survivors in

a public and collective initiative, and the response, mostly among the young, was ready, massive, and passionate.[11]

Primo Levi remembered an interesting episode in regard to this fact and discussed it in an article that he published in 1984 in *Rassegna Mensile di Israel*. To explain why the reprinting of *Se questo è un uomo* was so immensely successful, Levi says that the occasion for republishing the book was provided in 1956 by the exhibition in Turin about the deportation. Levi remembers that "The young... asked me questions. They seemed to know my book by heart. They asked me if I hadn't anything else to tell. Then I proposed the book to Einaudi, which reprinted it in 1958."[12] The exhibition actually took place after the book was published; Levi inverted the causes and the effects. As the historian Anna Bravo explains, the besieging of Primo Levi by the young was not the reason for the reprinting of the book but rather its consequence. It was evidence of the success that *If This Is a Man* encountered among groups of young people who were culturally and politically receptive and aware. The members of this new public did not have a past to defend or conceal. Even the little they might have known about the deportation and the extermination may have been very vague. However, they looked to recent history for ideas and models as they would to a fount from which they might derive the strength to face a present for which they had little affection. This sort of quest was one of the definitive traits of the ideological and civil formation of that generation. Another manifestation was the great interest shown in the lessons of history in the spring of 1960, when the Gallery of Modern Art in Turin hosted classes on "Thirty Years of Italian History (1915–1945)." The classes were so successful that the organizer decided to offer them again the following year and sought a larger place in which to hold them. Furthermore, while none of the classes in the first round was directly dedicated to the deportation and the extermination, in 1961 Piero Caleffi, the aforementioned survivor of Mauthausen, retold the camp experience of the Italian deportees for the first time since the end of the war. The new classes were held at the Teatro Lirico in Milan, which had a seating capacity of more than 3,000. Their success gave decisive evidence of the younger generation's new interest in the baggage of the past — the war, Nazism and fascism.[13]

This was the complex cultural and political soil into which Eichmann's arrest in Argentina and trial in Jerusalem were planted. This signal event should therefore be understood and interpreted in the context explained above.

The capture and prosecution of Adolf Eichmann immediately reverberated powerfully in Italian public opinion. It turned into one of the most important events in postwar Italy and a unique impetus for mobilization against the Right. Due to the Eichmann event, Italians were now able to consult newspapers, several books, and debates in prestigious journals in order to apprise themselves of the vicissitudes of the Italian and European Jewish communities during the war. Although people of any age could have done this, it was mainly the young who did so. Their elders, generally speaking, had been too involved in the fascist past to behave similarly.

After his arrest and even before the trial began, Eichmann appeared on the front pages of all Italian newspapers, especially those affiliated with the Left. The communist daily paper, *L'Unità*, launched its anti-Adenauer and anti-Eichmann campaign in March 1961, and the journalist Ruben Tedeschi became its correspondent in all phases of the trial in Jerusalem. *L'Unità* reported extensively on the man who had been in charge of Jewish affairs in the Third Reich, running a picture of the man in his prison cell in Haifa, articles against Bonn mingled with one against Nazi Germany, and so forth. The distinction among the prewar, war and postwar periods became blurred.[14] The daily newspaper *Il Messaggero* of Rome wrote about the complex method used to arrest Eichmann and explained how "Israeli agents" had delivered him to Israel clandestinely. The correspondent Matteo De Monte was sent afterwards to Jerusalem to cover the trial.[15] Three journalists with the *Corriere della sera* — Vero Roberti in Jerusalem and Dino Frescobaldi and Massimo Caputo in Bonn — wrote several editorials and articles about "Adenauer's Germany," the German psychosis of collective guilt, and Eichmann. They interviewed members of Eichmann's family, including Robert Eichmann, the brother of "the exterminator of the Jews," as the headline in the paper termed him.[16] Sergio Segre, a columnist for *L'Unità*, segued from the antagonistic coverage of Eichmann to an assault on the most prominent officials in Adenauer's government: Hans Globke, the Chancellor's undersecretary; Adolf Heusinger, chairman of forces at NATO; and Friedrich Foertsch, inspector general of the Bundeswehr, stating: "The real problem is not the problems of names... but rather the problem of why, fifteen years after, between the Rhine and the Elbe, the old, traditionalist, arrogant, conformist, deaf, irritating, and ambitious Germany still exists."[17] In fact, the press at large — not only its communist and socialist organs — mobilized to demonstrate a purported Hitler-Bonn nexus. Interestingly, nearly all of the most *engagé* journalists were Jews.

As noted, several books about the event were published. Two of them came out in March 1961, even before the trial started. The words on the cover of *Dossier Eichmann* proclaimed: "Six million victims — on the eve of the trial against the person directly responsible for the Jews' extermination, chilling documentation of his criminal activity." The cover of Moshe Pearlman's book, *It's Him, Eichmann*, showed a *Muselmann* — a camp prisoner who is as good as dead due to physical and psychological collapse — walking and pointing towards Eichmann, silently mouthing the words "It's him!" in a kind of *J'accuse*.[18]

The trial undoubtedly had the valuable and important effect of lifting the veil of silence and oblivion that had been drawn over the concentration-camp phenomenon for 16 years. However, if the public followed the phases of the trial painstakingly, day after day, on the front pages of the most widely circulated and important Italian newspapers; if books about the concentration-camp universe appeared concurrently, albeit at different levels of quality and engagement; if a public that steadily grew in size and involvement became informed of the Germans' extermination policy — none of this means that the public suddenly realized that its historical knowledge was lacking, that it wished to correct the deficiencies, or that it simply decided to demand its "share" in the truth that others had already acquired.

> To believe such a thing is to commit the sin of naïveté... but also to admit that the Eichmann trial was an excellent impetus for the publication of works that, in another time not long ago, had been bought by no one or had been even considered unsellable. Let us also admit that the current efflorescence of writing about the concentration camps is truly advantageous, irrespective of the factors that brought it about.[19]

In conclusion, the Eichmann event raised discomfiting questions and reopened old wounds that had never really healed. It could have served as a positive challenge to the prettified rhetorical image of fascism as having had absolutely nothing to do with the deportation and the extermination of the Jews, an affair that was individuated and defined as German-only. Italian Jews such as Hulda Cassuto Campagnano testified against Eichmann. The trial could also have demolished the mythical extraneity of fascism that had been proposed immediately after the war and that most of the Italian population still considered valid during the years at issue. The old Resistance-style formula of anti-fascism, which had become "synonymous with prejudice, ignorance, and obscurantism," was replaced by a kind of sterile and celebrative anti-fascism.[20] According to this dilutional way of thinking, the Resistance — and, with it, the extermination and the deportation — lost its role and risked becoming a mere "genre," susceptible to the tyranny of standardization.

Both the Jewish world and the non-Jewish world in Italy agreed that the trial was a historical necessity. As Primo Levi said very pointedly on the occasion of a survivors' reunion:

> It seems to me that even in a world that miraculously has been restabilized on the basis of justice, even in a world that, hypothetically, faces no more threats to its peace, [in which] any violence would disappear, any offense would be rectified, any evildoer would be punished and made to pay his price, even in this world, a world so unlike our own, it would be a mistake and an act of foolishness to maintain

silence about the past.... Everybody knows that "History" is not always
full of justice and that "Providence" does not always act. However,
everyone loves Justice. So why should we hide this great example of
historical justice from our children?[21]

The non-Jewish world, however, considered Eichmann as part of Nuremberg,
another cog in the process of bringing the Third Reich to justice. The Italian
Left, using the Cold War rhetoric that still characterizes Italian political
discourse, picked a fight with Eichmann as Adenauer, setting the event in the
old-fashioned context of the liberation war of 1945–47 — in the context of
anti-fascism as against the fascism of the present and the past.

The Eichmann event in Italy reverberated mainly on and in the world of
Italian Jewry. In the early postwar years, the Jews wished to accept the proposals
of the Resistance model in part, acquiescing in this representation of the Jews in
the context of European history and their participation in the war of liberation.
Sixteen years later came confirmation that the Jews, too, could claim their
Resistance and that the racial deportation could be considered a kind of political
deportation, as Primo Levi put it. At long last, the Jews' survival of the
concentration camps could be deemed the equivalent of active resistance to
Nazism. What happened now, it seems, was what Slavoj Zizek wrote about image
and gaze, about the relationship between imaginary and symbolic identification
or — to use a distinction made by Jacques-Alain Miller — between "constituted
and constitutive" identification.[22] The Italian Jews constituted themselves by
identifying with the image of the heroes whom they would like to have been, that
is, members of the Resistance, instead of passive victims of persecution. Thus,
they shaped their own version of the Resistance ethos. Symbolically, however,
they concurrently created an identification with the place from which — albeit
vicariously — they could be perceived, and perceive themselves, as heroes and
Resistance fighters. That place was the arrest, the trial and the execution of Adolf
Eichmann — in Jerusalem, not in Nuremberg.

From then on, Eichmann opened Israel's doors to the diaspora. Eichmann's
captors joined the heroes of the Warsaw ghetto as paragons of Jewish courage.
By virtue of his arrest, the Jews could claim a full place in the ethos of the Italian
and the European Resistance, without ambiguity and without shame.

NOTES

1 Ernesto Galli della Loggia, "Ideologie, classi e costumi," in Valerio Castronovo (ed.), *Italia
   Contemporanea, 1945–1975* (Torino, 1976), p. 397.
2 Piero Caleffi, *La personalità distrutta nei campi di sterminio* (Firenze 1955), p. 12.
3 Eloisa Ravenna, *Ha-Tikwà* (Gennaio 1965); Liliana Picciotto Fargion, "Sul contributo di
   ebrei alla Resistenza Italiana," *Rassegna Mensila di Israel*, Nos. 3–4 (1980), pp. 132–46;
   Fausto Coen, *Italiani ed ebrei come eravamo* (Rome, 1988), p. 137. Two thousand of the
   200,000 Italians who chose to fight as partisans were Jews, a very high percentage of Jews

in Italy and even a higher fraction of the remaining population in the part of Italy where the fight against Nazi fascism took place. On the Jewish resistance groups, see Manuela Consonni, "Giustizia e Libertà Organization," and Vittorio Foa, "An Interview with History," *Michael*, No. 16 (2004).

4   Giacomo Debenedetti, *Otto ebrei* (Milan 1959), pp. 88–9.

5   Roberto Battaglia, "La Resistenza," *Movimento di Liberazione*, 57 (1959), pp. 187–220.

6   Armanda Guiducci, "Sulla letteratura dei campi di sterminio," *Società*, No. 1 (1955), p. 118.

7   Ibid., p. 119.

8   Associazione Nazionale Ex-Deportati Politici in Germania, sezione di Milano (ed.), *L'oblio è colpa*, Pellegrinaggio di Devozione ai Campi di Eliminazione di Mauthausen, Gusen ed Ebensee, *Triangolo Rosso*, No. 1 (Milan, 1954).

9   Jorge Semprun, *Il grande viaggio* (Torino, 1960). The book was widely reviewed; see, for example, *Il Ponte*, No. 7 (1962); *Rinascista*, 9 May 1964; *Movimento di Liberazione*, Vol. 60 (1963). On the oblivion, see, among others, Yosef Haim Yerushalmi, "Riflessioni sull'oblio," in idem (ed.), *Usi dell'oblio* (Parma, 1990); and Charles S. Maier, "A Surfeit of Memory? Reflections on History, Melancholy and Denial," *History and Memory*, Vol. 5, No. 2 (Fall/Winter 1993), pp. 136–51.

10 Eduardo De Filippo, *Napoli milionaria* (Torino, 1950).

11 Anna Maria Bruzzone, "Testimoni dell'esperienza: I sopravvissuti ai campi di sterminio nel dialogo con le nuove generazioni," *Storia vissuta: Dal dovere di testimoniare alle testimonianze orali nell'insegnamento della storia della seconda guerra mondiale* (Milan, 1986), p. 49.

12 Primo Levi, "Itinerario di uno scrittore ebreo," *Rassegna Mensile di Israel*, No. 50 (1984), pp. 376–90; Anna Bravo and Daniele Jalla, *Una misura onesta* (Milan, 1993).

13 Franco Antonicelli, "Un ricordo di queste lezioni" and "Nota dell'editore," in idem (ed.), *Trent'anni di storia italiana (1915–1945): Lezioni con testimonianze* (Torino, 1961). Apart from Piero Caleffi, speakers included Mario Spinella, representing the military internees, and the historians Ernesto Ragionieri and Ferdinando Vegas. On the second event see *Fascismo e anti-Fascismo (1918–1936; 1936–1948)* (Milan, 1962); *Rinascita*, 20 July 1963; *Movimento di Liberazione*, No. 60 (1963); *Il Ponte*, No. 9 (1963).

14 Guido Conato, "Adolf Eichmann fu una creatura dei 'Konzern' tuttora potenti," *L'Unità*, 12 April 1961; "Globke collaborò con Eichmann nello sterminio," *L'Unità*, 15 April 1961; Reuben Tedeschi, "Al processo Eichmann si ascoltano i nomi di personalità della Germania di Bonn," *L'Unità*, 16 April 1961; "Un giornale israeliano rivela che Globke ordinò la deportazione e il massacro di oltre diecimila ebrei greci," *L'Unità*, 18 April 1961; "Un nuovo documento presentato al processo Eichmann conferma la complicità del dottor Globke con Hitler," *L'Unità*, 20 April 1961; *Rinascita*, 26 May 1962; T. H. Tetens, "I vecchi Nazisti e la nuova Germania," *Rinascita*, 21 July 1962; M. Argentieri, "I film di guerra tedeschi da West Front 1918 a Guerra Lampo," *Rinascita*, 30 June 1962.

15 Maurizio De Monte, *Il Messaggero*, 29 April 1961; Sergio Segre, "Adenauer sta diventando un alleato fastidioso," *Rinascita*, 26 May 1962.

16 *Corriere della sera*, 5 March–30 August 1961.

17 Sergio Segre, "L'esecutore dei crimini Nazisti di fronte ai giudici — Una lezione di storia," *L'Unità*, 9 September 1961.

18 *Dossier Eichmann*, preface by Léon Poliakov (Rome, 1961); Moshe Pearlmann, *Èlui, Eichmann* (Milan, 1961). But see also, Q. Reynolds, *Il ministro della morte* (Milan, 1961); and H. A. Zeiger, *Ecco le prove: Adolf Eichmann* (Milan, 1961).

19 Andrea Devoto, "Su alcuni aspetti della letteratura concentrazionaria," *Movimento di Liberazione*, No. 71 (1963), pp. 73–82.

20 Nicola Gallerano (ed.), *Fascismo e anti-Fascismo negli anni della Republica* (Milan, 1986).

21 Primo Levi, "Testimonianza per Eichmann," *Il Ponte*, No. 4 (1961), pp. 646–50.

22 Slavoj Zizek, *The Sublime Object of Ideology* (London and New York, 1989), pp. 105–8; and Jacques-Alain Miller, introduction to Jacques Lacan, *The Four Fundamental Concepts of Psychoanalysis* (Harmondsworth, 1977).

The Representation of the Holocaust in the Arab World

Meir Litvak and Esther Webman

The representation of the Holocaust has become a major criterion in the examination of attitudes to the Jews in general, and to Israel in particular. Radical right-wing movements in Europe and the US have adopted the denial of the Holocaust as an integral part of their political platforms. The number of Holocaust deniers has risen over the years, as well as their sophistication and daring. These ideas have found an echo in the Arab world with an additional component, that is, the price the Arabs had to pay. World War II is not perceived in Arab collective memory as a war between good and absolute evil. Rather, Arabs view it as a war in which they had no direct interest, while they had to bear the brunt in its aftermath and pay a price with the displacement of the Palestinians. Hence, the immediate context of the Holocaust for many Arabs has been the establishment of the State of Israel in the midst of the Arab world and its efforts to gain legitimacy. Stemming from the point of view that the scene of the disaster and the perpetrators were European, the dominant Arab approach contended that the Holocaust did not concern the Arabs. "The Arabs do not have Holocaust accounts in their wars with Israel. It's the opposite way around," wrote *al-Hayat's* editor 'Abd al-Wahhab Badrakhan.[1]

For many Arabs the Jews had been the real victors of World War II. Zionism is perceived as cynically using the Holocaust and even inventing it as a means of financial and psychological extortion by creating and cultivating a sense of guilt in the West. Various Arab circles have used Nazi symbols, terminology, and ideology to project them on Zionism and Israel. The Jews have thus been transformed from victims to culprits. Alternately, the Palestinians are often represented as the Holocaust's true victims. Consequently, various attitudes in the Arab world have developed since the end of the war. These attitudes were partly inspired by those in the West, but unlike the West, they are not confined to marginal or extreme groups. They are shared by political establishments and mainstream political and ideological movements.

The representation of the Holocaust in the Arab world was influenced and shaped mainly by the context of the Arab–Israeli conflict. The Holocaust serves as a means or another dimension in the construction of the image of the "other." We may contend, based on the sources we have reviewed, that this discourse is basically unanimous. Only in the last few years did different voices challenge the advisability of this discourse. Still, we would argue that a coherent narrative does not exist. We have constructed what we consider a narrative, from a reservoir of references, arguments and images that are scattered and intertwined in the vast literature on the conflict, Zionism, Judaism, World War II and the history of Arab attitudes to Nazi Germany and the National Socialist Party. This reservoir does not represent a specific intellectual trend, but rather serves Islamists, nationalists and leftists. Moreover, there is a high degree of continuity, and many motifs and terms used by authors during the 1950s are still used today.

Although over 50 years have passed since the Holocaust, the representation of the Holocaust in the Arab world has not been dealt with in any systematic and thorough study.[2] This study is part of a larger ongoing project seeking to fill this void. The purpose of our study is to analyze patterns of continuity and change in the representation of the Holocaust in the Arab world since the end of World War II, and examine the evolution of the Arab discourse, its characteristics and the causes that contributed to its construction. It will also try to establish whether a correlation exists between the varying ideological trends in the Arab world and the various aspects of the representation of the Holocaust.

The research we have already done allows us to conclude that the data on the Holocaust that shaped this discourse has been extremely selective and biased and that efforts have been exerted to prevent the free flow of information on this issue. This process has led to a certain vacuum, widespread ignorance and insensitivity, which has left the door open for extensive manipulation. The present study will focus on some of the themes that lie on the spectrum from justification to denial which typifies the dominant Arab discourse on the Holocaust, and will also introduce a new approach that has recently emerged, which breaks away from the traditional discourse.

Justification of the Holocaust

The demonization of the Jews, or the "other," as reflected in various Arab writings on European anti-Semitism was by and large a function of the Arab–Israeli conflict culminating in the justification of Nazi actions against the Jews. The justification motif was more prevalent well into the 1970s, when the conflict was perceived as an existential one that necessitated the annihilation of the State of Israel. However, it did not disappear even during periods of improved political atmosphere. It stemmed from the need to explain and justify the elimination of Israel, particularly after the occurrence of such a catastrophe to the Jews. Hence, similar actions against the Jews in former times were attributed to the evil character and criminal activities of the Jews themselves, and Jewish suffering during the Holocaust was explained as a just and deserving punishment for their actions in the past and present. This approach is exemplified by a caricature that appeared in the Christian Lebanese newspaper *al-Anwar* after the capture of Adolf Eichmann in May 1960. It showed Israeli Prime Minister David Ben-Gurion and Adolf Eichmann facing each other and shouting. Ben-Gurion says: "You deserve the death sentence for killing six million Jews," to which Eichmann replies: "Many argue that I deserve death for not completing the job."[3]

The justification of Hitler's actions falls into three categories: pseudo-historical descriptions of the activities of the Jews in Germany throughout history; short-term explanations focusing on the period preceding the war; and retroactive justification based on alleged conduct by the State of Israel. All of these writers focus on the Jews of Germany and their alleged activities against the Germans, ignoring the fact that most of the Jews who perished in the Holocaust lived outside Germany and had no direct link to the events in that country itself.

Most of the writers who pursued this line of argument were Egyptians from the nationalist and national-Islamic trends, but there were also Lebanese and Palestinians, including leftists. They expressed their understanding of Hitler's deeds against the Jews and interpreted them as a justified reaction to the Jews' malicious intentions and behavior. Agreeing with Hitler's claims about the Jews' devastating effect on Germany, some writers cited *Mein Kampf* as a historical proof. The Jews, explained Ibrahim Khalil Ahmad, an Islamist writer, whose book received the endorsement of the Ministry of Religious Endowments in Egypt, "treated humanity with hatred and enmity" and brought evil on society. Consequently, society "wanted to repel this evil from its midst by expelling them or by eradicating them as Adolf Hitler tried to do in Germany."[4]

The reason for Hitler's anti-Semitism, explained Dessouki and Salman, was the evil deeds of the Jews, enumerated in his book *Mein Kampf*. These included extortion of the people through usury, the control of banks, the stock exchange, trading companies and publishing houses, and intervention in state affairs against its interests culminating in treason and espionage. These deeds were the cause for the persecutions and expulsions of the Jews and for the confiscation of their money throughout Europe, until Hitler decided "to burn them in large crematoria in order to get rid of them."[5]

Another common theme is that Hitler was merely responding to Jewish provocation or manipulations. The resolutions of the Jewish Congress in Amsterdam in July 1933, for example, were considered as tantamount to a declaration of economic war against Germany, and the Jews were seen as responsible for the worldwide boycott against Germany and for America's entry to the war. Another reason behind the Jewish manipulations of the world's fate was their desire to encourage emigration to Palestine. Islamist writer Sai'd Banajah links the Arabs' fate with that of Germany. World War I, which resulted in Germany's defeat and the Versailles Treaty, also produced the Balfour Declaration and the beginning of the Zionist invasion of Palestine. World War II enabled the Jews to destroy Germany, to consolidate their control of the world, to expedite the emigration of Jews to Palestine and to advance the establishment of the State of Israel.[6]

Dessouki and Salman quote SS leader Heinrich Himmler's speech on 4 October 1940, in which he allegedly said that the Nazis had "the right and the duty to their own people to fight this people [the Jews] that wants to exterminate them." The truth, they conclude, is that Himmler's statements against the Jews were but a "minor observation" compared with the enormity of the Jews' crimes against others.[7]

'Asma' Fa'ur refers to the persecution of the Jews in all the countries they had lived in and attributes it to sedition and acts of destruction that they committed. The most prominent example, she argues, was the declaration of independence of Bavaria by Jewish Communist Kurt Eisener after Germany's defeat in 1918. Eisener, who appointed himself president of the new republic, congregated the Jews there, put the management of its affairs in their hands and turned it into a Jewish principality. It was only natural, Fa'ur adds, that subsequently the Jews suffered persecutions, killings and expulsions by Hitler.[8]

Anis Mansur, a prominent Egyptian journalist and confidant of former President Anwar Sadat, offered perhaps the most vehement Holocaust justification following the 1967 war. In an article published in the Egyptian semi-official daily al-Akhbar, he reviewed the change in Hitler's image. During the early years after the war Hitler and the Germans were accused of brutality, and Hitler was presented as a human savage whose "favorite food was Jews whom he had burned and drowned." Later, he said, a new approach emerged which conceded that Hitler had indeed been brutal, but not only towards the Jews. Similarly, the crematoria in Dachau, Buchenwald and Belsen were intended not only for the Jews, but for anyone who disagreed with him, Jews and Christians alike. These approaches, Mansur explains, reflected the compassion people felt towards the Jews. The Jews, however, are not poor people that deserve pity. They are the enemies of humanity and even Hitler could not commit the kind of crimes they perpetrate in the Occupied Territories. Therefore, people throughout the world began to feel sorry for the "genius man who did not burn the rest of the Jews." The whole world realized, he concludes, that "Hitler was right" since the Jews are "blood-suckers," who want to destroy the whole world.[9]

Left-wing writers generally refrain from justifying the Holocaust, but there are a few exceptions. Jurji Haddad, for one, who saw Nazism and Zionism as two movements that were born out of capitalism and competed for world domination, contends that the Nazis simply launched a war against the Jews as a defensive measure and as a first step in a war against other imperialist forces. In other words, while he does not justify their actions, he implicitly blames the fate of the Jews on themselves.[10]

Justifications of the Holocaust continued well into the 1990s, albeit with declining frequency. However, the recent outbreak of violence in September 2000 between Palestinians and Israel gave them renewed impetus. Unlike the early expressions, the later ones justify the Jewish disaster as retribution "in advance" for Israel's actions as a state.[11] Analyzing Jewish and Israeli distorted traits in the modern period, Anis Mansur wrote in al-Ahram, the leading Egyptian paper, that "it would become clear to the world that what happened to the Jews of Germany, Poland and Russia, was justified."[12] Ahmad Rajab, a columnist in al-Akhbar went even further, thanking Hitler, "who on behalf of the Palestinians, revenged in advance, against the vilest criminals on the face of the earth," and regretting that the revenge was "incomplete."[13]

Denial

Denial of the Holocaust in Arab political and intellectual discourse aimed primarily at demolishing the moral-historical basis of Zionism and delegitimizing the State of Israel. It is highly likely that the importance of the Holocaust in Israeli identity and psyche made it more difficult for Arabs to accept it. Accepting the victimhood of the "other" could mean granting the enemy some moral authority or justification and undermining one's own status of victimhood. Acknowledging the Nazis' systematic extermination of Jews might give implicit credence to Zionist claims and right to statehood.

Another reason for denial may have been the Arab difficulty in reconciling the absolute helplessness of the Jews during World War II with their victory over the Arabs only three years later in 1948. Admitting the weakness of the Jews would have required deep soul-searching regarding the Arab defeat, beyond the standard explanations given in the Arab world. It was, therefore, easier to present the Jews as a much more powerful force than they had actually been. This may also explain why the Zionists are presented as allies of the Nazis, and thus portrayed as a powerful Machiavellian force.

There are some major differences between Holocaust deniers in the Arab world and their counterparts in the West. The latter seek to redeem the reputation of Nazism and rehabilitate the past. By contrast, Arab deniers' main focus is the attack on Zionism and Israel. Some of them regard themselves as anti-Nazi.[14] Moreover, Holocaust deniers in the West usually belong to the political margins. They are generally racists who detest Jews as well as other ethnic groups, including Arabs. In the Arab world most of those who deny or even justify the Holocaust belong to the intellectual and political mainstream, including leading politicians and statesmen, and such writings constitute part of the dominant intellectual discourse. Unlike the European racists, these writers see themselves as members of the Third World who are hurt by the racism of the radical Right in the West. Still, often due to their common enmity towards Israel, they tend to ignore the racist views of Western Holocaust deniers and of the radical European Right and even cooperate with them. Like the European deniers, many of the Arab deniers tend to relativize the Holocaust and argue that the actions of the Nazis and the Allies were morally equivalent.

Denial is not a consequence of ignorance of historical facts, but rather an extreme example of selective reading. Arab writers were aware of the Western discourse on the Holocaust, but preferred to ignore the vast scholarly literature, which did not suit their ideological convictions, and to highlight the pseudo-scientific material that did.[15] Denial appeared in various forms: total rejection of the Holocaust as a historical fact and its description as a pure Jewish-Zionist hoax; admitting the death of Jews as any other group under war circumstances, but denying that they were murdered as Jews according to a specific plan of annihilation; and minimizing the number of Jews murdered.[16]

Unlike the situation in the West, politicians and statesmen also took part in denial. One of the earliest statements was Lebanese Foreign Minister Charles Malik's assertion during the 1955 Bandung Conference of Third World Countries that the massacre of the Jews was mere "Zionist propaganda."[17] In a similar vein, Egyptian president 'Abd al-Nasser told the German *National Zeitung*'s editor in 1964 that "no person, not even the most simple one, takes seriously the lie of the six million Jews that were murdered."[18]

Although there are abundant examples of denial, the work by Dessouki and Salman may be the most comprehensive, including several recurring motifs. Nazi persecution of the Jews, they wrote, has become the basis for laying historical responsibility on the entire German people and for attaining emotional support for world Jewry, for German Jews and for Israel, which was artificially implanted in the region a few years following that persecution. That persecution has become the "wailing wall" for the Jews to which they turn every time that their "treasures are depleted." It is on this basis that international Zionism inflated the so-called "guilt complex" among the Germans and the need to "atone" continuously for this sin through compensation and aid. Zionism, they charged, exploited the persecutions in the "vilest way" in order to mislead and to commit the most vicious crime of modern history — the usurpation of Arab Palestine.

In other words, occupying Palestine was a far worse crime than Nazi persecutions.

Dessouki and Salman minimized the numbers of Jewish victims by resorting to German documents and testimonies. Both authors conceded that Hitler's victims amounted to millions, but Jews were only a small fraction among them. They cite the testimony of Rudolph Höss, the commandant of Auschwitz, who said that 2.5 million people perished in the camp by gas and one million by hunger, but they insisted that only 100,000 of them were German Jews, implying that the others were non-Jews. Examining the number of Jews that were said to have lived in Europe before the war, Dessouki concludes that the numbers claimed by the Jews are "fallacious and imaginary, and that among the German documents there is not even one which points to these numbers."[19]

Many of the deniers base their claims on partial or fabricated statistical data. Mustafa Sa'dani, for instance, who put the number of the Jews in Germany at 600,000, asked rhetorically "where could the Germans bring 6,000,000 Jews from?" His second proof was that Hitler's plan to get rid of the Jews was realized gradually over a period of ten years, during which a large number of Jews were able to sell their property, smuggle their money abroad and emigrate to the US. The third proof he cited was the 100,000 Jews found in German detention camps at the end of the war.[20]

An exceptional attempt to provide a pseudo-scientific denial appeared in the Palestinian journal al-Istiqlal in 1989. The author, Khalid al-Shimali, did not rely on Western deniers of the Holocaust but on his own experience as an expert on incinerators. He claimed to have visited the Sachsenhausen concentration camp where he received the impression that living and sanitary conditions were far better than those of Palestinian prisoners in Israel, making him realize the fallacy of Zionist propaganda. Shimali cited the Encyclopaedia Britannica as allegedly claiming that between 18 and 26 million perished in the Nazi camps, half of them in Sachsenhausen. However, as an engineer he concluded that it would take 1,300 years to burn so many bodies. At the most, 30,000 Jews were killed rather than 6 million during the war; thus, the Holocaust was a Zionist hoax, designed to justify the occupation of Arab lands.[21]

Since the 1980s there has been a growing trend to rely on the so-called professional Western deniers. Some, like French denier Robert Faurisson, were interviewed by Arab newspapers to explain their findings, and their books were translated into Arabic.[22] The Jordanian government newspaper al-Dustur, for example, printed an interview with Faurisson that had appeared in an Italian journal. In the introduction attached to each part, al-Dustur explains that the "eminent" French historian "refuted decisively and emphatically in a clear scientific analysis and decisive proofs the existence of gas chambers and crematoria for burning corpses. This is a major myth, which the Jews launched at the end of the World War II, and the Allies' media supported and disseminated, thereby planting it in human consciousness."[23]

Henri Roque's doctoral thesis that "proved" the hoax of extermination of the Jews also enjoyed positive acclaim by Arab newspapers.[24] 'Arafa 'Abduh 'Ali, who discussed the acceptance and subsequent disqualification of Roque's dissertation in his article on the "Holocaust lie" stresses that the French Minister of Higher Education, who issued the directive rejecting the thesis, pointed to technical errors, but totally ignored the dissertation's content.[25]

Roger Garaudy's *The Founding Myths of Israeli Politics*, published in 1996, is another example of Arab receptivity of Holocaust denial. The book refers to the Holocaust as one of the so-called founding myths of Israel. Garaudy was put on trial in France and fined under the 1990 Gayssot law banning Holocaust denial, but was warmly embraced by Arab countries. Following the publication of the book, Garaudy toured the Middle East twice, in 1996 and on the eve of his trial in 1998. His trips received widespread coverage in Middle Eastern media. As the guest of Arab writers' associations, he gave numerous public lectures and met writers, intellectuals and politicians. Funds were raised to support him in his trial, and a team of Arab lawyers rallied to defend him. His book, as well as compilations of his lectures and articles written in his honor, was published in Arabic.

The commotion around Garaudy probably stemmed from his overall criticism of Israel and his determination to stand up against the so-called dominant Jewish-Zionist establishment as well as his views on the Holocaust. As a former Marxist who had converted to Islam, he also represented an additional angle — the superiority of Islam over the West. The Western attacks on him were perceived as part of the West's attack on Islam. In various newspaper articles published in early 1998 he was described as a second Dreyfus who was being unjustly persecuted for his views, or as an Emile Zola who had came out in defense of truth. Since he was a foreigner, who was not directly involved in the Arab–Israeli conflict, his work was considered unbiased, based on a wide array of Western and Jewish sources.[26]

Denial appeared in various contexts, not only in publications dealing with the Arab–Israeli conflict.[27] Overall, denial has become an extremely common theme used by all political trends, from the Islamist Right to the Left, appearing in various media such as books, journals and newspaper articles, Islamist radio stations in the West, and recently in the Internet. Denial may appear together with condemnation of Nazi crimes and with the attribution of Nazi conduct to parties opposed by the author. A recent example was provided by an article by the Islamist writer Rif'at Sayyid Ahmad, entitled "Guantanamo, the Auschwitz of the American era." Ahmad accuses the US of maltreating al-Qa'ida prisoners, creating "another Auschwitz, at the beginning of the new century" and exacerbating the crimes committed there. Auschwitz, he explains for those who do not know, was the detention camp in which, "Hitler allegedly burned Jews in gas chambers during World War II."[28]

Alleged Zionist–Nazi Collaboration

Allegations of cooperation between the Zionists and the Nazis, or even collusion, in the extermination of European Jewry has been a common theme among Arab writers from all ideological currents that referred to the Holocaust. The main argument revolves around the alleged joint interest between the Nazis who wanted to rid themselves of the Jews at all costs and the Zionists who wanted Jewish immigration to Palestine. This converged interest is described as driving the two parties to close collaboration, including the extermination of the non-Zionist Jews, who constituted the majority of European Jewry. Some writers go even further, claiming that "Zionist banks and monopolies" provided Hitler with "substantial financial support" which was instrumental in paving his way to power.[29]

As in the case of Holocaust denial, the allegations of Nazi–Zionist collaboration may be found in a variety of contexts and are not confined to publications devoted to the Arab – Israeli conflict. For example, two political science encyclopedias in Jordan and Syria assigned special entries to this issue, immediately following the entry on Nazism. Significantly, they gave more space and detail to this alleged collaboration than to the discussion of Nazism itself.[30]

While this theme appeared already in the late 1940s, it has become prevalent among Palestinian writers and particularly in PLO-sponsored publications.[31] Most important is the book published in the early 1980s by senior PLO official Mahmud 'Abbas, aka Abu Mazin, former Palestinian Prime Minister, based on his doctoral dissertation.[32] 'Abbas contends that the Nazis regarded the Zionists as their natural allies and wanted to establish a Zionist state in Palestine that would secure their regional imperialist interests. The collaboration between the two parties lasted until the end of the war, and even massacres of Jews were carried out under the joint planning of both parties. In return, the Nazis permitted the transfer of tens of thousands of Jews to Palestine through a selection process conducted by the Jewish Agency with the active help of the Gestapo.[33]

In contrast to writers who either justify or deny the Holocaust, writers who raise the theme of collaboration make a distinction between Jews and Zionists, and claim to identify with Jewish suffering caused by the Zionists. Thus, 'Abbas describes the Jews as the first victims of Zionism and stresses the need to sympathize with them. Secondly, all of these writers condemn the Nazis and portray their regime and policies negatively, partly because their policies eventually harmed the Arabs.

Like most Holocaust deniers, there is an effort to present this narrative as an academic one that provides an alleged factual basis based on common historical sources. However, unlike Western Holocaust deniers, they often rely on Soviet sources, Jewish sources (mainly those composed by anti-Zionist Ultra-Orthodox Jews), and on partial or distorted statements by Zionist leaders. As in the case of the previous themes discussed above, some major themes of this narrative also fit the typical conspiracy theory model.[34]

Some of those who emphasize the alleged Nazi–Zionist collaboration, simultaneously deny the Holocaust or minimize the number of Jews who perished. The most glaring example is Mahmud 'Abbas's book, which is devoted to proving Nazi–Zionist collaboration in the extermination of the Jews, but at the same time casts doubt on the figure of six million, citing Faurisson as a source and presenting it as a Zionist invention.[35] Contacts between Zionists or Jews with representatives of the Nazi regime were indeed held in the 1930s and during the war in an effort to save Jews, but their aim was distorted in the Arab literature.[36] The goal of these "so-called rescue operations" was not to save Jews, some writers claimed, but to win immigrants to the Zionist project of establishing a state.

The writers who raise the collaboration theme attribute to the Zionist leadership great foresight and cunning in devising its policies. They claim that the Zionists were the only group that welcomed the Nazi ascent to power and Nazi measures against German Jews, in the hope that these measures would drive many of them to immigrate to Palestine. One writer, Jawdat al-Sa'd, even argues that the Zionists were able to realize their racist ideals through this collaboration in order to implement the biblical promise that "God will exterminate the weak and the worthless."[37]

The 1933 "Transfer Agreement" signed between Dr. Haim Arlozoroff, head of the Political Department of the Jewish Agency, and the German government, facilitating the emigration of German Jews to Palestine, is presented by many writers as a cornerstone of the alleged Zionist–Nazi collaboration. They argue that the agreement helped Germany break the boycott organized by the non-Zionist Jews and other anti-fascist groups, thereby inflating the power of Jewish organizations worldwide. Moreover, it flooded the Palestine markets with German goods to the detriment of the local Arab economy. Thus while the non-Zionist Jews are presented as principled moral persons, the Zionists are portrayed as cynical manipulators who cared only for their narrow interests.[38]

Not surprisingly, many writers elaborate on alleged Nazi sympathy with or even enthusiasm for Zionism. A few quote Hannah Arendt's book, *Eichmann in Jerusalem*, to prove their point, claiming that Eichmann hated the assimilated and Orthodox Jews but admired the Zionists because they resembled the Nazis so much.[39] The most serious accusation against Zionists leveled by several Arab writers is the alleged cooperation in the extermination of European Jews. They claim that the Zionists agreed to the extermination of non-Zionist Jews or of Jews who were of no use to the Zionist project, in order to drive the remaining Jews — the young and the strong — to Palestine to take part in building the state. Hence, these writers charge the Zionists of intentionally thwarting all attempts to save Jews by sending them to other countries except Palestine, since the goal of Zionism, in their view, was not to save Jews, but to use them as "raw material" for building the Zionist state.[40] Some writers even accuse the Zionists of thwarting rescue efforts and British "sincere efforts" to save Jews during the war by sending hundreds of them to the island of Mauritius.[41] Munir Ma'shush asserted that Zionist leader Chaim Weizmann rejected a British offer made by the 1936 Peel Commission to save (the symbolic number of) six million Jews. Misquoting Weizmann's speech at the Zionist Congress, Ma'shush claims that Weizmann told the British: "Let the old people perish, anyway they are a moral and economic burden to the world, while we will save the young."[42]

Two writers affiliated with the Islamist trend attribute the idea of exterminating the Jews to the Zionists. Al-Sa'd contended that two persons, Carter Robin (sic) and Jacob Tehon, a leading Zionist figure in Poland, devised a plan with the Nazis to exterminate sick and elderly Jews. 'Abbas even claims that the Zionist leadership incited the Nazis to take revenge on the Jews and expand mass extermination.[43] In order to further the collaboration theme, Glubb and 'Abbas maintain that most heads of the Judenräte (Jewish Councils) in the ghettos were Zionists, who were driven by their Zionist ideology and collaborated with the Nazis to save themselves. They insist that the Zionists did not organize even one rebellion against the Nazis. Instead, they foiled the resistance attempts of non-Zionists, who were truly anti-fascist. Since both authors could not ignore the Zionist affiliation of some ghetto rebellion leaders, most notably Mordecai Anielewicz in Warsaw, they assert that these individuals acted in defiance of their movements' policies.[44] 'Abbas describes the Judenräte as thoroughly Zionist, charging that they were not forced to carry out their duties, but were volunteers whose conduct was the highest manifestation of Zionist–Nazi collaboration. He and 'Abduh 'Ali depict the Jewish police force set up by the Nazis as a "Zionist organization," thus making the case that the Zionists helped in practical terms to deport the Jews to the death camps.[45]

All writers refer to the activities of the Hungarian Jew Reszö Rudolf Kasztner, who headed the Aid and Rescue Committee in Budapest in 1944, as the most prominent manifestation of this alleged collaboration.[46] They all attribute Kasztner's activities to his Zionist ideology which sought to save a small number of Zionists, who would immigrate to Palestine, while helping the Germans to transfer hundreds of thousands of others to the death camps. Some of them even describe Eichmann's proposal to exchange "Jews for trucks" (for the German army) as a pro-Zionist scheme to enable the immigration of wealthy Jews and members of the Zionist youth organizations. As the whole affair elicited a fierce political controversy in Israel in the early 1950s, culminating in what came to be known as the Kasztner trial, several writers maintain that the Israeli Security Services killed Kasztner in order to "prevent the dissemination of more facts on the collaboration between the Jewish Agency and the Nazis."[47] Likewise, they claim that the Israelis abducted and executed Eichmann because he was the Nazi official who knew most about the Zionist–Nazi collaboration. Hence, the conspiracy theory concerning the Zionists finds its logical conclusion, and the plot, which had started during the 1930s, ends in 1962.[48]

Interestingly, while accusing the Zionists of collaborating with the Nazis, most of the Arab writers who discussed the history of their own societies during the war gloss over or justify the collaboration of Arab leaders, particularly Hajj Amin al-Husayni, the Mufti of Jerusalem, with Nazi Germany. Some deny this episode altogether as a Zionist slander. Most, however, excuse it by arguing that the Arab leaders or nationalists did not support Hitler's ideology but merely sought to liberate their countries from British and French imperialism. Islamist writers, however, explicitly justify this collaboration, asserting that the Allies were no better than Hitler and that the mission to save Palestine from the Zionist threat justified the means.

The New Approach

Only in the mid-1990s did the first Arab voices challenging aspects of the traditional Arab approach begin to be heard. The discontent with the Arab representation of the Holocaust gave rise to a new trend among Arab intellectuals, calling for a new approach to the Holocaust. The gist of this approach is the acknowledgment of Jewish suffering as a crime against humanity and the separation of its human aspects from its political repercussions. The Arabs, claimed Hazim Saghiya, a Lebanese author and commentator, could surely not be blamed for the Holocaust, but as members of the international community, they should not exclude themselves from responsibility for the calamity. Saghiya challenged the traditional Arab notion of "the Holocaust does not concern us," and claimed that in order to comprehend Western and world sympathy towards Israel, the Arabs should try to understand the Holocaust and show more sensitivity and empathy towards the Jewish tragedy.[49]

The importance given to the Holocaust in the West prompted prominent Palestinian American Professor Edward Said to reach the conclusion that the Arabs should "accept the Jewish experience in all that it entails of horror and fear.... This act of comprehension guarantees one's humanity and resolve that such a catastrophe should never be forgotten and never again recur." Said claimed that a link existed between what had happened to the Jews in World War II and the catastrophe of the Palestinian people.[50] The motif of mutual recognition of the Jewish and the Palestinian tragedies as a paramount element in any reconciliation between the two peoples is central to this new approach. Another theme is the universalization of the lessons of the Holocaust. Recently, asserted Saghiya and Salih Bashir, the Holocaust is being expropriated from limited Jewish possession, assuming universal moral values that serve as a bulwark for democracies against the threats of fundamentalism, extremism and racism.[51] This new Arab approach, which gradually gained the support of additional Arab intellectuals and writers, has evoked an intensive debate on the Holocaust in the Arab press since 1997.[52]

The taboo on the Holocaust has been lifted, at least in part. Calls for original Arab research and for spreading knowledge of the Holocaust, along with admissions by Arabs of visiting the death camps and the US Holocaust Memorial Museum in Washington, are a far cry from the ban on information of the past. This approach, however, may also usher in a revisionist reaction. Such was the case of Egyptian journalist Hasan Rajab who remained unconvinced that six million Jews were gassed even after his visit to Auschwitz,[53] and of Masiri, whose studies on Judaism and Zionism only reinforced his conviction of the alleged symbiotic relations between Zionism and Nazism.

The collapse of the Oslo Accords and the latest outburst of hostilities between the Palestinians and Israelis gave a further boost to this trend. At a conference held in Amman on 13 May 2001, a group of Arab journalists and members of anti-normalization associations openly discussed Holocaust denial and the alleged parallels between Zionism and Nazism. They criticized Arab intellectuals who promoted the new approach and called on Arabs to actively engage in Holocaust revisionism, since the Zionist narrative on the Holocaust could not coexist with the Palestinian right of return.[54] The views voiced during this event seem to prove again that the Arab discourse on the Holocaust is still dominated by the politics of the Arab–Israeli conflict and affected by the political realities of the Middle East.

NOTES

1 *Al-Hayat*, 21 January 1998.
2 For works treating the issue of the Arab attitude to the Holocaust, see Yehoshafat Harkabi, *Arab Attitudes toward Israel* (New York, 1972); Bernard Lewis, *Semites and Anti-Semites* (New York, 1997).

3 *Al-Anwar* (Beirut), 9 June 1960.

4 Ibrahim Khalil Ahmad, *Isra'il: fitnat al-ajyal: al-'usur al-qadima* (Israel: A Sedition for Generations: Ancient Times) (Cairo, 1969), p. 29. See also Husayn Tantawi, *Al-sahyuniyya wal-'unf falsafa wa-istratijiyya* (Zionism and Violence, Philosophy and Strategy) (Beirut, 1977), p. 8.

5 Muhammad Kamal Dessouki and 'Abd al-Tawwab Salman, *Al-sahyuniyya wal-naziyya: dirasa muqarina* (Zionism and Nazism: A Comparative Study) (Cairo, 1968), p. 71; 'Imad 'Abd al-Hamid al-Najjar, *Al-tatawwur al-ta'rikhi li-bani Isra'il* (The Historical Development of the Children of Israel) (Cairo, 1973), pp. 74–5; 'Abd al-wahhab Zaytun, *Yahudiyya am sahyuniyya* (Jewish or Zionist) (Beirut, 1991), p. 95; S. Naji, *Al-mufsidun fi al-ardh aw jarai'm al-yahud al-siyasiyya wal-ijtima'iyya 'ibra al-ta'rikh* (The Corrupted on Earth or the Jews' Political and Social Crimes through History) (Damascus, 1966), pp. 276ff.

6 Sa'id Banajah, *Nazra hawla al-mu'amarat al-dawliyya al-yahudiyya wa-asl al-thawrat* (A Glance at the International Jewish Conspiracies and the Origin of Revolutions) (Beirut, 1985), pp. 101ff.

7 Dessouki and Salman, *Al-sahyuniyya*, pp. 73, 94–5.

8 'Asma' 'Abd al-Hadi Fa'ur, *Filastin wal-maza'im al-yahudiyya* (Palestine and the Jewish Claims) (Beirut, 1990), p. 142.

9 *Al-Akhbar* (Cairo), 19 August 1972.

10 Jurji Haddad, *Al-mas'ala al-yahudiyya wal-haraka al-wataniyya al-'arabiyya* (The Jewish Question and the Arab National Movement) (Beirut, 1976), pp. 150–6.

11 See for instance a reader's letter in *al-Ahram* (Cairo), 8 March 1997, saying that after the "Zionists had declared their intention to build settlements in Jerusalem, I realized why the Nazis burned Jews in the gas crematoria."

12 *Al-Ahram*, 13 February 2001. A French translation of the article was published in the Cairo daily *Le Progrès Egyptien* on 14 February 2001. A "refined" version was published in the English-language *Egyptian Gazette* on the same day. In this version, however, the justification of the Holocaust was omitted, as were some of the anti-Semitic expressions.

13 *Al-Akhbar*, 18 April 2001. Lest he be misunderstood, Rajab repeated his statement a week later in ibid., 25 April 2001.

14 Deborah Lipstadt, *Denying the Holocaust: The Growing Assault on Truth and Memory* (New York, 1993).

15 Muhammad Kamal Dessouki, for example, wrote a doctoral dissertation in Germany on Hitler's attitude towards the Middle East and claims to have read "thousands of pages and hundreds of volumes" in German archives related to the war. Yet, he justified the fate of the Jews while denying the enormity of the Holocaust. See Muhammad Kamil Dessouki, *Al-harb al-'alamiyya al-thaniyya: sira' isti'mari* (The Second World War: An Imperialist Conflict) (Cairo, 1968), pp. 282–4.

16 See, for example, Ahmad 'Attar, *Al-yahudiyya wal-sahyuniyya* (Judaism and Zionism) (Beirut, 1972), p. 158, who acknowledges that perhaps several thousand Jews may have been murdered.

17 Godfrey H. Jasen, *Zionism, Israel and Asian Nationalim* (Beirut, 1971), p. 257.

18 *National Zeitung*, 1 May 1964, cited in Harkabi, *Arab Attitudes toward Israel*, p. 277. See also statements below by Palestinian leader Mahmud 'Abbas.

19 Dessouki, *Al-harb*, pp. 282–4; idem and Salman, *Al-sahyuniyya*, pp. 94–5.

20 Mustafa al-Sa'dani, *Al-fikr al-sahyuni wal-siyasa al-yahudiyya* (Zionist Thought and Jewish Policies) (Cairo, 1971), pp. 267–8.

21 *Al-Istiqlal* (Ghaza), 13 and 20 December 1989.

22 See Robert Fourisson, *Al-ukdhuba al-ta'rikhiya: hal fi'lan qutila sitta malayin yahud* (The Historical Lie: Were Six Million Jews Really Killed) (Beirut, 1988), and interviews with him in *al-Sha'b* (Cairo), 17 May 1994. See also articles on Henry Roque in *al-Musawwar* (Cairo), 6 June 1986; the translation of the "Leuchter Report," in *al-Ahram al-'Arabi* (Cairo), 24 April 1999; and *al-Manar* (Jerusalem), 3 May 1999, as well as Roger Garaudi's book, *The Founding Myth of Israel Politics* (see below).

23 *Al-Dustur* (Amman), 14–16 January 1986.

24 *Al-Musawwar*, 6 June 1986; *al-Dustur*, 14 June 1986; *Filastin al-thawra*, 5 July 1986. See also 'Arafa 'Abduh 'Ali, "Usturat al-hulukast: ta'awun mashbuh bayn al-sahyuniyya wal-naziyya" (The Holocaust Myth: Notorious Cooperation between Zionism and Nazism), *al-Katib* (Kuwait), No. 498 (May 2000), which discusses the thesis and its disqualification. For Roque's thesis, see Pierre Vidal Naquet and Limor Yagil, *Holocaust Denial in France: Analysis of a Unique Phenomenon* (Tel Aviv, n.d.).

25 'Ali, "Usturat al-hulukast," pp. 113–14.

26 For an extensive coverage of the Garaudy affair, see The Project for the Study of Anti-Semitism, *Anti-Semitism Worldwide, 1996/97* (Tel Aviv, 1997), pp. 193–204; Esther Webman, "Rethinking the Holocaust," in *Anti-Semitism Worldwide 1998/99* (Nebraska, 2000), pp. 16–30.

27 Magdi Sayyid 'Abd al-'Aziz, "Adolf Hitler," in *Mawsu'at al-mashahir* (Encyclopedia of Famous Personalities) Vol. 2 (Cairo, 1996), pp. 164–5. See also Dessouki, *Al-harb*.

28 Rif'at Sayyid Ahmad, "Guantanamo, the Auschwitz of the American Era," *Al-Liwa'* (Lebanon), 21 February 2002. See also Anis Mansur's statement that America's torture of al-Qa'ida prisoners is worse than Hitler's treatment of his Jewish and Christian "rivals," *al-Ahram*, 26 January 2002.

29 "Bank Ferenheim mawwala su'ud al-haraka al-naziyya" (Ferenheim Bank Financed the Nazi Movement), *Filastin al-thawra*, 1 June 1985; 'Ali, "Usturat al-hulukast," p. 110.

30 See "Al-naziyya" (Nazism) and "Al-naziyya wal-sahyuniyya" (Nazism and Zionism), in 'Abd al-Wahhab al-Kayyali et al. (eds.), *Al-mawsu'a al-siyasiyya* (The Political Encyclopaedia) (Amman, 1995), Vol. 6, pp. 545–8.

31 Salman Rashid Salman, "Almania al-naziyya wal-qadiyya al-filastiniyya" (Nazi Germany and the Palestinian Question), *Shu'un Filastiniyya*, No. 31 (March 1974); Mahmud al-Labadi, "Jawla fi al-'aql al-i'lami al-sahyuni" (A Tour of the Zionist Propaganda Mind), *Shu'un Filastiniyya*, No. 94 (September 1979); "Al-naziyya wal-sahyuniyya" (Nazism and Zionism), in *Encyclopaedia Palaestina* (Damascus, 1974), Vol. 4; Faris Yahya [Glubb], *Zionist Relations with Nazi Germany* (Beirut, 1978). *Shu'un Filastiniyya* published an abridged Arabic translation of the book in Nos. 78 and 84 (May and November 1978); Mahmud 'Abbas, "Al-sahyuniyya taw'am al-naziyya wal-yahud awwal dahayaha" (Zionism is the Twin of Nazism and the Jews are its first Victims), *Shu'un Filastiniyya*, No. 112 (March 1981); Yusuf Haddad, "Al-tamathul wal-ta'awun bayn al-sahyuniyya wal-naziyya" (Assimilation and Cooperation between Zionism and Nazism), *Shu'un Filastiniyya*, No. 209 (August 1990); "Al-jusur al-sirriyya: dirasa fi ta'rikh al-'alaqat al-sirriyya bayn al-sahyuniyya wal-naziyya" (The Secret Bridges: A Study of the Secret Relations between Zionism and Nazism), *al-Huriyya*, 28 January and 11 February 1990; Issa Nakhle, *Encyclopaedia of the Palestinian Problem* (New York, 1991), Vol. 2, pp. 892ff.

32 Mahmud 'Abbas, *Al-wajh al-akhar. al-'alaqat al-sirriyya bayn al-naziyya wal-sahuniyya* (The Other Face: The Secret Relations between Zionism and Nazism) (Amman, 1981).

33 'Abbas, "Al-sahyuniyya," p. 6

34 Glubb, *Zionist Relations*, p. 7.

35 Rafiq Natshah, *Ali-isti'mar wa-filastin: Isra'il mashru' isti'mari* (Imperialism and Palestine: Israel an Imperialist Project) (Amman, 1984), p.151; 'Ali, "Usturat al-hulukast." See also 'Abd al-Wahhab al-Masiri, "Al-ibada al-naziyya lil-yahud asbabuha al-ta'rikhiyya wal-hidariyya" (The Nazi Extermination of the Jews, Its Historical and Civilizational Causes), *Shu'un Filastiniyya*, No. 183 (June 1983), p. 61.

36 For discussions of these issues, see Yehuda Bauer, *Jews for Sale? Nazi–Jewish Negotiations, 1933–1945* (New Haven, 1994); and Francis R. Nicosia, *The Third Reich and the Palestine Question* (London, 1985), pp. 29–50, 126–40.

37 See, for example, William Fahmi, *Al-hijra al-yahudiyya ila filastin* (The Jewish Immigration to Palestine) (Cairo, 1974), p. 31; 'Abbas, *Al-wajh*, pp. 3–4, 43; Haddad, "Al-tamathul," p. 69; Nasar Shimali, *Iflas al-nazariyya al-sahyuniyya* (The Bankruptcy of Zionist Ideology) (Beirut, 1981), p. 118; Jawdat al-Sa'd, *Al-shakhsiyya al-yahudiyya 'Abr al-ta'rikh* (The Jewish Personality through History) (Beirut, 1985), p. 201.

38 Glubb, *Zionist Relations*, pp. 21ff. See also *Encyclopaedia Palaestina*, Vol. 4; Natshah, *Al-isti'mar*, p. 152; al-Sa'd, *Al-shakhsiyya*, p. 203; Munir Ma'shush, *Al-sahyuniyya* (Zionism)

(Beirut, 1979), p. 74; Kamal Sa'fan, *Al-yahud ta'rikh wa-'agida* (The Jews: History and Creed) (Cairo, 1988), p. 105; "Al-jusur al-sirriyya," 11 February 1990; 'Abbas, *Al-wajh*, pp. 13, 22; Haddad, "Al-tamathul," p. 69.

39 Salman, "Almaniya," p. 103; Hasan Qasim, *Al-'arab wal-mushkila al-yahudiyya* (The Arabs and the Jewish Question) (Beirut, n.d.), p. 103; Natshah, *Al-isti'mar*, p. 146; Glubb, *Zionist Relations*, p. 15; Masiri, "Al-ibada," pp. 68–9; Nakhle, *Encyclopaedia*, Vol. 2, pp. 873–4; 'Abbas, *Al-wajh*, pp. 18–19. 'Abbas relies on David Yisraeli's book, *Ha-raikh ha-germani ve-Eretz Yisrael: Be'ayot Eretz Yisrael ba-mediniyut ha-germanit ba-shanim 1889–1945* (The Third Reich and Palestine: The Palestine Problem in German Politics, 1889–1945) (Ramat Gan, 1974), pp. 160–1, but totally distorts his findings.

40 Haddad, "Al-tamathul," p. 72; Hasan Sabri al-Khuli, *Siyasat al-isti'mar wal-sahyuniyya tujah filastin fi al-nisf al-awal min al-qarn al-'ishrin* (The Policy of Imperialism and Zionism toward Palestine in the First Half of the 20th Century) (Cairo, 1973), p. 753; Masiri, "Al-ibada," p. 69; Glubb, *Zionist Relations*, pp. 51ff.

41 Glubb, *Zionist Relations*, pp. 53–5; 'Abbas, *Al-wajh*, pp. 48, 56–7, 69; Shimali, *Iflas*, p. 119, citing 'Abbas.

42 Ma'shush, *Al-sahyuniyya*, pp. 74–6. For the texts of Weizmann's statement to the Peel Commission, see *The Letters and Papers of Chaim Weizmann, Series B Papers* (New Brunswick, NJ, 1983–84), Vol. 2, pp. 276–87.

43 Al-Sa'd, *Al-shakhsiyya*, p. 202; Sa'fan, *Al-yahud*, p. 105; 'Abbas, *Al-wajh*, p. 48; see also Shimali, *Iflas*, p. 119.

44 Glubb, *Zionist Relations*, pp. 37–50; 'Abbas, *Al-wajh*, pp. 172ff.

45 'Abbas, *Al-wajh*, p. 192; 'Ali, "Usturat al-hulukast," p. 112; 'Abd al-Wahhab al-Kayyali, *Al-mawsu'a al-siyasiyya*, Vol. 6, p. 548.

46 For a discussion of this case, see Bauer, *Jews for Sale?*, pp. 145–71.

47 Sa'fan, *Al-yahud*, p. 105; al-Sa'd, *Al-shakhsiyya*, p. 206; Natshah, *Al-isti'mar*, pp. 150–51; Nakhle, *Encyclopaedia*, p. 875; Glubb, *Zionist Relations*, pp. 57–64 and "Al-naziyya wal-sahyuniyya," in *Encyclopaedia Palaestina*; 'Abbas, *Al-wajh*, pp. 56–7; 'Ali, "Usturat al-hulukast," p. 11. The defendant in the Kasztner trial was in fact Malkiel Gruenwald, who was charged with libel for having accused Kasztner of collaborating with the Nazis. Gruenwald was acquitted, and Kasztner was shot and killed by an assailant in March 1957, before the Appellate Court overturned the lower court's decision and cleared his name. See Yehiam Weitz, "Changing Conceptions of the Holocaust: The Kasztner Case," in Jonathan Frankel (ed.), *Reshaping the Past: Jewish History and the Historians, Studies in Contemporary Jewry*, Vol. 10 (1994), pp. 211–30.

48 Glubb, *Zionist Relations*, pp. 65–8; 'Abbas, *Al-wajh*, p. 59; al-Sa'd, *Al-shakhsiyya*, pp. 206–7; Haddad, "Al-tamathul," pp. 70–71.

49 Hazim Saghiya, *Difa'an 'an al-salam* (Defending Peace) (Beirut, 1995), pp. 63–94; *Ha'aretz*, 21 March 1997.

50 *Al-Hayat*, 5 November 1997; *al-Ahram Weekly*, 6 November 1997.

51 *Al-Hayat*, 18 December 1997.

52 Webman, "Rethinking the Holocaust."

53 *Al-Akhbar*, 14 July 1998.

54 *Free Arab Voice Online* (FAV), 15, 28 April 2001; *The Journal of Historical Review*, May/June 2001; *Jordan Times*, *al-Hayat al-Jadida* (Ramallah), 15 May 2001; al-Jazira TV (Qatar), 15 May 2001, in MEMRI, dispatch no. 225, 6 June 2001; *al-Sabil* (Amman), 1–22 May 2001.

Too Little, Too Late? Reflections on Britain's Holocaust Memorial Day

Tony Kushner

Memory Contexts

During the 1930s and World War II the British government and its state apparatus, for complex reasons relating to the dominant liberal ideology and culture, as well as diplomacy, generally downplayed the fate of the Jews under Nazi control. As Frank Roberts, a senior official in the Foreign Office put in May 1944: "The Allies rather resent the suggestion that Jews in particular have been more heroic or long-suffering than other nationals of occupied countries."[1] This was, of course, the point at which Hungarian Jews were being openly transported to Auschwitz and the gas chambers there were working at full capacity.[2] From the end of the war until at least the 1980s British society as a whole was, for the most part, at best indifferent and at worst antipathetic to recognizing that Jews had, in fact, been subject to specific treatment by the Nazis. The net result was that Holocaust commemoration and education in Britain was left to a small group of largely Jewish activists, including some survivors. It was thus manifested mainly in the private domain, such as memorials in Jewish religious and communal buildings, or as ideas, such as a Holocaust museum, that seemed, as late as the early 1990s, to be pipe dreams given that the major site of British memory in relation to World War II, the Imperial War Museum, hardly mentioned the fate of the Jews.[3] The approach the activists faced was summed up in the response to the proposal in the early 1970s for a national Holocaust memorial in a prominent space in London: "this is not the time, this is not the place."[4] From such comments it becomes apparent that the Eichmann Trial, as with other significant moments of memory work after 1945, may have put in the British public domain the historical details of the Holocaust, but its longer-term impact was no more than a minor ripple. In contrast, in the last decade of the twentieth century and beyond, the situation has changed markedly and remarkably. The Holocaust has been placed in the school national curriculum, war crimes legislation has been passed and implemented (if only successfully in one case), and the small but immensely successful private Holocaust museum at Beth Shalom in Nottinghamshire has been followed by the lottery-funded permanent Holocaust exhibition at the Imperial War Museum.[5] Lastly, and the specific focus of this essay, the government has implemented Holocaust Memorial Day (HMD) which now has been commemorated annually since January 2001.[6]

It is significant that some of these developments have attracted major controversy and others not. Whilst the Holocaust, for example, was largely ignored in the initial proposals for a schools national curriculum, the attempts by activists, particularly linked to the Holocaust Education Trust, to insert it were both successful and largely uncontroversial.[7] Similarly although the Imperial War Museum obtained one of the largest National Heritage lottery grants for its Holocaust exhibition, as against large awards for the Churchill papers and the Royal Opera House, it achieved absolutely no public and media criticism or even interest. This was in contrast to the grants given to the Churchill family and the Opera House — both on grounds of public money being given to privileged or elite causes.[8] Its contents and nature were almost universally praised when it was opened in June 2000 and it is now fully functioning without controversy: less than a year after it opened it received its 250,000th visitor.[9]

In contrast to what might be viewed as the uncontroversial entry of Holocaust memory in the pedagogic arena, its insertion in the legal and political realms through the war crimes legislation debate in the early 1990s and discussions about Holocaust Memorial Day have been heated and at times unsavory, suggesting greater resistance in what might be regarded as the less "soft" underbelly of British culture. There has been some ground in common between those who oppose the war crimes legislation and the Memorial Day — an antipathy to what is perceived as Jewish particularity and an argument that stressing it will lead to an anti-Semitic backlash.[10] There is also concern that it is inappropriate for Britain to have such things — in the one case it would lead to an admission that the country had knowingly or otherwise let in Nazi collaborators, and in the other that Britain had some connection to the "other war," that of genocide, carried out between 1939 and 1945. The opposition to particularity and the concern to preserve the mythology of British difference, in essence an immunity to the continental disease of violent racism, are far from specific to the 1990s and the first decade of the twenty-first century. Indeed, as I have argued elsewhere, they are fundamental to the reasons behind Britain's reluctance to engage with the subject from the 1930s onwards.[11]

Yet there are distinct features in some of the qualms expressed about HMD that, whilst related to earlier concerns, reflect new anxieties. Whether these are legitimate will be analyzed in the remainder of this essay. It will be necessary to explore the potential in Britain for engagement and disengagement with the Holocaust through the contents and debates generated by the first two memorial days: January 2001 when it was inaugurated and was a major national event and January 2002 when it had the theme of "Britain and the Holocaust" and the focus shifted towards more localized commemoration.

First it will be necessary to explain why the relative failure of campaigners in Britain to gain recognition of and engagement with the Holocaust for the 50 years after 1945 has been so quickly reversed thereafter. The impact of Holocaust awareness and activism elsewhere, particularly in the USA, cannot be dismissed — for example, the creation of a prestigious and part government-funded United States Holocaust Memorial Museum in Washington exposed the absence of one in its major wartime ally, Britain. I have argued, however, that there are also domestic factors at an ideological and cultural level that have enabled Holocaust issues to belatedly develop, especially the growth since the 1970s at an intellectual and political level of multiculturalism and anti-racism.[12] Yet if it was such forces, working against an exclusive definition of the British past and present, that enabled the Holocaust to become literally part of the national landscape, it is also within the dynamics of cultural pluralism that a serious critique of Holocaust Memorial Day can be located.

To illustrate this issue further, a case study drawn from the treatment of an article written by the author for the first Holocaust Memorial Day in the local Southampton newspaper, the *Southern Daily Echo*, will be examined. The piece is of no major consequence in itself, but the process through which it was written and then edited has a wider significance. First, it was written quickly in response to a very belated request from the paper to do something — clearly as late as three days before that day the *Echo* had not really thought through the issue but realized that national media interest was growing and that they also had to respond, especially if a local angle could be highlighted. The draft that was scrambled together was written in less than an hour and thus reflected a fairly crude instant response. It was also 300 words too long, not intentionally, but the editing process was itself very revealing.[13]

There are two major concerns relating to Holocaust Memorial Day in Britain. The first is that rather than making ordinary people face the issues of contemporary racism in Britain and elsewhere, it may, in fact, have the reverse effect. There has been a danger since 1945 that British society and culture will bask in the glory of having defeated the Nazis (or, more commonly, the Germans), who are perceived as the ultimate in racist and genocidal perpetrators and the reverse of the freedom-loving, tolerant and decent British.[14] At a most obvious level, there is the involvement of the Home Office in promoting Holocaust Memorial Day. At the start it must be highlighted that the sincerity, hard work and integrity of the Home Office personnel involved in developing and promoting HMD is not at question. Yet it is the Home Office which is also responsible for the reception and treatment of asylum seekers in Britain today, policies that have at very best the defense that they are designed to keep racism at bay in Britain but in fact are there to reassure middle England that undesirable people are being kept out.[15]

The left-liberal world, exemplified by *The Guardian*, in effect told its readers in the 2001 General Election to vote Labour in spite of its asylum policies.[16] Doing the right thing with refugees, however, cannot be seen as a luxury but as an absolute moral necessity, as the late Hugo Gryn argued.[17] The Home Office has the misfortune to administer the asylum policies of the government. Unfortunately, such work inevitably undermines its efforts to commemorate the Holocaust, especially in relation to the multicultural, anti-racist agenda of HMD and of the Home Office in general. The tendency to celebrate the alleged decency of the British present — we do not commit genocide — and the British past — we fought Nazism and were supposedly generous to refugees trying to escape the regime — has to be considered in the politics of commemoration. It is significant, therefore, that my attempt in the draft article for the *Echo* to connect the past to the present by asking "how can we remember with genuine sorrow the murder of Europe's Gypsies whilst we denigrate and attack their descendants fleeing as refugees their continuing persecution on the continent?" was totally edited out.[18] It should be remembered that the Race Relations (Amendment) Act, 2000, whilst outlawing institutional racism within all public bodies in Britain, and in this respect the strongest piece of such legislation in the world, remarkably exempts immigration policy.[19] Czech Roma, for example, are openly discriminated against by British officials, and through this very tough act, they are allowed to do so.[20] We can remember the brutal racist murder of that promising young man, Stephen Lawrence, by brutal white youths, the Macpherson Inquiry into his death being the direct cause of the Race Relations (Amendment) Act, but not apparently that of the far less acceptable Roma in our midst, almost all of whose claims for asylum are rejected.[21]

The second concern with regard to the problem of connecting Britain to the Holocaust through memory work relates to other victims of mass murder. Mass murder is not the exception in the modern world but the norm. The Holocaust, for so long ignored and marginalized, has now developed iconic status as the traumatic event of the twentieth century. Campaigners, including the gay rights activist Peter Tatchell, have criticized Jewish historians for ignoring the plight of other groups persecuted by the Nazis or for marginalizing the plight of other victims of genocide such as the Armenians.[22] In response, it could be countered that without the efforts of Jewish historians and others the Holocaust also would have been forgotten and that whilst some have not focused on other victims of the Nazis, Jewish writers from Raphael Lemkin, who coined the term, to Leo Kuper and Mark Levene, have also been prominent, much more than most, in writing about and confronting other genocides.[23]

There is a need to be concerned, however, if the Holocaust becomes safe and uncontested territory — as with the dominant media and popular response to the Imperial War Museum's exhibition of "we/you must go, this was terrible." The subject can act as a way into considering other genocides past, present and future. It can also lead to a feeling of being "morally cleansed" (as was a frequent reaction to those who felt they *should* go to see *Schindler's List*) and therefore as a barrier to greater engagement. Again, I refer to the editing of the author's article in which all references to other genocides and to other victims of the Nazis were removed by the local paper.[24] Can HMD link Britain to the genocidal history closer to home, that is, that linked to slavery and imperialism? I would argue that it is indeed possible for the link to be made, as could also be the case of making connections between restrictive immigration and asylum policies past and present, but only if HMD is defined in a more pluralistic way, one in which the particularity of the Jewish experience, for so long denied, is recognized, but not at the expense of wider connections. James Young has written that any form of Holocaust commemoration that leads to closure has ultimately failed — the aim he argues is to ensure "that study of the Holocaust continues in itself as a form of memorial work."[25] In his work on Holocaust memorials, he adds that it is not enough to ask whether they

> remember the Holocaust, or even how they remember it. We should also ask to what ends we have remembered. That is, how do we respond to the current moment in light of our remembered past? This is to recognize that the shape of memory cannot be divorced from the actions taken in its behalf, and that memory without consequences contains the seeds of its own destruction.[26]

From this point of view, the tensions generated by the first Holocaust Memorial Day can be seen in a positive light, as part of a process of balancing the particular and the universal, which I would argue is at the heart of the present and future liberal democratic dilemma as we confront the intolerance and denied pluralism of the past. The day, whether for good or bad, has been instituted, and that itself is an indication of the growth of awareness of ethnic, or at least some ethnic, sensitivities. The discourse surrounding the first day, however, suggested that British society and culture as a whole had still to come fully to terms with Jewish difference.

Remembering the Holocaust in Britain in 2001 was, on the surface, a safe political gamble for the Labour Party in power. If there is still confusion about the whens, hows and to whoms, the word brings to mind at a popular level horror and inhumanity. As one person put it in summarizing British attitudes towards Germany and World War II: Auschwitz "means a lot of very unpleasant things to a lot of people."[27] But it was, after all, long past and over "there." Moreover, careful government policing has limited the scope of HMD to cover references to "safe" genocides and not ones that would offend allies such as Turkey by mention of the Armenian genocide, or more contemporary mass killings by regimes with which Britain trades weapons of destruction.[28] If Tony Blair wanted to impress the Jewish electorate of his sincerity then his appearance at the national ceremony in 2001 gave him ample opportunity to do so, and it avoided the legal minefield of the election half-promise to ban Holocaust denial in 1997. That other ethnic minority groups, especially Armenians and Afro-Caribbeans, were empowered enough to demand their say — leading, incidentally, to a still ongoing possibility of a Slavery Day — was a (not necessarily welcome) surprise to the Home Office and those delegated to make Holocaust Memorial Day a success. But the official focus of the second day, on Britain and the Holocaust, had the potential, even if it was not fully realized, to become more challenging.

The Memory of Survivors

There are many different strands, some profound, others indirect, linking Britain to the Holocaust. The second part of this essay will focus on one specific aspect that has been relatively neglected both in historiography and wider memory — the survivors that came to Britain after the war and responses to them from state and society. The failure to engage critically with their story before or during the second Holocaust Memorial Day provides another indication of the progress, but also of some of the limitations, of Britain's engagement with the Jewish catastrophe in recent years.

Until recently, there was little awareness of or interest in the Holocaust survivors who made Britain their home, something that the Eichmann trial, whilst putting the survivor at the forefront of Israeli society, did little to change in a UK context. That marginality has been changed quite markedly in the last few years — three examples will be provided covering different cultural spheres. First, there is the late Rabbi Hugo Gryn's preface to the Macmillan version of *The Diary of Anne Frank* (1995), which seems unremarkable in itself given the prominence, affection and respect he achieved in the last stages of his life and career when he became one of the voices of moral authority and wisdom in the British media.[29] The significance is that earlier English-language editions of this most-read work relating to the Holocaust had prefaces written or ghosted by prominent righteous Christians who had campaigned on behalf of the Jews — Storm Jameson in the UK and Eleanor Roosevelt in the USA.

By 1995 it seemed right and fitting that an eloquent and much-loved survivor such as Hugo Gryn should be the person to introduce this text to the public.[30] Fifty years earlier when Hugo and several hundred other children arrived in Britain not even their most sympathetic supporters believed they had a place in society other than as useful artisans. As Leonard Montefiore, the person largely responsible for getting the children into Britain, stated categorically in 1946, in relation to his own synagogue, the West London Reform: "By no stretch of the imagination is it conceivable that any one of these children will become a member of [this] Synagogue."[31] With lovely irony, Hugo Gryn became the prestigious synagogue's senior rabbi in the 1980s and 1990s.

There is always a danger attached to defending refugees on the lines of what they contribute to receiving countries as opposed to the incontrovertible right of asylum. Nevertheless, it is fitting in the Southampton local context to recall the reflections of Perec Zylberberg about the committee set up to help the children: "[They] did not encourage anybody to take up studies. They forever complained of lack of funds. With very few exceptions everybody was directed to some sort of occupation."[32] One of those children was Ben Helfgott, prominent now as a leader of survivors in Britain and in the 1950s as an Olympic competing weightlifter, but more importantly for his material well-being, a graduate in Economics from what was still the University College of Southampton in 1951. Similarly, it is not too self-indulgent to refer, in relation to Britain's current underutilization of the immense skill reservoir of today's refugee population, to the case of Anita Lasker-Wallfisch, prominent musician in the English Chamber Orchestra, and survivor of, amongst other places, Auschwitz and Belsen, and the remarks again of Montefiore explaining the children under his charge to the wider Jewish public in 1946: "[they] would like to spend seven years in this country studying to be a doctor, or a professional pianist." His response to such requests was blunt: "Think of something else."[33]

The second example of the greater visibility of and respect for survivors was revealed through Ben Helfgott, Anita Lasker-Wallfisch and other less well-known figures and their prominence in the national televised commemoration of the first UK Holocaust Memorial Day in January 2001. It was one that was repeated, with the addition of refugees, and also contemporary victims of racism and homophobia, in the second event, which took place in Manchester in 2002. Their contribution in 2001, in what was a highly staged event was, performance-wise, uneven, but it would have been remarkable in 2001 had the survivors *not* been present at such an event. Yet even half a decade earlier, at an event at the Imperial War Museum to commemorate the 50th anniversary of the liberation of Belsen, survivors were marginalized in a discourse dominated by former members of the British forces who, as soldiers or medical workers, had confronted through the liberation of Belsen what was then seen as the nature of bestial Nazism and is now used as graphic illustration of the horrors of the Holocaust.[34]

But it is in the Imperial War Museum that the final example of the awareness and respect paid to survivors in Britain is to be found in its use of survivor testimony in the narrative provided in the permanent Holocaust exhibition. From a life-history analysis perspective, a critique can be provided of the way the survivor testimony is presented. What is relevant here, however, is that mainly British-based survivors are featured prominently through video interviews throughout the exhibition. Such extensive use was not initially intended when its planning was at an early stage — an indication of how quickly attitudes towards survivors have changed in the UK.[35]

The memory of survivors in Britain has thus developed with rapidity. It is still not, however, fully formed in contrast to the memory of the *Kindertransport* which has become remarkably institutionalized and official through organizations, official recognition, especially through a plaque at the House of Commons, unveiled in 1999 and more recently with the memorial at Liverpool Street Station (2004) and in a series of documentaries and films, including the Oscar-winning *Into the Arms of Strangers* (1999), almost all with the emphasis placed on gratitude to the lives saved. In this respect, the late W. G. Sebald's last novel, *Austerlitz*, published in autumn 2001, is an important corrective to the overwhelming trend towards nostalgia that has typified *Kinder* studies and representation in recent years — contrast, for example, the rawness of ambivalent emotion captured in Karen Gershon's *We Came as Children* (1966) with the anthology produced several decades later, *I Came Alone* (1990).[36]

There is, largely through the efforts of Ben Helfgott and the historian and chronicler Martin Gilbert, the makings of an official memory of the survivor experience in Britain. From the Primrose Club set up on behalf of the survivors in the 1950s emerged their own organization, the '45 Aid Group. Martin Gilbert, through his connections to Ben Helfgott and Hugo Gryn, was first stimulated to write his history, or more accurately, chronology of the Holocaust, published in 1986, and more recently, a history of the members of the '45 Aid Group, *The Boys*, published ten years later.[37] Biographies and autobiographies of other survivors who came to Britain, some through series such as that from Vallentine Mitchell and Beth Shalom, have added to a body of material, as have oral and video history interviews carried out by the National Life Story Collection at the British Library, the Spielberg Foundation, the Imperial War Museum and the Manchester Shoah Centre. Significantly, however, these life-history testimonies often furnish a counter-narrative to that provided by what might now be regarded as the official voice of this movement — Sir Martin Gilbert. Yet it is Gilbert's version of their history that provides the safe narrative that apparently meets the needs of British society if the sales and reviews of his work are to be regarded as an accurate measure of contemporary attitudes.

Survivors and British Immigration Policy

In the final section of this essay I want to highlight some of the areas of contention that remain unexplored or indeed may have been deliberately ignored in order to provide a palatable narrative of Britain and the survivors of the Holocaust. These are highlighted not to muckrake or otherwise sensationalize, but to add to the process of explaining rather than condemning/defending the past British record.[38] It is again a reflection of the immaturity of the debate that in January 2002 the media demanded a totally polarized debate on whether enough had or had not been done for the Jews of Europe by Britain. For the most part, self-reflexivity was absent. The questions that were rarely asked, for example, included: what were the roots of sympathy, antipathy and, more than anything, ambivalence that made up the British response to the plight of the Jews in the Nazi era and what was the overall relevance to issues of the moment?

For reasons of space I will limit the remaining discussion to five particular issues that are raised by Britain and the Holocaust survivors. First, to put it negatively, Britain had no legal necessity to take any survivors as such immediately after the war. The United Nations Convention on Refugees was created as late as 1951, and even if it had been in force there was no way, other than the spectacularly untypical case of Miklos Hammer, who came into Britain adopting the identity of a British citizen, how survivors could have arrived on British soil as illegal aliens.[39] Some did arrive legally through other larger movements, such as the later notorious landlord Peter Rachman and the Polish army.[40] It is significant that many hundreds of thousands of aliens were entering Britain at this time but it is so far undisputed in the limited existing scholarship on the subject that Jews were seen as undesirable newcomers — perceived as unassimilable, both religiously and racially, left-wing trouble makers and poor workers. At the same time the state was excluding for not dissimilar reasons those of color from the Commonwealth — a greater problem, however, legally, as in contrast they were British citizens. The quite blatant anti-Semitism of keeping out Jews in any numbers in the immediate postwar period should be recognized. It needs to be contextualized in postwar fears and racial thinking, but here there is an onus not just on the state and politicians today to recognize this informal but rigid policy, but also on those working on postwar race relations and immigration control who studiously ignore the work of myself, David Cesarani and Louise London which makes the connection to other forms of exclusion after 1945.[41]

There are those who argue that keeping out asylum seekers today from Eastern Europe cannot possibly be racist because they are not black. The case of the Jews after 1945 shows the falsity of such denials.[42]

Second, why then did Britain allow in any survivors? A comforting mythology has developed over the children who came to Britain in 1945, organized by the Committee for the Care of Children from the Concentration Camps. It was set up to find 1,000 child survivors from the camps to come to Britain to recuperate, not settle, but only 732 could be found — in other words the tiny number reflected the totality of the Nazi extermination campaign and not the meanness of the British state structure in keeping out the survivors. Unfortunately, there is little truth in this mythology, though it is understandable to all concerned why comfort is found in its belief. A very thick Home Office file in the Public Record Office gives a full bureaucratic history of the movement. It is a story of people of goodwill bending the official rules as much as possible, of genuine empathy, but underneath it reveals the clear philosophy of government policy of keeping Jewish permanent settlers out of Britain. So: the reality. The scheme was set up because Leonard Montefiore was desperately upset about the images coming out of Belsen and Buchenwald and, along with Otto Schiff, wanted up to a thousand orphans to come to Britain to recuperate from these two camps. The reason that the Home Office agreed was that it would have been in a desperately uncomfortable position not to — 10,000 young people from the continent, first Holland and then France and Belgium, came to Britain at the same time. To not allow a smaller number from the camps would have been hard to justify in the atmosphere of disgust generated by their images in spring/summer 1945. The Home Office insisted, however, that non-Jews should also be included. The children came on temporary permits, their numbers were limited because the scheme was limited to a few camps and not because there were not that number of Jewish orphans alive across the continent of Europe. The number was then restricted to 800 by the Jewish bodies that funded it, purely for financial reasons.[43] The fact that this history is not mentioned in Martin Gilbert's lengthy account is disturbing because in essence it distorts an account that is relevant not just to the commemoration of Britain and the Holocaust but to contemporary refugee questions. As referred to earlier, Gilbert's sanitized account is the one that has proved extremely palatable and he is, in the Jewish and non-Jewish world in Britain, the closest to an official voice of Holocaust memorialization.

Third, focusing on these children, like the *Kinder*, distorts other, messy, movements of survivors into Britain at that time and subsequently. Most did not come through this scheme, yet it is this scheme and its subsequent organizations that have dominated discussions and also issues of compensation and so on. There is, of course, a sexism at work in the description "The Boys," used in practice to exclude female survivors, who were numerous within it but marginalized at the time and now subsequently in memory work. Furthermore, many of those who were not part of this scheme or its later voluntary associations were, until recently, left outside power structures and official dialogue. The Hendon-based Holocaust Survivor group, formed a few years ago, provides greater depth, but it still does not include many isolated survivors outside London.[44]

Fourth, the largest group of survivors came through the Distressed Relatives scheme which was extremely limited in its scope — the survivors had to prove close relations in the UK and no other surviving family. The result, quite understandably, was that many survivors lied to get into Britain, killing off other family members on their forms. They also had to come to Britain as domestic workers or the like. Knowledge of this treatment is not to shock but just to state what was government policy, which was seen by the Ministry of Labour, but not the Home Office at the time, as far too severe.[45] It reflected the desire to normalize Jews and to remove the risk of anti-Semitism. It did not, of course, cater for the needs, either physically or psychologically, of the often damaged survivors.

Many other survivors came to Britain then and later through accident — such as Trude Levi who came to the country having been in South Africa immediately after the war.[46] In short, the survivors did not come in some neat humanitarian scheme but through muddle and meanness mitigated by many ordinary people, Jewish and non-Jewish, who looked after these damaged children, and some officials who turned a blind eye to 23-year-olds mascarading as teenagers to get into Britain. Many who came to Britain not as part of the scheme, such as Kitty Hart, were given very little help and support and in short had to get on with their lives without mentioning, as British comic tradition would have it, "the war."[47]

Fifth and finally, many of those who came to Britain were severely damaged. Many never recovered their mental or physical health. Even those who have "made it" are still affected today, and we of course hear little now of those who were unable to get on in a society that had no inkling of how to deal with trauma. Today one in six refugees has a severe physical health problem and many more suffer from the mental torment of their persecution. The memory of the survivors of the Holocaust in Britain, like the refugees from Nazism that preceded them, should start from the perspective of the damage done, rather than the contribution made. This is what links those that came to Britain then to those today, rather than, as is the case in general discussion, acting as a barrier between those we say retrospectively deserved asylum and those that allegedly abuse it now. Granting asylum is about us, the givers, not about them, whether they be child survivors of the Holocaust of the past or Afghans after 11 September 2001.

To conclude, Holocaust Memorial Day, alongside the Imperial War Museum exhibition, has shown on the one hand the ability of British society for the first time since 1945 to accept that the war, still the defining moment in British national identity, can at least begin to be approached pluralistically. The Queen, if not present on the first Holocaust Memorial Day, still opened a permanent exhibition in June 2000 whose size exceeded that devoted to World War II in what is Britain's official place of memory for the conflict, if not *the* museum of Britain itself during the twentieth century.[48] Yet it remains, aside from the inevitable platitudes about the evils of racism coming from the Prime Minister and the Home Secretary, that the first Holocaust Memorial Days have largely shown the persistence in the belief that Britain is somehow different from the racist continent/outside world. Britain, for example, we are often told, will always allow in genuine refugees. Those refugees, however, always tend to exist in the past, and in this respect the Jews escaping Nazi Europe to Britain are now the most highly prized and often cited genuine asylum seekers — not of course, how they were generally perceived at the time. We may well accept and indeed venerate the now aging Jewish refugees and survivors who settled in Britain but we still hesitate to accept the unedifying way they were allowed entry.

Holocaust Memorial Day has the potential to take the easier path of remembering in order to forget or to begin the difficult process of self-reflection. So far, not surprisingly, in what are still its early stages, HMD has yet to confront fully the prejudices of the past and present in British society, culture and politics that have affected and continue to affect Jews and other minorities in Britain — as well as the country's responses to the protection of such groups outside the UK. Returning to the local example, the newspaper chain that has been very positive towards HMD has also been at the forefront of the campaign against situating an asylum-seeker camp in the Southampton region.[49] Perhaps, however, to end on a note of cautious optimism, the very difficulties faced by the government in trying to contain Holocaust Memorial Day themselves reflect something of a success. To those concerned with the memory of the Holocaust, the phrase "Never Again" has become one of the most fatuous and meaningless. It is more likely that those in the Home Office with responsibility for running the event, with all the headaches it has caused, would be relieved if "never again" actually referred to HMD itself. Yet its problematic nature and the discussions it has generated are a minor triumph and themselves a justification for the day.[50] Whilst James Young's maxim in relation to the Holocaust — "Better abused memory . . . which might then be critically qualified, than no memory at all" — is debatable,[51] in a British context it has replaced the more basic dilemma of some memory being better than no memory at all — one that groups such as the Roma and the descendants of slavery still face. In that respect, by revealing that memory work can often be infectious and uncontrollable, Holocaust Memorial Day has served and continues to serve a valuable function.

NOTES

1 Frank Roberts, 11 May 1944, in Public Record Office (PRO) FO 371/42790 W7937.
2 David Cesarani (ed.), *Genocide and Rescue: The Holocaust in Hungary 1944* (Oxford, 1997).
3 Tony Kushner, *The Holocaust and the Liberal Imagination: A Social and Cultural History* (Oxford, 1994), ch. 7. See also idem, "The Holocaust and the Museum World in Britain: A Study of Ethnography," in Sue Vice (ed.), *Representing the Holocaust* (London, 2003), pp. 13–40.
4 Response from the (Catholic) Archbishop of Westminster, 13 February 1973 in Council of Christians and Jews papers, 9/84, University of Southampton Archive.
5 See Philip Rubenstein and Warren Taylor, "Teaching about the Holocaust in the National Curriculum," *The British Journal of Holocaust Education*, Vol. 1, No. 1 (Summer 1992), pp. 47–54; David Cesarani, *Justice Delayed*, 2nd edn. (London, 2002); Steven Cooke, "Beth Shalom: Re-thinking History and Memory," *The Journal of Holocaust Education*, Vol. 8, No. 1 (Summer 1999), pp. 21–41.
6 Already a lively academic discussion about Holocaust Memorial Day in Britain has emerged. See the debate between, on the one hand, Nira Yuval-Davis and Max Silverman and, on the other, David Cesarani, "Memorialising the Holocaust in Britain," *Ethnicities*, Vol. 2, No. 1 (2002), pp. 107–33; the shorter debate between Dan Stone and David Cesarani in *Patterns of Prejudice*, Vol. 34, No. 4 (2000), pp. 53–66; and at greater length by Donald Bloxham, "Britain's Holocaust Memorial Days: Reshaping the Past in the Service of the Present," in Vice (ed.), *Representing the Holocaust*, pp. 41–62.
7 Rubenstein and Taylor, "Teaching about the Holocaust."
8 See *Jewish Chronicle*, 13 December 1996, for the lottery grant and *The Guardian*, 12 May 2004, for lottery controversies in its first ten years.
9 Kushner, "The Holocaust and the Museum World in Britain"; idem, "Oral History at the Extremes of the Human Experience: Holocaust Testimony in a Museum Setting," *Oral History*, Vol. 29, No. 2 (Autumn 2001), pp. 83–94.
10 On the war crimes debate see Cesarani, *Justice Delayed*; Alan Robinson, "War Crimes, Old Soldiers and Fading Memories: The Serafinowicz Case," *The Journal of Holocaust Education*, Vol. 8, No.1 (Summer 1999), pp. 42–57; and Jon Silverman, "War Crimes Inquiries," *History Today* (November 2000), pp. 26–8.
11 Kushner, *The Holocaust and the Liberal Imagination*, chs. 1, 4 and 7.
12 Ibid., pp. 261–3.
13 Tony Kushner, "Horrors of Racism We Must Not Forget," *Southern Daily Echo*, 27 January 2001.
14 Paul Gilroy, *There Ain't No Black in the Union Jack* (London, 1987), develops this theme in relation to the limits of the anti-Nazi movement in Britain from the 1970s onwards.
15 Tony Kushner, "Meaning Nothing but Good: Ethics, History and Asylum-Seeker Phobia in Britain," *Patterns of Prejudice*, Vol. 37, No. 3 (2003), pp. 257–76; Liza Schuster, *The Use and Abuse of Political Asylum in Britain and Germany* (London, 2003).
16 It did, however, produce a series of articles defending refugees and attacking the anti-asylum-seeker campaign, published as a booklet: *Welcome to Britain* (London, 2001).
17 Hugo Gryn, *A Moral and Spiritual Index* (London, 1996).
18 Kushner, "Horrors of Racism." The longer version is still in the author's possession.
19 Home Office, *Race Relations (Amendment) Act 2000* (London, 2001), p. 40; and John Solomos, *Race and Racism in Britain*, 3rd edn. (London, 2003), pp. 73–4, for comment and analysis.
20 *The Guardian*, 30 July and 23 August 2001.
21 Figures in *iNexile: The Refugee Council Magazine*, August 2000. For Lawrence, see Brian Cathcart, *The Case of Stephen Lawrence* (London, 2000).

22 Peter Tatchell, quoted in *The Guardian*, 16 June 2001.
23 Leo Kuper, *Genocide: Its Political Use in the Twentieth Century* (New Haven, 1981). Levene, now the leading world authority on the history of genocide in the twentieth century, is working on a multi-volume history of the subject.
24 Kushner, "Horrors of Racism."
25 James E. Young, *Writing and Rewriting the Holocaust: Narrative and the Consequences of Interpretation* (Bloomington and Indianapolis, 1988), p. 149.
26 James E. Young, *The Texture of Memory: Holocaust Memorial and Meaning* (New Haven, 1993), p. 15.
27 Quoted in "The Media Show," Channel 4, 14 October 1990. See comment by Mark Steyn in *The Independent*, 15 October 1990.
28 Bloxham, "Britain's Holocaust Memorial Days."
29 Hugo Gryn with Naomi Gryn, *Chasing Shadows* (London, 2000).
30 Hugo Gryn, "Foreword," *The Diary of Anne Frank* (London, 1995), pp. vii–xi.
31 The details of Montefiore's involvement and advice are in Tony Kushner and Katharine Knox, *Refugees in an Age of Genocide: Global, National and Local Perspectives during the Twentieth Century* (London, 1999), pp. 207–12.
32 Ibid., p. 212.
33 Ibid., pp. 211–2. See also Anita Lasker-Wallfisch, *Inherit the Truth, 1939–1945* (London, 1996).
34 See Jo Reilly et al. (eds.), *Belsen in History and Memory* (London, 1997).
35 Kushner, "Oral History at the Extremes of the Human Experience."
36 Karen Gershon (ed.), *We Came as Children: A Collective Autobiography of Refugees* (London, 1966); B. Leverton and S. Lowensohn (eds.), *I Came Alone: The Stories of the Kindertransports* (Lewes, Sussex, 1990).
37 Martin Gilbert, *The Holocaust* (London, 1986); and idem, *The Boys: Triumph over Adversity* (London, 1996).
38 For a further elaboration of this perspective see Tony Kushner, "The Search for Nuance in the Study of Holocaust 'Bystanders'," in David Cesarani and Paul Levine (eds.), *"Bystanders" to the Holocaust: A Re-evaluation* (London, 2002), pp. 57–76.
39 Hammer's remarkable story is told in Gerald Jacobs, *Sacred Games* (London, 1995).
40 Shirley Green, *Rachman* (London, 1979).
41 Kushner and Knox, *Refugees in an Age of Genocide*; Cesarani, *Justice Delayed*; Louise London, *Whitehall and the Jews* (Cambridge, 2000).
42 Kushner, "Meaning Nothing but Good."
43 The relevant file is PRO HO 213/781. See also Kushner and Knox, *Refugees in an Age of Genocide*, pp. 206–8.
44 See the essays in "Family/History: Survivors and Their Children," special issue of *The Journal of Holocaust Education*, Vol. 4, No. 2 (Winter 1995).
45 See Kushner, *The Holocaust and the Liberal Imagination*, ch. 7, for details.
46 Trude Levi, *A Cat Called Adolf* (London, 1995).
47 Kitty Hart, *Return to Auschwitz* (London, 1981).
48 Kushner, "The Holocaust and the Museum World in Britain."
49 Kushner, "Meaning Nothing but Good."
50 Indeed, it now seems likely that Home Office control of HMD will be passed to a trust which will replace its administration of it.
51 Young, *Writing and Rewriting the Holocaust*, p. 133.

Nativization and Nationalization:
A Comparative Landscape Study of Holocaust Museums in Israel, the US and the UK

Tim Cole

There has been much recent interest in what has been dubbed the "nativization" of the Holocaust, a term which, for Isabel Wollaston, describes the reality that "memorials and museums, and discussion of issues relating to the Holocaust, take particular forms and have particular emphases depending upon their national context ..."[1] A good example of this approach can be seen in James Young's groundbreaking study of Holocaust memorial landscapes in Austria, Germany, Poland, Israel and America. There, Young suggested that the "national memory of what I might call the *Shoah* varies from land to land," and that, "in every nation's memorials and museums, a different Holocaust is remembered, often to conflicting political and religious ends."[2]

Through a comparative landscape study of three — to varying degrees — national Holocaust museums,[3] I want to examine not simply the nativization of the Holocaust, but also its nationalization, within museum space in Israel, the United States and the United Kingdom. I will not focus on the reception of the narratives offered in these museums — an area relatively under-researched by scholars writing on Holocaust representation — nor on the institutional and broader politics underlying the creation of the museums themselves.[4] Rather, I want to examine three Holocaust museums — Yad Vashem in Jerusalem (the present historical museum was opened in 1973, although currently a new museum is in the process of being created), the United States Holocaust Memorial Museum (USHMM) in Washington, DC (first opened in 1993) and the Holocaust Exhibition at the Imperial War Museum (IWM) in London (first opened in 2000) — in terms of two major themes.

First, I want to reflect upon the meanings conferred upon the Holocaust narratives offered in these museums by considering the siting of the museums themselves. These museums do not exist within a spatial vacuum, but in specific sites with their own layers of memory and their own meanings, which influence the memories and meanings given to the event — the Holocaust — being represented. The conferring of meaning in and through site, can be clearly seen in the way in which the same artifact — a World War II-era cattle car — has been variously exhibited at Yad Vashem, USHMM and IWM.

Second, I want to reflect upon the journeys that these museums take the visitor on. In any museum, but particularly in museums offering a historical narrative as Yad Vashem, USHMM and IWM all do, the visitor engages in an act of "organized walking" rather than aimless wandering.[5] A pathway is laid out for the visitor, and in the case of Yad Vashem, USHMM and IWM, an essentially chronological narrative is offered which has a clear sense of a beginning, middle and end. By examining these two elements of museum landscape, I want to suggest that these three museums offer rather different — nativized and nationalized — versions of the Holocaust to their respective audiences. Whether or not those audiences buy into those accounts, is of course another question entirely.

Siting the Holocaust

Yad Vashem

The siting of Yad Vashem is significant at a variety of scales — ranging from the national to the local. At the scale of the nation, the very locating of a Holocaust museum in Israel points towards the links between this historical event and the creation of the state. As James Young argues, Yad Vashem is, "a place where Holocaust history is remembered as culminating in the very time and space now occupied by the memorial complex itself."[6] The location of a Holocaust museum on Israeli soil suggests a dual relationship between the Holocaust and the State of Israel. On the one hand, the Israeli setting offers redemptive closure to the Holocaust. On the other hand, the events portrayed in the Holocaust museum offer a compelling argument for the continuing need for a Jewish state in Israel.

A clear example of the former can be seen in the recently erected Memorial to the Deportees. This memorial sculpture, with its cattle car perched precariously on severed rails, draws its meaning not simply from the authentic wartime cattle car (a gift of the Polish government) but also from its setting overlooking the hills of Jerusalem. This is made explicit in a leaflet explaining that, "Although symbolizing the journey towards annihilation and oblivion, facing as it does the hills of Jerusalem, the memorial also conveys the hope and the gift of life of the State of Israel and Jerusalem, eternal capital of the Jewish People."[7] In short, this cattle car means something very different here than the cattle car (also a gift of the Polish government) which is exhibited in the USHMM. The cattle car in Washington, DC, through which the museum visitor walks, is the means by which we transition in the historical exhibition from the ghettos to the concentration and death camps. It is quite literally the way by which we — and we are encouraged to merge our identities with those of the victims, or at least one victim — are taken to Auschwitz. Thus the cattle car is situated within the US museum as representative of deportation. A similar role is given to the cattle car (given by Belgian Railways) on display at the IWM. In both places, the journey the cattle car is taking is to Auschwitz.

In marked contrast, the cattle car at Yad Vashem is ultimately journeying to (and has journeyed to) Israel. There is recognition that it took Jews to the death camps — to the places of "annihilation and oblivion" — but it is seen as journeying beyond those places, to Israel. And that journey is not simply one which is metaphorical, but also one which is physically enacted with the siting of this European cattle car on a rail line jutting out from the Jerusalem hills. By placing it here, the cattle car speaks of emigration as well as deportation, of rebirth as well as destruction, of Jerusalem as well as Auschwitz. There is redemptive closure.

Alongside this reinvesting of the central symbols of the Holocaust with new meaning in this site, Yad Vashem reinvests Israel itself with new significance through its telling of the story of the Holocaust on Israeli soil. As Omer Bartov has suggested,

> the visitor [to Yad Vashem] should come out with the thought that had there been a Jewish state before the Holocaust, genocide would not have occurred; and since genocide did occur there must be a state. But also that just as the state can be traced back to the Holocaust, so too the Holocaust belongs to the state: the millions of victims were potential Israelis. . . . And more: that all Israelis are potential victims in the past, the present, and the future.[8]

Thus the siting of this historical museum and memorial space at the symbolic heart of the Israeli state, ensures that multiple connections are drawn between the event in the European past and the politics and society of the Israeli present.

But there is more to the site itself than simply a plot of Israeli soil. This is not simply any piece of land. Rather, Yad Vashem is sited on the Mount of Remembrance in West Jerusalem, in close proximity to the national cemetery where the father of Zionism, Theodore Herzl, is buried along with Israel's fallen soldiers. This geographical merging of the Holocaust and the War of Independence (in essence the events of the early 1940s in Europe and late 1940s in Israel) which takes place spatially on the Mount of Remembrance is echoed in the ceremonial calendar of Israel. Each year, Holocaust Memorial Day (with its televised opening ceremony at Yad Vashem) is followed a week later by Memorial Day (centered on the military cemetery on Mount Herzl) and Independence Day (centered in part on the tomb of Herzl on the summit of Mount Herzl).[9]

The spatial and temporal proximity of Israel's remembrance of the Holocaust and War of Independence was stressed by Israeli Prime Minister, Levi Eshkol, when he spoke at the ceremony held at Yad Vashem on the eve of Holocaust Memorial Day in 1964. He noted the link between the site where he stood and spoke — Yad Vashem — and the sites where Memorial Day and Independence Day would be observed a week or so later:

> The very struggle against the adversary and the victory which followed laid the foundations for the revival of our national independence. Seen in this light, the Jewish fight against the Nazis and the War of Independence were, in fact, a single protracted battle. The geographical proximity between Yad Vashem and Mount Herzl thus express far more than mere physical closeness.[10]

Eskhol's linking of the resistance during the Holocaust with the war for independence — and his making of these two historical events in very different places into essentially a single, continuous history of Jewish resistance — is one of the particularly striking aspects of Yad Vashem. It is made explicit in the inscription on the Pillar of Heroism — one of the many memorials located on the Yad Vashem site — which remembers "those who rebelled in the camps and ghettos, fought in the woods, the underground and with the Allied Forces," alongside those "who braved their way to Eretz Yisrael."[11] Thus the wartime history of Europe and the immediate postwar history of Israel are drawn together within a broader history of Jewish heroism, enacted in the symbolic space of the Mount of Remembrance.

United States Holocaust Memorial Museum

With its location just off the Mall in the nation's capital, Washington, DC, there can be little doubt that the USHMM is also a museum located in symbolic space. On one level, this was the conscious choice of Washington, DC, the national capital, over New York, which for the Jewish historian Lucy Dawidowicz was the obvious choice, being "the center of the Jewish population in the United States and the cultural crossroads of the modern world."[12] The decision to locate the museum in the nation's capital signaled that the Holocaust was perceived to be in some way a part of American history, and not simply American-Jewish history. This reflected the conclusions of the Presidential Commission, which reported back in 1978 on plans to erect some form of Holocaust memorial in the United States. They saw the Holocaust to be a part of American history because America had been an indifferent bystander during the 1930s and 1940s, American troops had liberated a number of concentration camps in 1945 and a large number of survivors had emigrated to the United States after the war. And thus the nation's capital was to be an appropriate location for retelling this part of America's history.

However, there is more to the location than simply the national capital. This museum is not just located within the boundaries of Washington, DC. It is located right at the very symbolic heart of Washington, DC. Now in one sense the Mall is museum space. The USHMM is after all located but a short walk from some of Washington's finest and most-visited museums. This museum joins the others within walkable tourist space. It becomes one more stop on a tourist itinerary. But there is more to the Mall than simply tourist space. It is also symbolic space which articulates the founding history of the nation, and thus says something about what America is, and isn't. And it is here that the setting adds a significant layer of meaning to the museum in Washington, DC. For if in a sense the decision to locate the museum in the nation's capital signaled giving the Holocaust an American history (America as bystander, liberator and refuge), the decision to locate the museum on the Mall, at the symbolic heart of the capital, signaled endowing the Holocaust with an exceptional and un-American meaning.

Situated as it is, close to the monuments to America's great presidents — Washington, Jefferson and Lincoln — the USHMM is juxtaposed with that history of the writing of the Constitution and the founding of the nation. It acts as a sort of counterpoint to the values enshrined in these presidents' memory. This was made explicit by chairman of the Museum Council, Miles Lerman, in a fund-raising letter in which he described what the experience of walking around the museum and then emerging again out into the familiar landscape of the Mall would be like. This familiar landscape would — he suggested — be seen afresh, because, "having witnessed the nightmare of evil, the great American monuments to democracy that surround each departing visitor will take on new meaning as will the ideals for which they stand."[13]

As these words suggest, the museum was envisaged to offer the very antithesis of American values and America's founding history. Thus, whilst in one sense this is a national museum telling of America's involvement — or lack of involvement — in the Holocaust, in another sense the entire museum tells an alien narrative, which sits almost intentionally uncomfortably within this symbolic space. Thus the museum tells a story which Americans can relate to because they were bystanders, liberators and ultimately a refuge, but it also tells the most un-American story imaginable. This paradox is one ultimately settled with the means of framing the permanent exhibition, which I will explore in more detail below

Imperial War Museum

Something of this duality of meanings can also be seen in the siting of the IWM Holocaust wing. At one level, the location is a consciously "national" one within the nation's capital, London. As the exhibition itself shows, the connections between Britain's national history and the Holocaust are made explicit. In a sense then, like in Washington, DC, the Holocaust is incorporated into the nation's history, within the nation's capital.

However what is most striking in the case of the IWM Holocaust wing is the situating of this exhibition within existing museum space, rather than — as was the case in Washington, DC — the creation of an entirely new and separate museum to house a Holocaust exhibit. The Holocaust exhibition in London therefore draws upon the history and meanings given to the IWM. First founded in 1917, and opened to the public in 1920, the IWM was created to record the events and sacrifice of the Great War. It finally transferred to its present — and third — site in 1936, and with the outbreak of World War II was charged to record British and Commonwealth involvement in all wars since 1914.[14] The museum therefore has a history tied inextricably into British war memory, and thus the siting of the Holocaust exhibit here situates the events of the Holocaust within the events of World War II and the memory of the Holocaust within British war memory.

For many, such situating made good historical sense. Rather than treating the Holocaust as an event detached from its wartime history, the placing of a Holocaust gallery in the IWM situated the Holocaust within its historical context as an event perpetrated during wartime. For Edgar Samuel, writing to the *Jewish Chronicle*, "Holocaust history needs to be taught in the context of European and Second World War history. If there is to be a Holocaust museum in Britain, the Imperial War Museum is the right place for it."[15] This perception that the "right place" for a Holocaust exhibit was within a museum devoted to wartime history was joined by the parallel perception that a museum devoted to wartime history needed to have a Holocaust exhibit. As Ben Helfgott expressed it: "The Imperial War Museum is about war, and they now realize that the Holocaust took place in war, and that it wouldn't be the Imperial War Museum if they did not highlight what were the effects of war."[16]

By placing the exhibition here, in the military museum space of the IWM, the Holocaust is placed within the context of World War II. But it is also clear that the Holocaust is being cited (sited) as the very thing that the Allies were fighting against. For Field Marshall Lord Bramall, chairman of the Museum's Board of Trustees, speaking when he launched the project to build a permanent Holocaust exhibition, it was the discovery of the camps by the Allies that had convinced them that they were fighting a just war "and that Hitler and his most evil regime had to be beaten once and for all."[17] And in the words of

Robert Crawford, director-general of the museum, it was appropriate that in a museum devoted to showing "the efforts and sacrifice of many people, including those Allied servicemen and women who gave their lives to defeat Nazism," the "Holocaust Exhibition now depicts also the nature of the evil which they helped to defeat."[18]

Thus in a sense, the Holocaust acts as evidence of the justness of the Allied cause in World War II, exhibited throughout the museum. The Holocaust stands as the Hitlerite and Nazi crime, and thus the very antithesis of the Britishness central to this museum devoted to Britain's military record in the twentieth century, and specifically its "finest hour." The Holocaust is established as the crime that Britain fought against, and ultimately defeated as witnessed by the liberation of the camps. Now of course, as in Washington, DC, that sense of the Holocaust as the crime of the Other is tempered with critical self-reflection upon Allied inaction. As a number of historians have noted, the Allies showed a seeming disregard for Jewish fate during World War II.[19] Both the IWM and the USHMM permanent exhibitions relay this critical historiography.[20] However they do this within the broader context of exhibitions framed — in part through location — as representing the crime of the Other, and thus the very antithesis of Britishness and Americanness. Of course, such framing is not limited to location alone, but also through the content of the exhibitions themselves, and the narratives of the Holocaust that they construct for the visitor.

Journeying through the Holocaust

Yad Vashem

At Yad Vashem, the visitor's approach to the historical museum is framed through a series of encounters with Holocaust heroism. This begins with the non-Jewish heroism of the "righteous Gentiles" who are remembered and celebrated in the avenue of carob trees the visitor walks down (passing a boat used by Danish fisherman to take Jews to neutral Sweden) before entering the Warsaw Ghetto Square where Jewish heroism is remembered and celebrated in a reproduction of Nathan Rapoport's Warsaw Ghetto monument.[21] Such framing of the Holocaust in terms of heroism is entirely intentional, fitting with the early emphasis in Yad Vashem — and Israeli society more widely — upon the Holocaust as a period of heroism as well as martyrdom. From its inception in 1953, Yad Vashem was created as a site of remembering and celebrating Holocaust heroism. Of the nine objectives of this newly created "Memorial Authority for the Holocaust and Heroism," only three were concerned with remembering Jewish destruction, while five focused on remembering Jewish "heroism," "fortitude" and "struggle," and one on remembering the actions of "high-minded Gentiles." As I have written elsewhere, at Yad Vashem, "heroism outnumbered destruction two to one."[22]

Once at the doors of the historical museum, a second major framework overlays that initial framework of heroism. Through Naftali Bezem's Memorial Wall which stands at the entrance to the historical exhibition, the concept of rebirth is added to that of heroic resistance. As I have already suggested, this notion of rebirth is suggested by the very siting of this museum in Israel. The redemptive closure offered by Israel is made explicit in Bezem's four sculpted panels entitled "From *Shoah* to Rebirth" (*Me-shoah le-tekumah*). In the first of these, destruction is depicted through, amongst other symbols, the smokestack of the crematoria. In the second, resistance and revolt are depicted, drawing upon the linkage of martyrdom and heroism so central to Israeli tellings of the Holocaust. In the third and fourth panels, immigration to Israel and the rebirth of the nation are depicted, thus creating a sense of redemptive closure to the story that follows, prior to that story being told.

Whilst Jewish resistance is stressed in this opening encounter with the museum, there is clearly the suggestion, implicit in the siting of the museum and explicit in the third and fourth panels of Bezem's work, that resistance in the diaspora was not a sufficient guarantee of safety. This juxtaposition of recognizing and celebrating resistance, and yet also acknowledging its limitations by dint of the fragile nature of the diaspora, is made clear in the opening plaque in the historical museum which signals the uniqueness of the Jewish experience of the Holocaust. In framing the historical exhibit through both notions of heroism and rebirth, this entry text reminds us that Jewish resistance was only a partial victory, necessitating the ultimate victory of the State of Israel:

> This merciless denial of an entire people's right to live is what singles out the fate of the Jews from all other victims of Nazism. The response of the masses of Jews under Nazi domination ranged from the individual's struggle to survive to community-wide attempts to protect Jewish lives, to armed resistance. Nonetheless, an underlying element of the Jewish tragedy was their fundamental powerlessness, as an isolated people bereft of a sovereign state, in the face of the Nazi onslaught.

The historical museum adopts a roughly chronological approach exhibiting "Anti-Jewish Policy in Germany 1933–1939" and life in "The Ghettos 1939–41," before shifting to examine the implementation of "Mass Murder 1941–1945." However, the climax of the exhibition does not come here, in the section on "Mass Murder," as for example I think it does in Washington, DC and London. Rather, the visitor walks up a sloping tunnel — "symbolizing the sewers which served as hiding places and escape routes for Jewish fighters in the Warsaw Ghetto"[23] — from the depths of destruction into a brighter lit exhibition space dealing with "Jewish Resistance 1941–1945." This emphasis upon Jewish resistance and heroism, so central to the framing and content of the present historical museum, is set to continue in the newly created historical museum. As the museum plan puts it, "the new museum will emphasize Jews as subjects rather than as objects in the hands of the Nazis as has been presented until recently."[24]

If the section on "Jewish Resistance 1941–1945" can be seen as the climax of the exhibition, the ending comes with the final section on "Liberation and Aftermath 1945." The exhibition does not suggest that safety came with liberation by Allied troops — as is the case in Washington, DC — but rather highlights, as the text states, "the escape routes to *Eretz* Israel" attractive to "the Jewish survivors of the Holocaust [who] refused in most cases to return to their former homes in lands that had become for them only graveyards." It is Israeli Independence and the symbolic significance of trying Eichmann in Jerusalem that offer closure to the events of the Holocaust.

But, as Young suggests, ultimately the ending of the exhibition comes only once the visitor leaves the exhibition space and reenters Jerusalem. He reflects:

> In fact, as we exit the last room of the exhibition, the hall of names, we pass alongside the Baal Shem Tov's words, gilded in gold lettering, a distillation of this memorial's *raison d'être* in Israel: "Forgetting lengthens the period of exile! In remembrance lies the secret of deliverance." With these words in mind, we walk outside into the blindingly bright light of Jerusalem, the present moment. The memorial message is reinforced further still: "That has all come to this," the museum seems to be saying. "That was the *galut*, where Jews had no refuge, no defense only death and destruction; this is Israel, its people alive."[25]

United States Holocaust Memorial Museum

That sense of juxtaposition which Young points to in the case of Yad Vashem — between the Jewish experience then in the diaspora and the Jewish experience now in Israel — is, as I've suggested, mirrored — although in an entirely different way — in Washington, DC. Here the juxtaposition is between a European past (Nazism) and an American past (of the founding fathers) and present (democracy). The Holocaust is constructed as the most un-American of crimes and the very antithesis of American values, and that understanding is framed by the visitors' entry to the museum, at least from one of the museum's entrances.

Entering the striking building designed by James Freed to house the exhibition, from the Raoul Wallenberg Place side (closest to the Jefferson and Lincoln Memorials), the visitor reads the well-known words from the Declaration of Independence pledging all citizens the right to "life, liberty, and the pursuit of happiness." Alongside these words, are those of George Washington to the Hebrew congregation in Newport, assuring them that "the government of the United States... gives to bigotry no sanction, to persecution no assistance." These words frame what we are about to encounter, which is set up as nothing less than the very antithesis of the values enshrined in these documents penned by the founding fathers celebrated a short walk away. What we will see is a history of "bigotry" and "persecution" and the story of a regime which took away "life, liberty, and the pursuit of happiness" from millions of European Jews. In short, the history of a time and place when American values were turned on their head.

But visitors entering from the 14th Street side (closest to the other museums on the Mall) do not encounter these words from the founding fathers. Instead, they are greeted by the flags of the US army units involved in the liberation of the camps. Their framing of the Holocaust is thus as a part of American history, although with America's role shaped as that of liberator, not of bystander. In essence they encounter the other story — the Holocaust as part of American history, rather than the Holocaust as the antithesis of American history. Now what is striking is that these two different stories and these two different framing devices come together in the elevator which all visitors take up to the museum's fourth floor and the start of the Permanent Exhibition.

In both this elevator and the initial images of the Permanent Exhibition, the Holocaust is framed *both* in terms of an American history of liberation *and* as the most un-American of crimes. As the elevator doors close in the museum lobby, we are taken back to 1945 through images of US troops liberating the camps and the testimony of one US serviceman who tells us:

> The patrol leader called in by radio and said that we have come across something that we are not sure what it is. It's a big prison of some kind, and there are people running all over. Sick, dying, starved people. And you take to an American, uh, such a sight as that, you... you can't imagine it. You, you just... things like that don't happen.[26]

He is clearly lost for words, on discovering something quite simply unimaginable for an American mind. Here is evidence of the most un-American of crimes. Here is something that doesn't happen in America, and yet is witnessed by an American.

And as the elevator doors open, we confront a photograph of a pile of half-burnt corpses at Ohrdruf Concentration Camp. We form the other half of a circle, joining the servicemen caught by the camera on the other half of the pyre, staring with disbelief. Not only do we join them as liberators — co-Americans who encounter the camps. We also join them as witnesses of an alien scene, of the most un-American of crimes. That sense of sheer unbelief when confronted with this different world is echoed in Dwight Eisenhower's words placed close to this opening photograph. But there is more to Eisenhower's words than simply unbelief; there is also a prophetic utterance of the realities of late-twentieth-century American Holocaust denial:

> The things I saw beggar description.... The visual evidence and the verbal testimony of starvation, cruelty and bestiality were... overpowering.... I made the visit deliberately in order to be in a position to give firsthand evidence of these things if ever, in the future, there develops a tendency to charge these allegations merely to "propaganda."

These words provide us with another framework with which to view the Holocaust. We are not only to share the perspective of the American liberators viewing this un-American crime, but we are also going to be witnesses encountering "firsthand evidence." And the museum offers a wealth of authentic artifacts to convince us of the historicity of this event that the so-called "revisionists" deny.

Another major element of the framing of this exhibition is the issuing to each visitor of gendered identity cards as they enter the elevator that takes them up to the start of the exhibition on the fourth floor. Through these cards, we are being asked not only to see through the eyes of the liberator, but also to identify in some way with the victim. Of the 558 individual victims featured on the cards, the majority are Jews — 364 from Eastern Europe and 115 from Western Europe. But in this national museum, other victims of Nazism are included. We are encouraged also to identify with other victim groups: Polish prisoners (47 cards), Jehovah's Witnesses (20 cards), Homosexuals (9 cards), Gypsies (3 cards) and those killed during the T4 Euthanasia program (2 cards).[27]

This is a museum which, unlike Yad Vashem, focuses much more on victimhood than resistance. We are taken chronologically through "The Nazi Assault — 1933 to 1939" on to the "Final Solution — 1940 to 1945" And it is here that the climax of the exhibition comes. This is not the rise out of the Warsaw ghetto sewers into the light of resistance and heroism, as in Jerusalem, but rather the experience of spiraling down — quite literally given the museum's layout — through ghettoization and deportation into the very heart of destruction. We are taken on a journey through a cattle car and under the gates of

Auschwitz, before coming face to face with the horror of medical experimentation and the industrialized mass killing of the gas chambers and crematoria at Auschwitz-Birkenau. The climax of this exhibition is destruction, rather than resistance. And this makes sense, given that this exhibition narrates the story of an Other. It does not aim to bridge resistance in the Jewish past and present as Yad Vashem does, but rather reveals an antithetical history of destruction and victimhood on the one hand, and American liberation and refuge on the other.

As already suggested, the story of America as liberator and refuge is tempered with self-critical reflection on American inaction and indifference. Thus the failed Evian Conference of 1938, the turning back of the SS *St. Louis* from US shores and the vexed question of the Allied failure to bomb Auschwitz are all dealt with during the historical narrative dominated by Nazi German persecution of the Jews.[28] As I have argued elsewhere, "these stand as an explicit judgement on past inaction, and an implicit call to America (as self-styled 'policeman of the world') not to stand idly by in the future."[29]

But ultimately we are left with an ending that is hopeful at least in part. The exhibition closes with the showing of a film lasting one hour and 17 minutes and entitled *Testimony*, in which 20 survivors "recount their experiences of loss, suffering, and anguish, as well as rescue, resistance, compassion and hope."[30] Shown in an amphitheater whose walls are clad with Jerusalem stone, thus hinting at Zionist redemption, this ending is intended to be upbeat. These are not only survivors, filmed in their ultimate refuge in the contemporary United States, but they are also survivors whose stories were chosen to reflect the themes of "resistance, rescue, and defiance."[31] They are Americans whose tales of horror are tempered both by our knowledge that they lived to tell the tale and by their words of faith and hope. Their placing at the ending of this exhibition is striking. The survivors are given the last word, reflecting I think the significant changes wrought by the Eichmann trial. This offered up survivor testimony as the voice through which the Holocaust would be told. It was a trial that not only did much to shape the narrative of the Holocaust, but also to shape the dominant means of relaying that narrative.

Imperial War Museum

In London, the survivor's voice is given an even more prominent role. Not only do the survivors have the last word, offering their post-Holocaust reflections on the impact of this event upon their personal lives. They also have the first word, telling us of life before the Nazis. And we hear their voices throughout the IWM exhibition, describing their own experiences of the historical events being relayed to us.[32] As the museum's current director, Suzanne Bardgett, has noted, "their voices are almost constantly within earshot throughout the display as they remember being deported to ghettos and camps hundreds of miles from home." The survivors' voices, which accompany us throughout the exhibition, play the same role of "humanizing the narrative" intended by the identity cards we carry with us in Washington, DC.[33] We are thus encouraged to identify with the victim/survivor, although we are also called to reflect upon the roles of bystander, liberator and perpetrator.

But the beginning of the exhibition at the IWM is not just framed through the voice of the survivors recounting their experiences of "Life before the Nazis." Ultimately the exhibition is framed as we enter the main museum and walk through the entrance hall with its display of military hardware. As we come to the permanent exhibition itself, we are shown imagery of World War II and see Adolf Hitler's words informing us that "War is the origin of all things." And then we encounter the Holocaust, which the exhibition text introduces for us as an event within the broader history of war:

> Under the cover of the Second World War, for the sake of their "New Order", the Nazis sought to destroy all the Jews of Europe; for the first time in history, industrial methods were used for the mass extermination of a whole people, 6 million were murdered, including 1,500,000 children. This event is called the Holocaust.

Thus we do not encounter the Holocaust specifically as the liberator as is the case in Washington, DC. We are on the other side, but we are on the side of the combatant, fighting a just war against the enemy willing to perpetrate such war crimes. The Holocaust is integrated — *ex post facto* — into Britain's "finest hour."

In an essentially historical narrative, the nature of these war crimes unfolds, interspersed with the ambivalent contemporary reactions as the news of them "reaches Britain." Much more is made of native collaboration than in Washington, DC, and in perhaps the most striking room in the entire exhibition a lone typewriter represents the bureaucratic nature of this crime which involved such a massive array of state organizations and personnel in Nazi Germany, whose names are displayed "Hilberg-style" on the walls.[34] As with Washington, and unlike Jerusalem, it is destruction which is the climax of this exhibition — the bureaucratized and industrialized mass killings at Auschwitz-Birkenau, displayed in a large-scale model of the gas chambers and crematoria which mirrors in some ways the model on display in Washington, DC.

Auschwitz is again present at the close of the exhibition, although this time it is contemporary Auschwitz. On one screen, we see images of the contemporary remains at Auschwitz-Birkenau, while on another screen "our 'survivor-witnesses' deliver their thoughts on how the experience of surviving the Holocaust has affected them and what lessons it has for the world at large."[35] Their multiple voices (there are 18 of them) offer multiple responses to the Holocaust: "People get carried away by isms," "I feel very privileged to live in a free country," etc. However this multiplicity of lessons is overlaid with what is presented as the authoritative curatorial lesson which the Holocaust is deemed to offer — Edmund Burke's dictum that "for evil to triumph it is only necessary for good men to do nothing." Given the location of this exhibition within the context of a museum dedicated to British warfare, these words come as a reassurance that we were the "good men" who did something in 1939–45, as well as a warning to continue being "good men." Presumably "good men" may find themselves fighting just wars, which is the theme central to the whole of the IWM.

Nativization and Nationalization

In these essentially national museums, it would seem that something more than simply the nativization of the Holocaust has taken place. These are not only national museums, but in some senses at least, nationalist museums. They are museums where the Holocaust is exhibited as the radical Other and the very antithesis of the contemporary nation state.[36] There is a degree of self-critical reflection, in particular on the question of being an inactive bystander at the USHMM and IWM. But that sense of self-critical reflection in these two museums is joined with a less self-critical nationalist discourse, which might even be seen to be celebratory. However, there is surely something deeply ironic about the Holocaust of all historical events being utilized as a tool of nationalism. Even more: there is also something disturbing about such instrumentalization of this particular past.

NOTES

1 Isabel Wollaston, "A War against Memory? Nativizing the Holocaust," in John K. Roth and Elisabeth Maxwell-Meynard (eds.), *Remembering for the Future: The Holocaust in an Age of Genocides* (Houndmills, UK, 2001), Vol. 3, p. 507. For examples of studies of "nativization," see, in the case of the United States, Peter Novick, *The Holocaust in American Life* (Boston, 1999); and Hilene Flanzbaum (ed.), *The Americanization of the Holocaust* (Baltimore, 1999).

2 James E. Young, *The Texture of Memory: Holocaust Memorials and Meaning* (New Haven, 1993), pp. viii–ix. And as Young makes clear, these differences can be — and are — within nations as well as between nations (p. xi).

3 In the case of Yad Vashem and USHMM, these national museums are explicitly state-sponsored. The IWM Holocaust Exhibition is supported by the UK national lottery "Heritage Lottery Fund."

4 On the politics behind Yad Vashem, see Tom Segev, *The Seventh Million: The Israelis and the Holocaust*, trans. Haim Watzman (New York, 1994), pp. 421–45; on the US museum, see Edward T. Linenthal, *Preserving Memory: The Struggle to Create America's Holocaust Museum* (New York, 1995); on IWM, see Steven Cooke, "'Your Story Too?' The New Holocaust Exhibition at the Imperial War Museum," in Roth and Maxwell (eds.), *Remembering for the Future*, Vol. 3, pp. 590–606.

5 Tony Bennett, *The Birth of the Museum: History, Theory, Politics* (London, 1995), p. 6.

6 Young, *The Texture of Memory*, p. 244.

7 Yad Vashem, *The Memorial to the Deportations* (undated pamphlet).

8 Omer Bartov, *Murder in Our Midst: The Holocaust, Industrial Killing, and Representation* (New York, 1996), p. 178.

9 See Don Handelman, *Models and Mirrors: Towards an Anthropology of Public Events* (Cambridge, 1990) pp. 191–233, and Young, *Texture of Memory*, pp. 263–81.

10 Cited in Handelman, *Models and Mirrors*, p. 201.

11 Reuven Dafni (ed.), *Yad Vashem: The Holocaust Martyrs' and Heroes' Remembrance Authority, Jerusalem*, 5th edn. (Jerusalem, 1990), p. 26.

12 Cited in Linenthal, *Preserving Memory*, p. 57.

13 Cited in Alvin H. Rosenfeld, "The Americanization of the Holocaust," in idem (ed.), *Thinking about the Holocaust: After Half a Century* (Bloomington, 1997), p. 127.

14 Gaynor Kavanagh, "Museum as Memorial: The Origins of the Imperial War Museum," *Journal of Contemporary History*, Vol. 23, No. 1 (1988), pp. 77–97; and Sue Malvern, "War, Memory and Museums: Art and Artefact in the Imperial War Museum," *History Workshop Journal*, Vol. 49 (2002), pp. 177–203.

15 Cited in Cooke, "Your Story Too?" p. 598.

16 Cited in ibid. Although, as Cooke points out, there was also criticism of siting a Holocaust exhibition in a museum whose very name contained a reference to imperialism.

17 Cited in Imperial War Museum, *Report* (Winter 1996/97), p. 1.

18 Robert Crawford, "Foreword," in Imperial War Museum, *The Holocaust: The Holocaust Exhibition at the Imperial War Museum* (London, 2000).

19 See, for example, Tony Kushner, "The Meaning of Auschwitz: Anglo-American Responses to the Hungarian Jewish Tragedy," in David Cesarani (ed.), *Genocide and Rescue: The Holocaust in Hungary 1944* (Oxford, 1997), pp. 159–78; Bernard Wasserstein, *Britain and the Jews of Europe, 1939–1945* (Oxford, 1979); Louise London, *Whitehall and the Jews: British Immigration Policy, Jewish Refugees, and the Holocaust, 1933–1948* (Cambridge, 2000). For a counter-view, see William D. Rubinstein, *The Myth of Rescue: Why the Democracies Could Not Have Saved More Jews from the Nazis* (London, 1997).

20 Suzanne Bardgett, "The British Perspective on the Holocaust," in Imperial War Museum, *The Holocaust: A Major Permanent Exhibition for the New Millennium* (London, undated manuscript), pp. 6–7; cf. Tony Kushner, "The Holocaust and the Museum World in Britain: A Study of Ethnography," *Immigrants and Minorities*, Vol. 21, Nos. 1–2 (2002), p. 27.

21 In the newly planned Yad Vashem, visitors will exit a newly created Visitors' Center which will "create the appropriate atmosphere at the start of the visit," "either directly to the museum, or to the Avenue of the Righteous Among the Nations which will lead to the memorial square at the entrance of the Hall of Remembrance." See Yad Vashem, *Yad Vashem 2001 — Masterplan: The New Museum Complex and the Visitors' Center* (undated booklet), p. 19.

22 Tim Cole, *Selling the Holocaust: From Auschwitz to Schindler: How History is Bought, Packaged and Sold* (New York, 1999), p. 122.

23 Dafni, *Yad Vashem*, p. 8.

24 Yad Vashem, *Yad Vashem 2001*, p. 21.

25 Young, *Texture of Memory*, p. 253.

26 Cited in Linenthal, *Preserving Memory*, p. 167.

27 For further discussion on the use of identity cards, see Cole, *Selling the Holocaust*, pp. 161–4; and Andrea Liss, *Trespassing through Shadows: Memory, Photography and the Holocaust* (Minneapolis, 1998), pp. 13–26.

28 See Linenthal, *Preserving Memory*, pp. 217–24 for a discussion of the question of Allied bombings of Auschwitz. This section of the permanent exhibition has been revised.

29 Cole, *Selling the Holocaust*, p. 151.

30 Jeshajahu Weinberg and Rina Elieli, *The Holocaust Museum in Washington* (New York, 1995), p. 148.

31 See Linenthal's discussion in *Preserving Memory*, pp. 253–4.

32 Cf. USHMM, where the only other use of survivors' voices is in the "Voices from Auschwitz" section, set back from the main exhibition route.

33 Suzanne Bardgett, "The Holocaust Exhibition at the Imperial War Museum," http://www.iwm.org.uk/lambeth/pdf files/hol_bardgett.pdf, p. 3.

34 The display is reminiscent of the charts in Raul Hilberg, *The Destruction of the European Jews* (Chicago, 1961)

35 Bardgett, "The Holocaust Exhibition."

36 Although, as I have noted, at Yad Vashem, heroism does provide a link between Jewish resistance during the Holocaust and the more recent history of the Israeli state.

The Depiction of the Holocaust at the Imperial War Museum since 1961

Suzanne Bardgett

In reviewing this aspect of the Imperial War Museum's history, I should make it clear at the start that for very nearly three of the four decades under consideration this means addressing an absence, rather than a presence, of material on public display relating to the Nazi persecution of the Jews. This omission partly reflects the wider lack of public awareness with which we are all now familiar. It also reflects the narrower self-image that the Museum had in earlier decades, and shows the difficulties — as they were perceived at the time — of addressing the subject of the Nazi concentration camps in exhibition form.

At the time this account begins, 1961, the Museum's public displays presented a depressing picture. In his memoir, Dr. Noble Frankland, IWM director from 1960 to 1982, recalled a visit to the Museum he had made in 1955:

> the galleries had a dingy and neglected air. They were crowded with masses of mostly quite small items arranged in congested groups unrelated to each other and disconnected from any discernible historical themes.... Amongst the debris, it is true, there were numerous stunning exhibits such as the Sopwith Camel in which Lieutenant S D Culley had shot down a German Zeppelin over the North Sea, a German V1 flying bomb, an Italian human torpedo and the forward section of a Lancaster bomber. But the historical impact of these and many other remarkable objects was lost in the crush of matter which gave the impression of having been dumped in a warehouse rather than installed in a museum.[1]

Under Frankland's direction, the Museum modernized considerably, developing the curatorial, educational and display functions which would serve it for the next four decades. The Museum's staff increased from just 70 on his arrival to 343 when he retired in 1982 — a measure of its enormous expansion during his time.

Like his successors, Frankland recognized the problem of integrating the enormous legacy of large weapons of war — aircraft, tanks, guns and rockets

— into historical displays that were inevitably smaller in scale. Drawing up a blueprint for a modernized museum, he accepted that what he called "the three heavy galleries" of weaponry should remain, but he envisioned a museum which looked at war through generic themes: casualties, medicine, technology, the political, social and economic effects, and the power of devastation and recovery.[2] This plan seems to have been modified in practice, but the principle was now in place of offering the public displays dealing with historical subjects, rather than a series of curios to look at.

By the mid-1970s, there was a permanent narrative display on Trench Warfare and an educationally very useful exhibition on the origins of World War I. So-called "special exhibitions" started to be mounted, embracing cultural and social topics like *Poets of the First World War* and *The Occupation of the Channel Islands*. And television tie-ins became a regular feature, with a newly TV-enthused public, drawn — often in enormous numbers — to exhibitions such as *The Real Dad's Army* and *Danger UXB*.

It is not especially surprising that there was no examination of the Nazi persecution policies at this time, for the Museum at this stage had a much narrower focus than today. What mention there was of the Nazis tended to focus on the military strength of their war machines or the inventiveness of their scientists. Much of what was on display had been captured (like the Fockewulff and Heinkel aircraft, and the Wurzburg radar), and so soon after the end of World War II it is not surprising that the main thrust of the exhibitions was on how the war had been won, rather than on the beliefs of the defeated regime.

The only major special exhibition to deal with a Nazi theme during this period was the 1974 *Colditz* exhibition, but this centered on the experiences of the British POWs at Colditz castle and had little to say about Nazi ideology, nor about other groups imprisoned at this time.

I can think of only three items illustrative of Nazi persecution on permanent display in the late 1970s. One — and this was an oblique connection — was Dame Laura Knight's officially commissioned large oil painting of the court scene at Nuremberg, a reminder of who-was-who among the Nazi elite, and of their eventual bringing to justice. Hitler's Last Will and Testament, displayed in the Documents Room, contained a reference to his hatred of the Jews. The V2 rocket — in those days displayed lying on its side — *could* have been used to remind visitors of the 20,000 slave laborers who had died working on its production in the Dora concentration camp, but the facts had yet to be properly assimilated, and the caption concentrated mainly on the weapon's technical specifications and its impact on London and the South East of England in the closing stages of the war.

But if the public displays were as yet thin on this subject, in the Museum's reference departments, records were starting to be amassed which told the German story. A significant development initiated shortly after Frankland's arrival was the setting up of the Foreign Documents Centre in 1963. The Treasury could not be persuaded to fund such an enterprise, so it was paid for instead with a three-year grant from the Leverhulme Trust. Large quantities of Captured Enemy Documents were transferred into this Centre from the Foreign Office, including the official papers of the Nuremberg Trials.

The keeper of the Foreign Documents Centre, Leo Kahn (who had previously worked at the Wiener Library), oversaw the cataloguing and conservation of such material. He also started to cement links with archivists overseas, making visits in 1965 to several repositories in France (including the Centre de Documentation Juive Contemporaine in Paris), Germany and the Netherlands, and in 1966 visited the US National Archives in Washington.[3] The Museum's Film Department also organized several international film conferences at this time — often embracing Third Reich themes.

*

Then in 1973 the Museum partnered a major TV history of World War II — Thames TV's acclaimed series *The World at War*, directed by Jeremy Isaacs. A full episode — there were 26 in all — was devoted to the plan to annihilate the Jews. Moreover others — "A New Germany," "Occupation" and "Inside the Reich" — dealt with the subject as part of related themes. Jeremy Isaacs, who felt too close to the subject to make the program himself, gave it to his colleague Michael Darlow to direct. Darlow has described how he read up avidly on the subject, Gerald Reitlinger and Raul Hilberg becoming his "twin Bibles."[4] This immersion in the key texts of the time paid off. For a popular, as distinct from academic, treatment, the program — following as it did the steps of racial discrimination, forced emigration, through to the story of organized persecution — was distinctly ahead of its time.

*

In November 1977 the idea was put forward for a major exhibition at the Museum on the history of the Third Reich to occupy the former Naval Gallery — the central of the three oblong galleries occupying the old Bethlem courtyard. Three main sections were proposed: the first, dealing with the years 1919–33, explaining the Nazis' rise to power; the second, dealing with the years 1933–42, on the policies, personalities and organization of the Nazi Party; and the third (1942–45) on the consequences of the Nazis' policies. This last section would cover the party's racial policies and illustrate the concentration camps and their numerous uses and purposes.

The exhibition was to have drawn heavily on two extensive private collections of German militaria: the Sweeting collection — some 2,500 items purchased from an American collector — and the Brownlow collection, also originating in America and offered to the Museum on loan for five years. Donald Brownlow had been an Intelligence Officer in the US Army and, during the immediate aftermath of the war, had collected large quantities of relics of the Nazi period. The 84-page catalogue lists numerous artifacts belonging to key personalities, some very prosaic like cutlery and table linen, but others — the keys to the Berghof, a portrait of Geli Raubal, birthday greetings to Hitler from various diplomats in Berlin from 1933 to 1938, Göring's monocle and hunting trousers — more displayable, though obviously requiring the backup of photographs, film and text. There was a tapestry from the Nuremberg Congress Hall, some 40 Nazi flags, and scores of Nazi uniforms. Just two pages of the catalogue were devoted to concentration camp artifacts. They included antisemitic propaganda, a French Yellow Star, examples of currency from Terezin and Lodz, the key to a cell in Dachau, and various whips and clubs taken from the camps.[5]

It was easy to envisage the striking effect which such a rich cache of material would have. However, the director and the senior staff of the day were aware of the huge sensitivity of putting on such an exhibition, particularly in view of the appeal the Nazi memorabilia was suspected to have for National Front members and other extremists — at that time a worryingly prominent force in Britain.

Unusually for that time, staff's opinions were canvassed on the wisdom of pursuing "the German Exhibition," as it was known. The reaction was extremely guarded. Was such a thing justifiable in a museum that was essentially British? What three-dimensional objects would be available? There was concern that to concentrate on the phenomenon of the Nazis without giving due space to the strongly liberal strain in German culture was "surely to perpetuate many myths about Germany, its militarism, authoritarianism etc." "Certain manifestations of Nazism, notably its paraphernalia" were thought to exert an unhealthy fascination. One staff member, addressing specifically the question of the Nazis' attitude to the Jews, warned that the exhibition might

> appeal to a certain section of the public for very dubious reasons . . . the main problem is that Nazism was very successful in presenting a glamorous image and in humiliating its victims. To present that humiliation as a counterweight to Nazi glamour does not unfortunately always evoke the response of shock and horror, especially in the unsophisticated mind, but can simply reinforce the Nazi view of themselves as heroic and their enemies as degraded and deserving of their fate.[6]

Very unfortunately for the Museum, details of the exhibition were leaked to the press, and The Guardian ran a piece that cast the whole project in a very unfavorable light.[7] The Brownlow collection was known to contain a particularly gruesome and upsetting item — a book allegedly bound in human skin. It goes without saying that this would never have gone on display, but *The Guardian* put the worst possible interpretation on it, and the upshot — to cut a long and tortuous story short — was that the German Exhibition was postponed indefinitely.

The difficulties inherent in a display on the Third Reich might have been avoided if it had instead focused on the Nazis' persecution policies, an angle that would have given the clear message to the public that the regime was a pernicious one, rather than risk an exhibition whose message could be taken ambiguously. This option appears not to have been considered. Why? Such a notion was not unthinkable, especially after *The World at War* had provided such a fine model of how the story *could* be told.

Firstly, there is no doubt that the subject of the Holocaust was considered well to the margins of the Museum's terms of reference at this point. Indeed, it was still very much to the margins of the study of World War II in Britain generally. Although accounts by Reitlinger and Hilberg and, by the late 1970s, Karl Schleunes's *The Twisted Road to Auschwitz* and Lucy Dawidowicz's *The War against the Jews* were in the Museum's library, there was of course nothing like the volume of historical discourse on the theme which would appear over the next ten years.[8] The Museum's historians, moreover, would generally have been more attuned to the more "mainstream" works of British historians like A. J. P. Taylor and Alan Bullock — writers who, as Dawidowicz has pointed out, tended to concentrate on Hitler's diplomacy and give less attention to his antisemitism.[9] And even if the thought had occurred, it is probable that the paucity and grim nature of the concentration camp material in the Brownlow collection — probably the first the Museum's staff had ever seen — convinced curators that the subject was just a "non-starter" as an exhibition. The Museum occasionally got wind of some fairly dubious displays and tended to keep its distance from such enterprises. Moreover, collectors offering material were usually enthusiasts for Nazi memorabilia, and this gave the subject a rather grubby, unsavory reputation.

Loans from behind the Iron Curtain would have been thought impractical. Photographs and documents would probably have seemed too one-dimensional and abstruse to furnish an entire exhibition. And although the Museum's staff had interviewed a number of camp survivors, the notion of survivors' memories as a source of information had yet to become as concrete as it is today. Finally, the general climate in Britain was quite simply less favorable to such a display at this point. Tony Kushner — and Peter Novick writing on America — have in their different ways expounded on this phenomenon. The high level of interest in the Holocaust that had developed by the mid-1990s reflected the emergence of a more pluralistic society, more willing to accommodate the narratives of people who had been oppressed or whose suffering had brought them to this country as refugees.[10]

*

But if the Museum's displays had yet to embrace the subject of the Holocaust, behind the scenes two significant developments took place in the late 1970s, both of which helped lay the foundations for the Holocaust Exhibition which was eventually created from 1996 to 2000 and which will be discussed below.

In 1978 the Museum's Department of Sound Records embarked on an oral history project to record the experiences of refugees who had fled Nazi Germany in the 1930s. The project was conceived by Margaret Brooks, deputy keeper of the Department of Sound Records. Her intention was initially that the Museum should interview refugees about their internment by the British government as so-called "enemy aliens" during the invasion scare of 1940. But once the interviewing began, it became clear that the scope should be broadened to include their prewar lives. Some 155 hours of reminiscence were recorded, and a catalogue published in 1982.[11] The contacts made at this point — chiefly through the Association of Jewish Refugees — led to further interviews with camp survivors, work that continued steadily over the next two decades.

In the same year, Anita Ballin, at that time deputy head of the Museum's Education Section, developed an illustrated talk on "Life in Nazi Germany," which she and I gave to 15- to 16-year-olds on school visits as part of their history studies. The talk used film clips, sound recordings of witnesses, artifacts and documents to tell the story of Hitler's coming to power in Germany and the changes this brought for the German people. The talk included topics such as Nazi race theory, and used propaganda of the time such as *The Poisoned Mushroom*, and artifacts such as the Yellow Star, to show the kinds of measures taken against the Jews of Germany.

Schools attending the talk generally went on to screenings of one or other of the relevant *World at War* programs in the Museum's cinema. Thus while the Museum at this time offered little on Nazi persecution in its public galleries, many thousands of teenage schoolchildren had a solid day's learning on the history of Nazi Germany.

Interestingly, both Margaret Brooks's and Anita Ballin's fathers had fled to Britain from Austria and Germany in the 1930s. In fact one of the recordings that was played in the Nazi Germany talk was of Anita's aunt, remembering how her uncle had been sent to a concentration camp, and the terrible state in which he had returned.

In the mid-1980s two temporary exhibitions took place which broke new ground in the way they addressed the Nazi phenomenon. *Resistance* (1984), curated by Mark Seaman, was a large multimedia exhibition providing the first detailed account in the Museum of Nazi oppression in occupied Europe. Ration cards, travel permits, German proclamations and posters spoke of the curtailment of freedom in each of the occupied countries, and Gestapo truncheons and coshes of the brutal way in which rule was enforced. It was widely praised, but initially failed to deal specifically with Jewish resistance and in fact drew letters of protest from several Jewish organizations.[12] The Museum acknowledged that the subject had been under-represented, and a section on the Warsaw Ghetto Uprising was added to remedy this.

Then in the following year Mike Moody, the Art Department's poster expert, curated *Towards a New Europe,* a show of printed ephemera and magazines illustrating how the Nazi dream of a prosperous Europe, purged of all alien elements, was packaged for the people of occupied Europe. Strikingly designed posters showed how Frenchmen had been persuaded to travel to Germany to work and how Norwegians had been persuaded to join the SS. In table-top showcases, spreads from *Signal* showed the building of new waterways, motorways, bridges and housing developments for the German Labor Front. Actual persecution was not the main theme, of course, but in examining Nazi ideology, it was an important step.

Among the favorable reviews was one from the London *Evening Standard*'s critic Brian Sewell: "Forty years on," he wrote, "the horrors of war have faded and half the nation knows nothing of them. The War Museum's show could have been ten times its size. . . . Perhaps in ten years time (if we are still here) the authorities (whoever they may be) will put their heads together and give us the real exhibition — the real reminder and the real memorial."[13] Sewell had evidently forgotten this impassioned plea when he struck out so forcefully against the notion of a Holocaust Museum in 1999.[14]

In 1986 work began on the first stage of the Museum's redevelopment scheme, a long-awaited replacing of the 1930s infill of the old hospital courtyard with a new complex comprising the Atrium, new art galleries and an upgrading of the lower ground floor. It was this last space which was now allocated to the Museum's core First and Second World War galleries, opened in 1989. For the first time, the subject of the concentration camps was given its own section towards the end of the Second World War Exhibition. (It can still be seen today.) A life-sized photograph of the horrifying aftermath of the burning of the barn at Gardelegen sat adjacent to a showcase containing, among other things, the order for the punishment of a Russian prisoner at Gross Rosen; a Star of David, a tin of Zyklon B, part of a concentration camp uniform, and messages smuggled out of Auschwitz. The main-line caption made the point that six death camps had been established in Poland for the purpose of systematically killing the Jews of Europe.

In 1991 the Museum opened a special exhibition on the liberation of Belsen. The then director-general, Alan Borg, had become aware of the strength of the IWM's holdings in this area and decided that a special exhibition should be made, to be sited at the end of the new Second World War Exhibition. The display told the story of the camp's liberation, using photographs, film, sound recordings, paintings and artifacts — including the jumper worn by Auschwitz survivor Anita Lasker-Wallfisch, the Hanna Sachsel drawings, and several letters and diaries by relief personnel. In a central showcase, four bronze maquettes of a bound and gagged prisoner by the Frankfurt-born sculptor Fred Kormis offered a universal symbol of oppression. Drawing as it did solely on material held in the Museum at that time, the Belsen Exhibition told little of the camp's history before April 1945. Nor did it try to place the liberation in the broader context of Hitler's war against the Jews. But it was an important step and drew many comments from a public clearly moved by its content.

This was followed in 1993 by a small photographic exhibition on the Warsaw Ghetto. Two years later the Museum's art department collaborated with the South Bank Centre in a large touring exhibition, *After Auschwitz: Responses to the Holocaust in Contemporary Art.*[15]

*

The decision to mount a major Holocaust Exhibition was announced at a press conference in April 1996. In his speech Robert Crawford, who had recently succeeded Alan Borg as director-general, spoke of the centrality of the Holocaust in the history of the Second World War and the fact that there was now a "black hole" in the Museum's coverage of its story. "As the perspective of history lengthens, so that black hole will grow larger and larger. This project aims to ensure that that omission is finally put right."[16]

Support for the exhibition came in large measures from numerous quarters. The IWM's chairman at the time, Field Marshal Lord Bramall, wrote personal letters to the leaders of all three main political parties asking them to endorse the scheme, which they did. In December we learned that our application to the Heritage Lottery Fund to extend the Museum's building and create the exhibition had been successful. We wrote with details of what we were planning to likely supporters — many of whom became patrons of the project — and to those organizations which we knew were already working in the field. Last, but not least, we found help of a very tangible kind in our Advisory Group.

But not everyone felt that the time had come to have a Holocaust Exhibition at the Imperial War Museum:

> We want none of your proposed Holocaust Exhibition — absolutely scandalous. Your museum was built as a dedication to BRITISH war history, not these other fanciful things.

I believe the Board of Deputies [of British Jews] is behind all this —
need I say more. Yours disgustedly.

There were some dozen or so other letters in a similar vien. The press reported
the decision largely without comment, but I did take a call from a leader
writer on a national newspaper who wanted me to fax him a copy of the
Imperial War Museum Act. I can only assume that he was going to question
the validity of what we were planning, but that it got spiked.

On a practical level, the curating of the exhibition's content was a team
effort with a group of five curators taking responsibility for different sections
of the display. The first two years of the four-year project were spent mainly
identifying material for display — a process in which my colleague Terry
Charman played a major role — and the second two years working up the
detail of each of the 29 sections. The five curators thus had the satisfaction of
seeing the artifacts, photographs and documents they had researched in
1996–97 eventually make their way into showcases in 1999, and became
expert on the detail of their sections. James Taylor, my deputy, curated a
particularly large number, including the Auschwitz section with its huge and
detailed model. Steve Paulsson, a Canadian historian whom we employed in
the last two years of the project, ensured that the texts were historically
watertight and that there was balance across the whole display.

We also drew heavily on the guidance and thoughts of the Advisory
Group, in particular, in matters of content and interpretation, on the
filmmaker Martin Smith, who had also been a key player in *The World at War*
series and who later was director of the Permanent Exhibition at the United
States Holocaust Memorial Museum (USHMM) for two crucial years in its
development, and historian David Cesarani who helped us through numerous
historical questions. Among the numerous issues we addressed during that
time, I will address here those that relate specifically to the exhibition's siting
within this Museum.

Deeply conscious of the massive expectations that there would be of the
exhibition, we thought hard about the kind of ambience it should have and
what rules should govern its creation. Our feeling was that it should not
involve pretense or reconstructions, that its prime duty was to inform visitors
of what happened rather than tell them how to feel, and that a
straightforward, uncomplicated treatment would serve the subject best.
Colleagues at the USHMM had shared many of their thoughts on this theme,
and their maxim that "the story is so strong that it needs no embellishment"
was one which definitely struck home.

There was skepticism from several quarters over how such an exhibition
would fit into the rest of the Museum. Some people — especially academics
and some of our Jewish supporters — seemed anxious that it should have

a separate entrance: in other words that visitors to the Holocaust Exhibition should not have to cross the Atrium with its uncomfortable prelude of massed weapons. There was also anxiety over whether, as a national museum, we would be free to comment objectively on Britain's role.

Within the Museum too there were worries. Some staff wondered whether the whole thing would be too harrowing for the public, or whether they would come at all. The Museum had staged a series of highly successful exhibitions on topics that appealed to the British public's nostalgia for the era of World War II: *Wartime Kitchen and Garden, Wartime Fashion, From the Bomb to the Beatles* — dealing with the postwar years — and so on. These were exhibitions that could be relied upon to bring in large numbers of visitors. Would the same people be drawn by an exhibition on a genocide?

The exhibition had to sit happily with the rest of the Museum, yet needed its own special identity and to be sealed away from elements that might intrude on what clearly needed to be a special ambience. It was with this in mind that we conceived the large introductory space — a space for visitors to be settled and given some sense of the gravity of what lay ahead. The exhibition ends with a similar space, to allow the visitor time to reflect before leaving. Its time-frame and layout helped "bed it down" into the rest of the Museum: to start in 1918 and end in 1945 had an obvious logic; to make a physical descent from one floor to another on the outbreak of World War II further strengthened the notion of "the Holocaust Exhibition within the Imperial War Museum."

There was also the question of the British angle and how it should be shown. The perspective of the exhibition needed to be a European one, but at the same time we knew it would be important to show how news of the Nazi treatment of the Jews was received in Britain — an important strand of the story. The solution was the four *News Reaches Britain* windows: showcases that punctuate the story of what happened in occupied Europe, showing the visitor how news of atrocities reached the West and how this news was received.

Finally there was the problem of filling a 1,200-square-meter exhibition with artifacts, when our existing collections were so lopsided, with plenty on the liberation of Belsen, but little on the Jewish experience, and absolutely nothing to illustrate topics such as ghettos or mass shootings on the Eastern Front. We listed the kinds of artifact we hoped we might be able to find — a toy owned by a hidden child, a funeral cart, a sewing machine used in a ghetto. Astonishingly, with time, luck and perseverance we did manage to find many of these. An appeal through our newsletter brought material from survivors in this country, and field trips to museums overseas eventually produced a long list of promised loans. We got used to the strange scenario where the appearance in the Project Office of an especially "good" Yellow Star or a piece of striped uniform was a source of jubilation. The marble dissecting table we found in the psychiatric hospital at Kaufbeuren in Swabia is a deeply disturbing object, but one, we immediately realized, which would provide exactly the right physical and historical "crisis point" between the exhibition's two floors.

The exhibition was finally opened by HM the Queen in June 2000. To our intense relief, it appeared to satisfy most critics, both in the press and in academe, including several who had been openly skeptical at the start. The Holocaust Exhibition has brought the Museum new audiences, and has infused the whole Lambeth Road site with a more serious atmosphere. It has given us an important new dimension as a place where issues such as racism and persecution can be addressed. (Recently, for example, the local police launched a new initiative to combat race crime and used the exhibition as a focus.) And it has allowed the present generation of schoolchildren to learn — *for themselves* — the full story of Nazi persecution, a process enhanced by the carefully thought-through support for schools provided by Paul Salmons, Holocaust Education coordinator. The exhibition has also sent out a clear message that the Imperial War Museum is very much more than its name suggests, though I suspect it will be many years before *that* is changed.

NOTES

1 Noble Frankland, *History at War* (London, 1998), p. 160.
2 IWM past central files, Frankland series, 1960–63, 24a, Reorganisation of galleries.
3 IWM past central files, Frankland series, 1963–66, Foreign Documents Centre.
4 Typescript of talk given by Michael Darlow at the film conference held at the IWM in April 2001.
5 IWM Department of Exhibits and Firearms, Brownlow collection catalogue.
6 IWM past central files, Exhibition Planning, 15 (b)iii The German Exhibition.
7 Peter Millmore, *The Guardian*, 23 February 1978.
8 Karl A. Schleunes, *The Twisted Road to Auschwitz: Nazi Policy toward German Jews, 1933–1939* (Urbana, IL, 1970); Lucy S. Dawidowicz, *The War against the Jews, 1933–1945* (London, 1975).
9 Lucy S. Dawidowicz, *The Holocaust and the Historians* (Cambridge, MA, 1981), p. 32.
10 Tony Kushner, *The Holocaust and the Liberal Imagination: A Social and Cultural History* (Oxford, 1994); Peter Novick *The Holocaust and Collective Memory* (London, 2000).
11 *Britain and the Refugee Crisis, 1933–1947* (IWM, Department of Sound Records, 1982).
12 IWM past central files, Temporary Exhibitions, 15 (d)v The Resistance Exhibition.
13 Brian Sewell, *Evening Standard*, 10 July 1985.
14 Brian Sewell, "Manchester's Big Mistake," *Evening Standard*, 27 April 1999.
15 See Monica Bohn-Duchen (ed.), *After Auschwitz: Response to the Holocaust in Contemporary Art* (London, 1995).
16 Press conference, 23 April 1996.

Looking into the Mirrors of Evil

James E. Young

A notorious Nazi once said that when he heard the word "culture," he reached for his revolver. Now it seems, every time we hear the word "Nazi," we reach for our culture. Thus would we seem to protect ourselves from, even as we provide a window into, the terror of the Nazi Reich. It is almost as if the only guarantee against the return of this dreaded past lay in its constant aesthetic sublimation — in the art, literature, music, and even monuments by which the Nazi era is vicariously recalled by a generation of artists born after, but indelibly shaped by, the Holocaust.

Until recently, however, this has also been an art that concentrated unrelievedly on the victims of Nazi crimes — as a way to commemorate them, name them, extol them, bring them back from the dead. By contrast, almost no art has dared depict the killers themselves. It is as if the ancient injunction against writing the name of Amalek, or against hearing the sound of Haman's name, had been automatically extended to blotting out their images, as well. Of course, such blotting out was never about merely forgetting the tormentors of the Jews. For by ritually condemning our enemies to oblivion, we repeat an unending Jewish curse that actually helps us remember them.

As the New York Jewish Museum's 2002 exhibition, *Mirroring Evil: Nazi Imagery/Recent Art*, revealed, however, a new generation of artists sees things somewhat differently. In my reflections here on this exhibition and its extraordinarily fraught reception in the weeks before and after its opening, I should like to explore both the questions such art raises for us now, as well as this art's limitations for plumbing the generational breach between what happened and how it now gets passed down to us.

In December 2001, almost three months before the exhibition itself was scheduled to open on 17 March 2002, an intrepid *Wall Street Journal* reporter got wind of it at a New York dinner party. Even though there was no exhibition yet to review, a biting article soon appeared in the *Journal* that compared the Jewish Museum's *Mirroring Evil: Nazi Imagery/Recent Art* to the Brooklyn Museum's *Sensation* exhibition, which included incendiary images of Catholic icons, and which, as is generally well known, was actually a self-promoting Saatchi collection on tour. Only this new exhibition at the Jewish Museum, the article implied, would now be a Holocaust or Nazi sensation.[1] With a little push from *The Wall Street Journal*, it would also become a journalistic sensation, as reporters from across the city began showing a handful of the show's more provocative images to survivors and their children for reactions. The reactions were predictably mixed, with some survivors glad that if Nazi imagery in recent art was going to be shown anywhere, it would be in the context of a responsibly thought-through exhibition at the Jewish Museum. Other survivors and their families, having been shown these images without any accompanying context, were provoked into condemning an exhibition that was still months away from opening. Still others, Jews and non-Jews, survivors and their families, simply had little interest in seeing how Nazi imagery was used in any context, artistic or not. When asked what he was going to do about the exhibition, the new mayor Michael Bloomberg simply answered, reasonably enough, that it was not the mayor's job to say what should or should not be shown in the city's great museums. But suddenly a meticulously conceived and prepared exhibition on Nazi imagery in recent art was officially deemed "controversial" — months before anyone had even had a chance to see it.

The charge was led by someone I have long known and admired, Menachem Rosensaft, the founding chairman of the International Network of Children of Jewish Holocaust Survivors and a member of the United States Holocaust Memorial Council. He was soon joined by Brooklyn Assemblyman Dov Hikind, representative of the largest population of Jewish Holocaust survivors in America. Having viewed some of the most disturbing images from the exhibition, Rosensaft pronounced the show an irredeemable desecration and trivialization of the Holocaust. This exhibition, he wrote, "is in excremental taste. There can be no excuse," he continued, "aesthetic or otherwise, for the crude desecration of the Holocaust inherent in the display." He went on to say that he was not shocked that there were "artists, novelists, filmmakers and other pseudo-intellectuals who ridicule the Holocaust and demean the suffering of its victims." But the main outrage for him was that "a respected, mainstream Jewish cultural institution should be legitimizing the trivialization of the Holocaust."[2] At the end of this piece, which he wrote for the *Forward*, he promised that loud demonstrations and pickets would be the least of the Museum's problems were they to go ahead with the exhibition, and that the Museum's superb reputation would be irreparably compromised.

As one of the exhibition's academic consultants, I was invited by the *Forward* to write a companion piece for Rosensaft's essay defending the exhibition and providing a rationale for it. Though neither of us had read the other's article, they were twinned nonetheless, printed side by side, and entitled, "Demystifying Nazism, or Trivializing Its Victims? A Debate." For my part, I asked everyone with half an interest in this show, pro or con, to step back and consider an old curatorial axiom: "Hot topic, cool treatment." The aim of this sober-minded show, I said, was not to inflame the already viscerally charged passions evoked in images of the Nazis and their mass murder of Jews, but rather to explore very critically the ways a new generation of artists has begun to integrate images of the killers themselves into their work, much of it conceptual and installation art.[3] But in this piece I did not address a fundamental difference between audiences for this exhibition, which slice at least two ways. For many survivors, whose families were murdered and whose lives were permanently scarred by the Holocaust, it is impossible to see images of either the killers or the victims without their literal and visceral connection to their personal experience of events. But for the next generation, and for all who were not there, such experiences remain forever and only vicariously imagined and remembered. When these generations overlap, the breach between them is clear and perhaps unbridgeable. As the survivors' generation passes, however, these events will pass out of the realm of personal experience and into that of imagination only. If nothing else, this show exposes this generational fault line as never before, and for us in the next generation, part of what we recall must be just this divide, so that we never mistake our experiences for those of the survivors themselves.

"You can't shock us, Damien," say the words that artist Elke Krystufek has pasted over one of her collage-works, referring to artist Damien Hirst's provocative installations of vivisected animals. "That's because you haven't based an entire exhibition on pictures of the Nazis." Is this to say that the point here is merely to shock? Or that in a culture inured to the images of vivisected animals, only the images of Nazis can still shock? It seems to me that the artist has quite a different intention. Rather than repeating the degrading images of murdered and emaciated Jewish victims, thereby perpetuating the very images the Nazis themselves left behind, artists like Krystufek now turn their accusing gaze upon the killers themselves. For these artists, the only thing more shocking than the images of suffering victims is the depravity of the human beings who caused such suffering. To the traditional art that creates an empathetic nexus between viewers and concentration camp victims, these artists would add an art that brings us face to face with the killers themselves. Rather than allowing for the easy escape from responsibility implied by our traditional identification with the victims, these artists would challenge us now to confront the faces of evil — which, if the truth be told, look rather more like us than do the wretched human remains the Nazis left behind. In the process, we are led to ask: Which leads to deeper knowledge of these events, to deeper understanding of the human condition — images of suffering, or of the evil-doers who caused such suffering? Which is worse — the cultural commodification of victims or the commercial fascination with killers? These artists let such questions dangle dangerously over our heads, and in the end, I have to say, over their own. At the same time, it may also be true that not all of this art or the artists can bear the weight of the questions they have posed.

On the one hand, victimized peoples have long appropriated their oppressors' insidious descriptions of themselves as a way to neutralize their terrible charge. But what does it mean to appropriate images of the Nazi killers into the contemporary artistic response to the terror they wrought? Is this a way to normalize such images, making us comfortable with them, bringing them back into the cultural conversation, denying to them the powerful charge that even the killers themselves hoped to spread? Or is it merely to redirect the viewers' attention away from the effects of such terror to its causes?

Alas, these are the easy questions articulated so disturbingly by this exhibition of Nazi imagery in recent art. Tougher, more unsettling, and yes, even more offensive questions are also raised and openly addressed by both the works in this exhibition and by the catalogue essays written by curator Norman Kleeblatt and others, including Lisa Saltzman, Ernst van Alphen, Sidra Ezrahi, Reesa Greenberg and Ellen Handler-Spitz.[4] To what extent, for example, are we even allowed to consider the potential erotic component in the relationship between Nazi murderers and their Jewish victims? What does it mean to "play" Nazis by building your own model concentration camp out of LEGO? Is this different from "playing" Nazis in the movies? Were Nazis beautiful? And if not, then to what aesthetic and commercial ends have they been depicted over the years in the hunkish movie-star images of Dirk Bogarde, Clint Eastwood, Frank Sinatra, Max von Sydow and Ralph Fiennes? What does it mean for Calvin Klein to sell underwear and cologne in the Brekerian images of the Aryan ideal? And if this is possible, is it also possible for the son of survivors, British artist Alan Schechner, to imagine himself standing amidst emaciated survivors at Buchenwald, drinking a Diet Coke? Is he merely adhering to the Passover refrain that enjoins us to remember these events as if we were there, as Michael Berenbaum has suggested? Or is this an extension of the artist's other work, *Holocaust Bar-code*, which would critique the potential for commercial exploitation of the Holocaust by anyone, anywhere, including the artist himself?

Indeed, just where are the limits of taste and irony here? And what should they be? Must a depraved crime always lead to such depraved artistic responses? Can such art mirror evil and remain free of evil's stench? Or must the banality of evil, once depicted, lead to the banalization of such images, and become a banal art? As The Jewish Museum has made very clear in the dissenting (and affirming) voices of survivors included as part of the show's installation, such questions constitute the very reason for this exhibition. These questions are asked explicitly in wall panels by survivors, artists and rabbis in a talking-heads video, and they are implied in a fascinating compilation of popular cultural film and television clips, from *The Producers* to *Hogan's Heroes*, to *The Twilight Zone*. What is worse, Mel Brooks's song from

The Producers, "Springtime for Hitler," or art that self-consciously examines such a phenomenon? On Broadway in New York in spring 2002 it was possible to pay $150 for the right to laugh at Hitler's shenanigans in *The Producers*, but it was not possible to laugh at art that questioned this cultural conversion of terror into entertainment.

Neither do the artists always help themselves. On the eve of the 17th March opening, a disastrous interview between art critic Deborah Solomon and artist Tom Sachs appeared in *The New York Times* Sunday Magazine. "Tell me about your 'Prada Deathcamp,' one of the more incendiary works in the show," asked Solomon. The creator of "Prada Deathcamp," Tom Sachs, answered agreeably, "It's a pop-up death camp. It's a sort of best-of-all-worlds composite, with the famous Gate of Death and Crematorium IV from Auschwitz. I made it entirely from a Prada hatbox." He went on to describe what Prada meant to him: mainstream hipness and a place where you meet everyone you've ever known in your life. To which, Deborah Solomon responded, "What does that have to do with Hitler?" And here the artist Sachs did his best to suggest that the Emperor of Contemporary Installation Art was as naked as its crankiest critics had long suggested. With queasy stomach, I quote:

> I'm using the iconography of the Holocaust to bring attention to fashion. Fashion, like fascism, is about loss of identity. Fashion is good when it helps you to look sexy, but it's bad when it makes you feel stupid or fat because you don't have a Gucci dog bowl and your best friend has one.

To which an incredulous Solomon could only say: "How can you, as a presumably sane person, use the Nazi death camps as a metaphor for the more coercive aspects of the fashion industry? It makes me think you have failed to grasp the gravity of the Holocaust." I could not have said it better myself.

But in fact, Sachs's work and approach to it, as puerile as it may be, also provides that negative benchmark of kitsch and shallowness against which the rest of the show's art might be measured and, I think, more seriously considered. Much more compelling, even haunting, are the fantasies of Israeli artists Roee Rosen and Boaz Arad. In the former, Rosen's unfettered novelistic imagination asks us to put ourselves in the place of Eva Braun during her last moments in the bunker in Hitler's embrace — not a place many of us would want to go — but a suspension of judgment that allows us to get an intimate look at evil incarnate. Boaz Arad's fantasy is of an entirely different order. It is not about Hitler the seducer of a woman or an entire nation, but about an Israeli Jew's simple need for an apology from Hitler for what he did. By cutting and remixing original film-clips of Hitler's speeches, the artist literally forces Hitler's own guttural utterances into a Hebrew sentence, so that we see Hitler gesticulate and proclaim in his own voice, "Shalom Yerushalayim, ani mitnatzel" (Shalom, Jerusalem, I apologize.). People laughed when the American artist Bruce Nauman proposed that Germany's Holocaust memorial simply be composed of a tablet with the words, "We're sorry for what we did, and we promise never to do it again."[5] I do not think any of us should be ashamed for fantasizing about an apology from Hitler, especially not the artists whose job it is to show us what we were only imagining.

Another work, Polish artist Zbigniew Libera's LEGO concentration camp, also attracted more than its share of negative attention. But in fact, having been widely shown in exhibitions around the US and Europe (one even co-sponsored by the New Jersey State Holocaust Education Commission), this piece has already done much more than provoke outrage among viewers: it has also provoked dozens of thoughtful reflections on just how Auschwitz is ever going to be imagined by anyone born after the terrible fact. Like Art Spiegelman's *Maus*, it has also taken a seemingly "low form" of art and used it to address the artist's own tortured relationship to a place and events he never knew directly. And like David Levinthal, who when asked why he took photographs of Nazi toys instead of the reality itself replied that the toys, fortunately, were his only reality of Nazis, Libera similarly recognizes that his only connection to Auschwitz is an imagined one. Outraged critics like Menachem Rosensaft asked what's next, a LEGO recreation of the World Trade Center's destruction? What would the families of the murdered firefighters think of that?

At which point, I recalled how I had stumbled upon my two young boys, then ages 5 and 7, up early one morning at work on a LEGO memorial to the World Trade Center, this after we had taken pains to protect them from nearly all the media's images of the destruction. I also recalled here the night some two weeks after the September 11 attacks, when I heard our 7-year-old, Asher, screaming at his younger brother from the other room, "But Ethan, you have to fall down when I crash into you — that's the tragedy of the World Trade Center, that the towers fell down when the planes crashed into them." Do our children trivialize these events the moment they all too reflexively try to get their imaginations around them? Do we therefore proscribe such events altogether, thereby relegating them to the unimaginable, despite the historical fact that someone, somewhere had to imagine such events in order to perpetrate them?

If these questions are problematically formalized in this exhibition's art works, they are also carefully elaborated in the exhibition's catalogue essays. In this vein, art historian Ellen Handler Spitz explores the perilous border between inviolate childhood and absolutely violated children, that inner-world terror of children devastated by a cruelty whose name they cannot pronounce. What can children do with such trauma? Ernst van Alphen persuasively argues that to some extent the child has come to stand "for the next generations, who need to learn a trauma they have not directly lived," who instead of talking about such terror, or looking at it, will necessarily "play-act" it as a way to know and work through it.[6]

In fact, all of the writers in the catalogue are acutely aware that exhibiting and writing about works such as these may be regarded by some to be as transgressive and disturbing as the art itself. In this vein, both the exhibition curator, Norman Kleeblatt, and literary historian Sidra Ezrahi have probed deeply into what Ezrahi presciently calls the "'barbaric space' that tests the boundaries of a 'safe' encounter with the past." Here, in fact, cultural critic Reesa Greenberg reminds us that "playing it safe" is no longer a viable option for museums, curators, critics, or viewers when the questions at hand are necessarily so dangerous. For as art historian Lisa Saltzman shows in her reconsideration of the avant-garde, since "All the verities are [now] thrown into question," such transgressions require an art that makes excruciating demands on both critics and viewers. It is almost as if the more strenuously we resist such art, the more deeply we find ourselves implicated in its transgressions.

For a generation of artists and critics born after the Holocaust, their experience of Nazi genocide is necessarily vicarious and hyper-mediated. They have not experienced the Holocaust itself but only the event of its being passed down to them. As faithful to their experiences as their parents and grandparents were to theirs in the camps, this media-saturated generation thus makes as its subject the blessed distance between themselves and the camps, as well as the ubiquitous images of the Nazis and their crimes they find in the commercial mass media.

Of course, we have every right to ask whether such obsession with these media-generated images of the past is aesthetically appropriate; or whether by including such images in their work, the artists somehow affirm and extend them, even as they intend mainly to critique them and our connection to them. But then, this ambiguity between affirmation and criticism, too, seems to be part of the artists' aim here. As offensive as such work may seem on the surface, the artists might ask, is it the Nazi imagery itself that offends or the artists' aesthetic manipulations of such imagery that is so offensive? Does such art become a victim of the imagery it depicts? Or does it actually tap into and thereby exploit the repugnant power of Nazi imagery as a way merely to shock and move its viewers? Or is it both, and if so, can these artists have it both ways? By extension, can a venerable institution like the Jewish Museum ever just hang such work on its walls without creating a space for it in the high-art canon? Can a museum ever show art in order to critique it without also implicitly affirming it as somehow great art that had to earn a place on the museum's walls?

In some ways, these questions have assumed a greater prominence in the minds of both viewers and critics after September 11. The ever-collapsing line between gallery and museum exhibitions, encouraged by so much conceptual and installation art (and inspired by Duchamp many years ago), much of it brazenly anti-commercial, suddenly seemed like an indulgence we could no longer afford. Critics who had been harping on for years that the museum's role as arbiter of what was worthy and deserving of cultural preservation had all but been eviscerated by showing art whose essence openly negated such curatorial aims have dug in their heels. Their patience had been exhausted both by such shows and by what they regard as a self-absorbed generation of artists more preoccupied with their handiwork than with a world outside of themselves. Some critics like Michael Kimmelan at *The New York Times* grumpily admit to having reached the end of their patience with the repetitive plumbing of shock value for its own sake, with contemporary installation art repeatedly saying "look what I can do." One week, Kimmelman extolled the retrospective of Gerhard Richter's work at MoMA, one of the main conceptual forebears for this show, and the next week, he excoriated the artists in *Mirroring Evil* who came after Richter for having taken their cue from him.[7]

Clearly, something in all these works resonated deeply with Norman Kleeblatt, the Jewish Museum Curator who conceived and organized this exhibition. As the child of German-Jewish refugees who barely escaped with their lives, and the grandson and great-grandson of Jews murdered in the camps, he had the courage to face the images of an evil that has defined his truncated family legacy and continues to shape his identity as an American and as a Jew, whether he likes it or not.

In mounting this exhibition, the Jewish Museum showed similar courage in the way it openly faces equally fraught institutional issues: Where is the line between historical exhibition and sensationalistic exhibitionism? Can any exhibition, even the most rigorously framed, or the artists or curators, or even we as viewers objectively critique sensationalist imagery without participating in the sensation itself? In the end, viewers of the exhibition and readers of its catalogue will have to decide for themselves — but only after they have actually seen the exhibition. Though even here, the answers may depend on just how self-aware each of us is when it comes to understanding our own motives for gazing on such art, our own need to look evil in the face even as we are repelled by what we see.

In reference to Germany's Holocaust memorial problem, I once wrote that after the Holocaust, there could be no more "final solutions" to the dilemmas its memory posed for contemporary artists; there can be only more questions.[8] For these artists, the issue was never whether or not to show such images, but rather how to ask, through these images: to what extent do we always re-objectify a victim by reproducing images of the victim as victim? To what extent do we participate in their degradation by reproducing and then viewing such images? To what extent do these images ironize and thereby repudiate such representations? Or to what extent do these images feed on the same prurient energy they purportedly expose? To what extent does any depiction of evil somehow valorize or beautify it, even when the intent is to reveal its depravity?

For artists at home in their respective media, questions about the appropriateness of their forms seem irrelevant. These artists remain as true to their forms and chosen media as they do to their necessarily vicarious "memory" of events. But for those less at home in the languages of contemporary art, the possibility that form — especially the strange and new — might overwhelm, or even become the content of such work, will lead some to suspect the artists' motives. Some may wonder whether such work seems more preoccupied with being stimulating and interesting in and of itself than with exploring events and the artist's relationship to them afterward. Some may be leery of the ways such art may draw on the very power of Nazi imagery it seeks to expose, the ways such art and its own forms are energized by the Nazi imagery it purports only to explore.

Even more disturbing may be the question historian Saul Friedländer raised several years ago in his own profound meditations on "fascinating fascism," in which he asks whether an aesthetic obsession with fascism is less a reflection on fascism than it is an extension of it. Here Friedländer asks whether a brazen new generation of artists bent on examining their own obsession with Nazism adds to our understanding of the Third Reich or only recapitulates a fatal attraction to it. "Nazism has disappeared," Friedlander writes,

> but the obsession it represents for the contemporary imagination — as well as the birth of a new discourse that ceaselessly elaborates and reinterprets it — necessarily confronts us with this ultimate question: Is such attention fixed on the past only a gratuitous reverie, the attraction of spectacle, exorcism, or the result of a need to understand; or is it, again and still, an expression of profound fears and, on the part of some, mute yearnings as well?[9]

As the artists in this exhibition suggest, the question remains open, not because every aesthetic interrogation of Nazi imagery also contains some yearning for "fascinating fascism," but because they believe that neither artist nor historian can positively settle this question. In fact, by leaving these questions unanswered, these artists confront us with our own role in the depiction of evildoers and their deeds, the ways we cover our eyes and peek through our fingers at the same time.

No doubt, some will see such work as a supremely evasive, even self-indulgent art by a generation more absorbed in its own vicarious experiences of memory than by the survivors' experiences of real events. Others will say that if artists of the second or third generation want to make art out of the Holocaust, then let it be about the Holocaust itself and not about themselves. The problem for many of these artists, of course, is that they are unable to remember the Holocaust outside of the ways it has been passed down to them, outside of the ways it is meaningful to them 50 or 60 years after the fact. As the survivors have testified to their experiences of the Holocaust, their children and their children's children will now testify to their experiences of the Holocaust. And what are their experiences? Photographs, film, histories, novels, poems, plays, survivors' testimonies. They are necessarily mediated experiences, the afterlife of memory, represented in history's after-images.

Why represent all that? Because for those in this generation of artists, to leave out the truth of how they came to know the Holocaust would be to ignore half of what happened: we would know what happened to the survivors and victims but miss what happened to their children and grandchildren. Yet, is not the important story what happened to the victims themselves? Yes, but without exploring why it is important, we leave out part of the story itself. Is it self-indulgent or self-aggrandizing to make the listener's story part of the teller's story? This generation doubts that it can be done otherwise. These artists can no more neglect the circumstances surrounding a story's telling than they can ignore the circumstances surrounding the actual events' unfolding. Neither the events nor the memory of them take place in a void. In the end, these artists ask us to consider which is the more truthful account: that narrative or art which ignores its own coming into being, or that which paints this fact, too, into its canvas of history?

NOTES

1 *The Wall Street Journal*, 10 January 2002.
2 Menachem Z. Rosensaft, "How Pseudo-Artists Desecrate the Holocaust," in "Demystifying Nazism, or Trivializing Its Victims? A Debate," *Forward*, 18 January 2002, p. 18.
3 James E. Young, "Museum Show Truthfully Probes Society's Fascination with Evil," in "Demystifying Nazism, or Trivializing Its Victims?", *Forward*, 18 January 2002, p. 18.
4 Norman L. Kleeblatt (ed.), *Mirroring Evil: Nazi Imagery/Recent Art* (New Brunswick, NJ, 2001).
5 Cited by Peter Schjeldahl, "The Hitler Show," *The New Yorker*, 29 March 2002.
6 Ernst van Alphen, "Playing the Holocaust," in Kleeblatt (ed.), *Mirroring Evil*, p. 69.
7 Michael Kimmelman in *The New York Times*, 15 February and 15 March 2002.
8 See James E. Young, *At Memory's Edge: After-Images of the Holocaust in Contemporary Art and Architecture* (New Haven and London, 2000) for a study of these issues as they arise in more public art and architecture.
9 Saul Friedlander, *Reflections of Nazism: An Essay on Kitsch and Death* (New York, 1984), p. 19.

INDEX